GERMANY'S LIGHTNING WAR

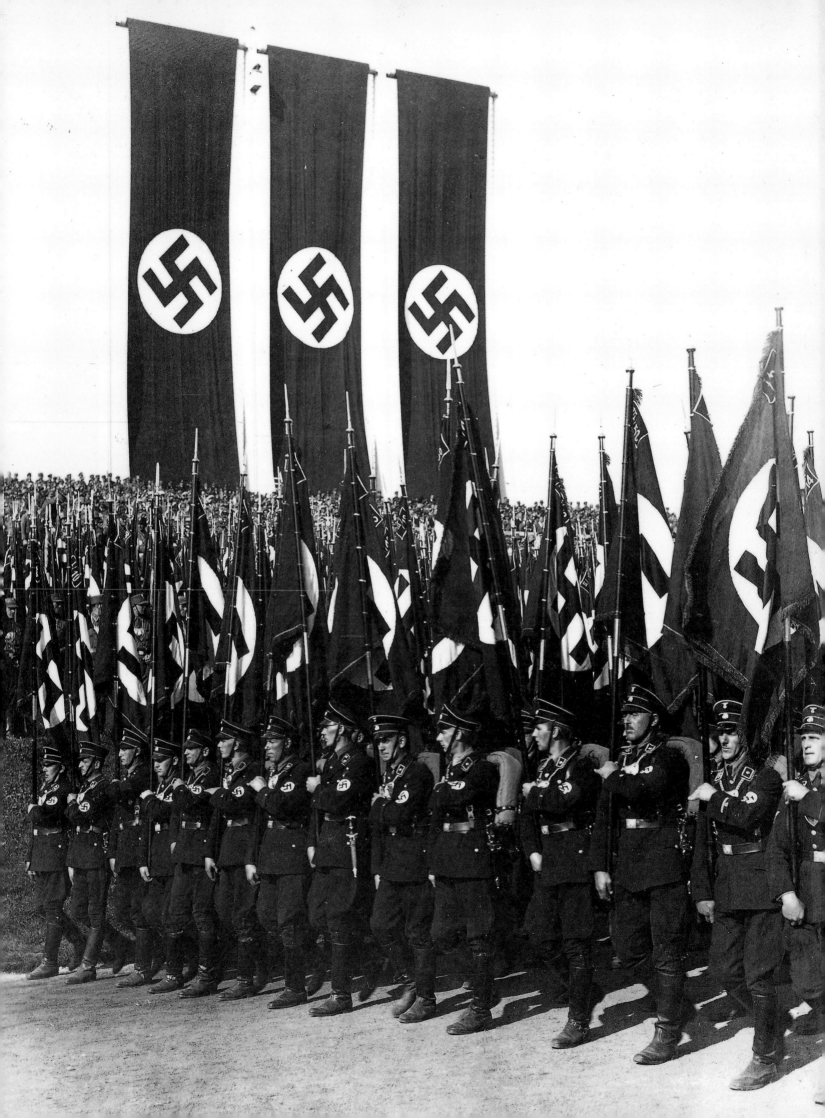

THE CAMPAIGNS OF WORLD WAR II

GERMANY'S LIGHTNING WAR

Adrian Gilbert

MBI Publishing Company

This edition first published in 2000 by
MBI Publishing Company,
729 Prospect Avenue, PO Box 1, Osceola, WI 54020-0001 USA

MBI Publishing Company books are also available at discounts in bulk quantity
for industrial or sales-promotional use. For details write to Special Sales Manager
at Motorbooks International Wholesalers & Distributors, 729 Prospect Avenue,
PO Box 1, Osceola, WI 54020-0001 USA.

Library of Congress Cataloging-in-Publication Data Available.

ISBN 0-7603-0845-4

Editorial and design: Amber Books Ltd
Bradley's Close, 74-77 White Lion Street,
London N1 9PF

Editor: Stuart MacReady
Design: Stylus Design, www.stylus-design.com

Picture credits
The Robert Hunt Library: 11, 14, 15 (b), 30, 32-33, 48, 49 (t), 51, 59, 65, 68, 72, 79, 84, 90, 91 (b), 92-93, 98, 100, 101, 102-103, 108, 136 (t), 144, 145, 146 (both), 179, 180, 182 (both), 185 (r), 186, 187 (t), 199 (t), 206, 212-213, 214, 231.

TRH Pictures: 6, 8, 9, 12, 13, 15 (t), 16, 17, 18, 19, 20, 21 (both), 22 (IWM), 24, 25, 27, 28-29, 32 (t), 35, 36, 37, 39, 40, 41, 42, 43, 45, 49 (b), 50, 52, 53, 54, 56, 57, 58, 60, 61, 62, 64-65, 66, 69, 70, 71 (IWM), 73, 75, 76-77, 78, 80, 81, 82-83, 86, 89 (b), 89 (t) (IWM), 94, 95, 97, 105, 106, 106-107, 110 (IWM), 112, 113, 114, 115 (IWM), 116 (IWM), 118, 119, 120, 121 (t), 122, 123 (IWM), 124, 125, 126, 127 (IWM), 128, 128-129 (IWM), 130, 131 (IWM), 132 (both), 133 (IWM), 134 (IWM), 135, 136-137, 138, 139, 140, 142, 143 (t), 143 (b) (IWM), 147, 148 (both), 149 (both), 150, 151 (t) (IWM), 151 (b), 152, 154 (US National Archives), 155, 156, 157, 158, 159, 160, 161, 162, 163, 165 (IWM), 166, 167, 168, 170-171, 171 (b), 172 (t), 173, 175 (IWM), 176 (IWM), 177 (IWM), 183, 184-185, 187 (b), 188, 189, 190 (both), 191, 192, 193, 194 (both), 195, 196, 197, 198 (IWM), 199 (b) (IWM), 201, 202 (t), 202 (b) (IWM), 203 (IWM), 204, 207 (IWM), 209, 210 (t), 211 (IWM), 213, 215 (mr), 216, 217, 218 (IWM), 219, 221, 222, 223, 224 (IWM), 225, 226 (b), 227, 228, 229 (IWM), 230, 232, 232-233, 234 (IWM), 236 (both), 237, 238 (IWM), 239 (t) (IWM), 240 (IWM), 241 (b), 242-243, 243, 244 (IWM), 245 (t), 246 (b)(IWM), 247 (IWM), 248, 249 (both), 250 (IWM).

Artwork credits
Aerospace Publishing: 31, 34, 38, 91, 96, 102, 121 (b), 169, 172 (b), 174, 181 (t), 208, 220.
Orbis Publishing: 26, 29, 44, 46, 55, 63, 71, 74, 76, 82, 87, 88, 92, 104, 111, 117, 164, 181 (b), 184 (b), 200, 210 (b), 215 (t & ml), 222 (bl), 226 (t), 233 (b), 239 (b), 241 (t), 246 (t).

Printed and bound in Singapore

Page 2: SS and SA standatds are paraded at the 1934 Nuremberg Party rally. (TRH Pictures)

CONTENTS

CHAPTER ONE

COUNTDOWN TO WAR

Europe in the 1930s was a continent dominated by the activities of Hitler and Mussolini. As the power of the Fascist governments grew, they began to flex their newly-acquired muscle.

When Adolf Hitler was appointed chancellor in January 1933, he promised the German people that he would reverse the humiliations imposed on the nation by the Versailles Treaty and return Germany to a dominant position in Europe. In direct contravention of the terms of the treaty, Hitler instigated a vast expansion of the armed forces and started the process of rearmament, concentrating on the production of aggressive instruments of war: tanks, bomber aircraft and U-boats.

By 1936, the growing strength of Germany's armed forces emboldened Hitler to adopt an increasingly belligerent foreign policy. Despite the presence of the League of Nations, Hitler was helped by the refusal or inability of other major powers to put a brake on his territorial ambitions. The Soviet Union and the United States were not members of the League, and both nations adopted a policy of non-intervention in world affairs. Britain and France were the two major powers within the League, but – weakened by their efforts in World War I – neither country had the will to act decisively against Hitler.

Hitler's foreign policy proved to be highly successful. Germany reoccupied the demilitarised Rhineland in 1936, without opposition from France or Britain. German troops were then sent to Spain to aid General Franco's forces fighting against the Spanish Government. The Spanish Civil War (1936–39) provided the German army and air force with valuable lessons in the conduct of modern warfare. In March 1938, German soldiers marched into Austria, which now became an integral part of the German Reich. Later in 1938, Hitler put pressure on Czechoslovakia to cede those of its territories in the Sudetenland region which contained large numbers of ethnic Germans.

Munich

The British prime minister, Neville Chamberlain, was fearful that the growing crisis in Central Europe would lead to all-out European war which, he believed, Britain must avoid at almost any cost. During September 1938, he attempted to placate Hitler's demands by encouraging the Czech Government to surrender the border regions of the Sudetenland to Germany. On 29 September, a conference was called in Munich to attempt to resolve the problem, attended by Hitler, Chamberlain, the French prime minister, Edouard Daladier, and Benito Mussolini. From their meetings came the infamous Munich Agreement, the first stage in the destruction of the Czechoslovak state. The Czechs were bluntly told by the Western powers to accept the German occupation of

OPPOSITE
A German panzer commander surveys the terrain from the turret of his PzKpfw IV tank. The earlier marks of the Panzer IV were armed with a low-velocity 7.5cm gun, and were intended to provide support for armoured operations led by the Panzer III.

the Sudetenland; if they refused they would face Germany alone.

Hitler's ability to force concessions from Britain and France encouraged him to go a step further. Formerly, his demands had been to restore lands inhabited by German-speaking majorities back to the German Reich, and in this he received grudging acceptance from Britain and France. This line was crossed, however, in March 1939 when Hitler exploited the break-up of the rump Czechoslovakia into separate Czech and Slovak entities. While Slovakia was allowed limited autonomy, German troops marched into Prague and established the 'Protectorate of Bohemia–Moravia'. This act finally alerted the Western powers and opened their eyes to the true nature of Hitler's foreign policy: the domination of Europe.

Although Chamberlain still hoped for peace, he began to adopt a more robust policy in the hope of deterring Germany from further aggression. Poland had come under pressure from Hitler to concede former German territories, and on 31 March 1939 Britain unconditionally promised to come to Poland's aid if it was attacked by Germany. France soon followed suit. But the Western alliance with Poland did not have its intended effect of curbing Hitler's demands. The German leader was convinced that Britain and France would not risk war in order to save Poland, and in April his generals began to prepare an invasion plan.

The Soviet threat to Hitler

The main problem in Hitler's mind was the attitude of the Soviet Union. He knew that Stalin had become concerned by German expansion into Eastern Europe, and that any German incursion into Poland would probably lead to Soviet intervention against Germany. Putting aside his pathological hatred of the Soviet Union, Hitler instructed his diplomats to negotiate a deal with Stalin which would divide Eastern Europe into mutually-recognised spheres of influence. On 23 August 1939, the Nazi–Soviet Pact was signed in Moscow, which included a secret clause agreeing to divide Poland between Germany and the Soviet Union. The way was clear for Hitler to go to war.

The power that underpinned Hitler's foreign policy was the German armed forces, of which the army was the key element. The army was the most powerful force in Germany, and consequently was deeply mistrusted by Hitler he worked hard to ensure that its potential for independent action was minimised. Ever since his accession to power in 1933, Hitler had steadily undermined the army's political influence. In 1938, Hitler dismissed the war minister, Field Marshal Werner von Blomberg, on trumped-up charges of sexual disgrace, and dissolved the war ministry in favour of the Oberkommando der Wehrmacht (OKW, or armed forces high command), with Hitler taking the role of supreme commander. Although OKW was

BELOW

Adolf Hitler, the German Chancellor, harangues the crowd at the 1934 Nuremberg Rally. By 1939, Hitler was sufficiently confident of his power to risk a European war.

responsible for all the armed forces, the heads of service of the army, air force and navy reported directly to Hitler and did not work together to formulate policy. The formation of OKW was essentially a device for Hitler to impose control over his armed forces.

During 1938, generals of an independent cast of mind were dismissed or sent to other posts, and more pliable commanders appointed in their place. They included General Wilhelm Keitel, promoted to OKW chief of staff, and General Alfred Jodl, who ran the operation section. Both men were besotted by Hitler and followed his every order, regardless of consequence.

Hitler's domination of the army was facilitated by three further factors. First, the army had traditionally concerned itself with matters of tactics and operational strategy, and rarely dealt with matters of grand strategy and other wider international concerns. Consequently, the generals were slow in understanding Hitler's motives and actions. Second, the old Prussian tradition of unswerving loyalty to the monarch continued to influence the German officer corps. During the period of the Weimar government, soldiers swore to uphold the state, but in 1934 they swore a direct oath of loyalty to Adolf Hitler. This personal bond to Hitler would have a powerful controlling force over the German officer corps, even when it was clear that he was leading Germany to destruction. Lastly, Hitler was astute in flattering his senior officers, bribing them with promotion and even with gifts of money and land.

Organisation of the army

The army had its own high command (*Oberkommando des Heeres*, or OKH), with Colonel General Walther Brauchitsch as its commander and General Franz Halder as its chief of staff. Below OKH were six army groups which controlled various military districts (*Wehrkreisen*) responsible for the recruitment and training of the army as a whole. The basic building block of the German army was the division which, besides being an organisational formation, was a means of forging a sense of solidarity, and

ABOVE
The British prime minister, Neville Chamberlain, waves the agreement signed at Munich in 1938, which Chamberlain hoped would bring 'peace for our time'. Rather than respecting Czech sovereignity after gaining the Sudetenland, Hitler soon set about undermining what was left of Czechoslovakia.

RIGHT

The German Panzer I was effectively obsolete by the outbreak of war. The first mass-produced Panzer, it entered service in 1934 and saw action in the Spanish Civil War. It was only thinly armoured and armed with two 7.92mm machine guns. Despite this, 1445 Panzer Is were still in service in 1939, and it was only withdrawn from front-line duties in 1941.

Panzer I
Germany

often had a strong regional identity (broadly similar to the British regimental system). The different divisions were designated as panzer (armoured), light, motorised, mountain and infantry, the latter forming the vast bulk of the army. On the eve of the invasion of Poland, the German army could muster more than 100 active and reserve divisions from a total force of 2.5 million trained soldiers.

In 1939 the German army employed the Wellen (waves) system to raise and deploy its infantry divisions; the divisions of each wave varied in terms of size, equipment, quality and potential deployment. The 35 divisions of the first wave were the largest (around 18,000 men each) and best equipped, and, being mobilised first, would also be the first into action. The 16 divisions of the second wave deployed around 15,000 men, and were drawn from reservists. The 21 third-wave divisions were reservists with only limited training or older men, and lacked a full artillery complement and other support services. The 14 fourth-wave divisions were raised from reinforcement battalions drawn from the regular army. The third and fourth wave divisions would follow up the main advance as reinforcements, or be used in secondary defensive operations.

The fact that the army had been restricted to 100,000 men by the Versailles Treaty was both a source of strength and weakness. The size restriction had ensured that only the best men were recruited, and the men of the former Weimar army acted as the training staff for the vastly increased force decreed by Hitler. On the debit side, the vast and hasty expansion of the army from 1934 onwards caused problems, especially with the introduction of equipment for the mechanised forces. Motorised transport remained in short

supply, and the bulk of the army relied on horses for basic transport.

Shortages of weapons and equipment had to be made good by the widespread use of captured stock. In 1939, for example, the great Skoda arms factory in the former Czechoslovakia was used to provide tanks for the new light divisions (which would be up-rated to panzer divisions for the 1940 campaign). Arms procurement was never one of the strengths of the German military system, as there were always too many small, competing projects producing too wide an array of equipment. This in turn placed great strain on the supply system, which found it difficult to cope with the multiplicity of weapons in use at any one time.

Superior German training

The real strength of the German army lay in its human material. Despite Allied propaganda claims that the German soldier was an unimaginative semi-automaton who only obeyed orders, the German soldier was, in fact, both a disciplined and imaginative soldier capable of complex and improvised operations. Backed by a fighting tradition which went back to the days of Frederick the Great, the ordinary German soldier was better trained than any of his opponents and, crucially, understood the 'leadership principle' which had become a part of basic German training in the 1920s. This system encouraged the soldier to be able to take over command at one or two grades above his own. Thus, if the immediate commander was killed or put out of action, the soldier was expected to be able to take over command and carry out the mission to a successful conclusion.

The officer corps was also expected to show high levels of initiative – in stark contrast to the systems prevalent in the Allied armies whether Polish, British or French. Once a common plan had been agreed upon, junior officers were given a wide degree of latitude in making decisions. Indeed, subordinate commanders were expected to demonstrate initiative at all times in furtherance of the general aim. Called *Auftragstactik* (roughly translated as goal-orientated tactics), this system of personal initiative was an essential component in the workings of the blitzkrieg philosophy.

Officers in the field were helped by a superb general staff system which ensured that the army as a whole operated as effectively as circumstances allowed. The old Great General Staff of the Prussian army formed the basis of the system, and was continued with the opening of the War Academy in Berlin in 1935. The antagonism that existed in the West between staff officers and the men on the ground was relatively absent in the German army, and accordingly ensured higher levels of cooperation between both parties.

Existing in an uneasy relationship with the army were the units of the military SS (which became the Waffen-SS or fighting-SS in 1940). Formed as Hitler's protection guard by Heinrich Himmler, the Waffen-SS expanded dramatically as the war progressed and became a major part of the German armed forces. In 1939, however, the military SS consisted of a few battalions of infantry operating alongside army units. The problem for the army lay in SS's ability to circumvent army discipline by appealing directly to Himmler. There was also a certain amount of jealousy on the army's part in having to operate with a competing organisation who, it believed, received superior arms and equipment. But as

BELOW
Czech infantry engage in manoeuvres along the border with Germany. In 1938, the Czech Army was well trained and generally well equipped, and deployed behind strong border defences; it could have posed serious problems for the German armed forces.

An SS soldier stands guard on a Prague street corner following the German takeover of the remains of the Czech state in March 1939. This marked a turning point in European international relations, as the western Allies reluctantly began to accept war was likely to be inevitable.

the war progressed, the army worked better with the Waffen-SS and began to respect its fighting abilities.

Role of the Luftwaffe

A further organisational complication for the army was the role played by the air force (Luftwaffe) in ground operations. Thanks to the influence of Herman Göring in the rise of the Nazis during the 1930s, the Luftwaffe had assumed a disproportionate importance within the Wehrmacht. The Luftwaffe was responsible for all parachute forces and controlled the bulk of the antiaircraft arm of service (later in the war it would even field its own infantry and armoured divisions). Although under nominal army control within a theatre of war, Luftwaffe formations retained their own chains of command and had right of appeal to Göring or the Luftwaffe high command.

Although possessing complete organisational autonomy, the Luftwaffe was closely tied to the conduct of ground operations, a fact reflected in the aircraft developed in Germany prior to the outbreak of war and in the tactics the air force adopted. German air power was based around the light and medium bomber with fighter support. Its role was to support the army operations at a tactical level and to spread fear and confusion amongst the civilian population by attacks on urban areas. The Luftwaffe never developed a long-range strategic bomber along the lines of the American B-17 or British Lancaster, as its prime function was to conduct the short, decisive wars that Hitler demanded of his military commanders.

During the 1930s, the Luftwaffe had been given priority in manufacturing production, so that on the eve of the invasion of Poland it could field an impressive force of 2564 operational aircraft comprising light and medium bombers, dive-bombers and fighters. Göring considered his men to be an elite force within the Wehrmacht, and, certainly, the men who crewed the Luftwaffe aircraft were exceptionally well trained and led. The morale and motivation of the Luftwaffe was exceptionally high during the early years of the war, helped by the fact that the air crews knew their aircraft were generally far superior to those of Germany's enemies.

The theory behind blitzkrieg

Central to Germany's military philosophy was the close integration of all military arms, especially its air and land forces. This cooperation formed the basis of *blitzkrieg* (lightning war), a term used to describe the highly successful offensive tactics employed by the Wehrmacht in the early years of World War II. The origins of the blitzkrieg philosophy dated back to the end of World War I, when the German army pioneered the use of infiltration tactics to bypass Allied strong points and maintain the momentum of the advance.

Training in mobile shock tactics developed further in the 1920s under the guidance of General Hans von Seeckt, commander of the 100,000-strong *Reichswehr* (Army). Tactically far-sighted, Seeckt emphasised the role of mobility and shock action using motorised vehicles, and he sent tank and air crews (forbidden in Germany under the terms of the Versailles Treaty) to the Soviet Union, where they trained in secret. On a theoretical level, the Germans were influenced by the teachings of two maverick British military thinkers, Major-General J.F.C. Fuller and Basil Liddell-Hart, who both espoused the use of fast-moving mechanised forces to achieve deep penetration into and behind enemy positions.

Blitzkrieg was more than just an operational system: it was part of a wider military philosophy aimed at destroying an enemy's total ability to resist. Hitler used the expression in a political speech given in 1935, and for the Nazis, blitzkrieg involved the use of subversion in enemy territory prior to the advent of open hostilities. Thus, the large German minorities in Czechoslovakia and Poland were used to conducting subversive activities, including sabotage, and to creating a general climate of fear and apprehension through a campaign of lies and half-truths.

The use of fear as a military weapon had been used by the Germans extensively in World War I in order to cow the civilian populations of the countries they had conquered. Called *Schrecklichkeit* ('frightfulness'), this policy was incorporated into blitzkrieg: towns and cities were deliberately bombed, and columns of refugees machine-gunned to add to the general confusion of invasion and so

BELOW
A Nazi stormtrooper escorts a German policeman through the streets of Berlin. By 1939, the Nazi party had imposed tight discipline over all German state institutions.

interrupt the movement of enemy forces. Surprise and speed were the other two essential factors behind blitzkrieg. In order to secure surprise, mobilisation was to be kept secret and declarations of war were to be avoided if possible. Speed would be provided by fast-moving mechanised forces – spearheaded by tanks – which would dispense with preliminary artillery bombardments and instead rely on close support from the Luftwaffe.

This combination of armour and air power was crucial to the tactical success of blitzkrieg, but they would require good communications and dynamic leadership to be effective. These were provided primarily by the lightweight radio and by a new generation of officers who understood armoured warfare. Radios were fitted into individual tanks, enabling them to maintain contact with each other and with command vehicles at all times. Also, radios enabled the commanders to leave their headquarters in the rear and move up to the front line. There, they could assess the military situation as it was happening, and yet still remain in touch with other units and rear headquarters. It was no coincidence that the great pioneer of Germany's armoured forces, General Heinz Guderian, had begun his military career as a signals officer.

German planning

The campaign against Poland would be the first test of blitzkrieg. The flat, open terrain that was characteristic of most of Poland was ideal for mechanised warfare, although roads were generally poor, and the great rivers that crossed through Poland could become real obstacles. A more serious factor, however, was the weather: during October and November the autumn rains would turn much of the Polish countryside into a sea of mud. This mud – called *raputitsa* by the Poles – was particularly sticky and clinging, and would bring military operations to a virtual standstill. Consequently, when Hitler ordered OKH to prepare a plan of attack in April 1939, the generals knew that the invasion could begin no later than the end of August. If that date were missed, then the campaign would have to be called off until spring of 1940.

The German planners started with one great geographical advantage, in that by 1939 German-controlled territory virtually surrounded Poland on three sides. This allowed them the option of launching the offensive in a wide range of places of their choosing, and correspondingly forced the Poles to defend a wide frontier area. Only in the east, where

Poland butted up to the Soviet Union, did the Poles feel safe from attack.

During the summer of 1939, OKH drew up its blueprint for invasion. The team responsible for planning was called *Arbeitsstab Rundstedt*, named after its presiding light, Colonel General Gerd von Rundstedt, who, in 1939, was Germany's most senior general. Rundstedt, in fact, left the detailed work to two of his most brilliant staff officers, Major-General Erich von Manstein and Colonel

Equipped with PzKpfw II light tanks, a German panzer unit parades through the streets of Prague, following the invasion of the Czech state in March 1939. The Czech presidential palace can clearly be seen in the background.

Günther von Blumentritt. Manstein would also play a major role in the planning of the 1940 offensive against the Western Allies, before taking up major command positions on the Eastern Front.

'Fall Weiss'

Crucial to the German plan was the need to defeat Poland quickly and decisively. If Britain and France did come to Poland's aid, then the Poles would have to be crushed before the Allies could initiate offensive operations against Germany from the west. The dangers of a two-front war traditionally remained uppermost in the minds of all German strategists. The bulk of the German army (55 medium and high-quality divisions) would be deployed against Poland, while reserve formations would be assigned to man the defences

on the Siegfried Line to counter any possible intervention by the Allies in the west.

The German invasion would be led by its five (later six) panzer divisions (with a nominal strength of 560 tanks each, but typically around 300 in the field), its four light divisions (equipped with fewer tanks but soon to be converted into full panzer divisions) and four motorised divisions (infantry formations fully equipped with motorised transport). These divisions would batter through the frontier defences and then race deep into the country to begin the encirclement of the slow-moving Polish army.

Code named *Fall Weiss* (Case or Operation White), the German plan envisaged the destruction of the vast bulk of the Polish army west of the line formed by the Narew, Vistula and San rivers, as a result of concentric attacks launched by two German army groups. The forces of Army Group North (General Fedor von Bock) comprised two armies. Third Army (Lieutenant-General Georg von Küchler) fielded eight infantry divisions plus a panzer brigade and a cavalry brigade, and was deployed in East Prussia. Fourth Army (General Günther Hans von Kluge) was stationed in Pomerania and consisted of four infantry divisions, two motorised divisions and a panzer division. Both armies were to act together to eliminate the Polish Corridor (which separated Pomerania from East Prussia) and trap as many Polish troops as possible in the process. In addition, Third Army had the role of advancing on Warsaw from the north and of cutting off the retreat of Polish forces from the west.

The main thrust

Army Group South (Rundstedt) was assigned the bulk of the German forces: three armies deployed in Silesia, Bohemia and parts of Slovakia. Eighth Army (General Johannes Blaskowitz) comprised five infantry divisions; Tenth Army (Lieutenant General Walther von Reichenau) comprised six infantry, two panzer, two motorised and three light divisions; Fourteenth Army (General Siegmund List) deployed five infantry, two panzer and one light division. Befitting its greater size, Tenth Army was the main strike force which would drive directly towards Warsaw, protected on its flanks by the other two armies. The mechanised (and therefore fast) formations of the Fourteenth Army would also be responsible for outflanking the Polish forces in the south of the country, before driving northwards to meet up with advance units from the Third Army fighting its way south from East Prussia.

The Luftwaffe deployed two air fleets (*Luftflotten*), one each in support of the two army groups. The cutting edge of the air offensive would be provided by 897 bombers and 426 fighters, plus a variety of reconnaissance, air/ground cooperation and transport aircraft. The Luftwaffe tasks were to destroy the Polish air force, disrupt road and rail communications, eliminate Polish army command posts and spread terror amongst the civilian population. The German navy would play a subsidiary role in the campaign, but its vast resources enabled it to support coastal operations with little interference.

Poland's armed forces were dominated by the army, an institution that also played a dominating role in Polish society (many Polish political leaders were senior army officers). Under the overall command of Marshal Edward Smigly-Rydz, the peacetime Polish army comprised 30 regular infantry divisions (plus a further nine reserve divisions), 11 cavalry brigades, two motorised brigades and a number of heavy artillery, tank, engineer and signals units. Peacetime strength was around 280,000 men which could be increased by up to three million reservists after full mobilisation. Whereas the German system allowed its troops to be mobilised swiftly and in conditions of near secrecy, the Polish mobilisation

BELOW
German Junkers Ju 87 Stuka dive-bombers in flight. The German armed forces used Stukas to act as aerial artillery in direct support of the panzer divisions, whose tank units lacked sufficient heavy guns to destroy enemy positions by themselves.

system was relatively slow and cumbersome – a fact that the Germans would use to their advantage when war broke out.

The Polish armed forces

The air force came under direct army control and consisted of 15 fighter, 12 reconnaissance/bomber, four medium bomber and 12 army cooperation squadrons. Total strength was 400 aircraft, but the vast majority were obsolete models which could not offer serious resistance against the latest aircraft deployed by the Luftwaffe. Similarly, the small Polish navy was no match for the German forces arrayed against it, consisting of just four destroyers, five submarines and six mine-sweepers.

Although Poland had a well-established military tradition, its generals were not well versed in the skills of high command and failed to understand the dangers posed by Germany's mechanised forces. The Polish army was essentially a force of infantry and cavalry, although during the late 1930s attempts were made to modernise the force. Priority had been given to anti-aircraft and anti-tank guns, with many of the latter motorised. But the 48 artillery pieces assigned to each infantry division compared poorly with the firepower that a first-wave German infantry divisions could muster, the Germans possessing more guns overall, and of a heavier calibre with greater range.

Poland's cavalry forces were in the process of converting from their role as mounted infantry/reconnaissance troops to becoming a mechanised force. In 1939 the transformation was only beginning and the Poles were only able to deploy a few TP light tanks. The bulk of Poland's small armoured force relied on the hopelessly outclassed TK/TKS tankettes.

In the all-important area of communications, the Polish army compared poorly with its German adversary. Although a radio system

BELOW

Heavily-laden German soldiers march through an Austrian town during the Anschluss celebrations. Although the panzers represented the cutting edge of Germany's blitzkrieg philosophy, the infantry still formed the backbone of the German Army.

**TKS
Poland**

LEFT
*The Polish TKS tankette
only had a crew of two, and
was so lightly armoured that
it could be easily destroyed
by anything more powerful
than the Panzer I. It was
armed only with a 7.9mm
machine gun.*

was being introduced, communication within units was based on hand signals and runners, while communication between divisions and the high command was dependent on the civilian telegraph and telephone networks. These would not survive the coming onslaught, leaving both small units and larger formations isolated within hours of the German offensive, and thus unable to respond in a coherent manner to the invasion.

Until Hitler began to issue direct threats against the Polish in 1939, Poland had generally maintained good relations with Germany. For the Polish general staff, the main potential enemy had always been the Soviet Union, and so it was not until March 1939 that detailed defensive plans ('Plan Z') were drawn up to repel a potential German invasion. The Polish staff were aware of the overwhelming material strength of Germany, and implicit in the plan was the necessity of military aid from outside Poland.

In May 1939, Smigly-Rydz stated: 'The plan is a defensive one. Its aim is to prevent the destruction of our forces before the start of the Allies' offensive in the west by inflicting on the Germans the greatest possible losses... I must accept at the beginning of the war the loss of certain parts of Polish territory which will later be regained.' Unfortunately for the Poles, Allied assistance would be too little and too late in coming to affect the outcome of the campaign.

The defence plan

As the western half of Poland was the most populous and economically developed, the Polish plan was based on a stubborn defence of these areas. Whereas, from a purely military perspective, the Poles' would have been better advised to defend deeper within the interior of the country, political considerations dictated a frontier defence. Another influencing factor was the perceived need to pay particular importance to the defence of Danzig and parts of the Polish Corridor. In the minds of Poland's leaders, it was quite possible that the Germans might just seize these border areas as a *fait accompli* and then attempt to negotiate a settlement from a position of strength. Consequently, more Polish troops were pushed further towards the frontiers with Germany. In hindsight, all these measures just played into the hands of the German planners at OKH; the greater the numbers of Polish troops stationed near the frontier, then the easier it would be for the panzer columns to outflank and then encircle them.

Defending the Polish Corridor was the Pomorze Army (General W. Bortnowski) with five infantry divisions and one cavalry brigade. To the south was the Poznan Army (General Taduesz Kutrzeba) comprising four infantry divisions and two cavalry brigades; support was provided by the Kutno Group of two reserve divisions. Facing the main German force in Silesia was the Lodz Army

(General Juliusz Rommel) of four infantry divisions and two cavalry brigades, and the Cracow Army (General Antoni Szylling) with seven infantry divisions, a cavalry brigade and a mechanised brigade. Guarding the southern flank was the Carpathian Army (General Kazimierz Fabrycy) consisting of two mountain brigades, and the Tarnow reserve group of two infantry divisions.

Along the border with East Prussia were deployed the Modlin Army (General Emil Przedrzymirski-Krukowicz) with two infantry divisions and two cavalry brigades, and, further to the east, the Narew Group (Major-General Czeslaw Mlot-Fijalkowski) with two infantry divisions and one cavalry brigade. A reserve force for these two formations consisted of the Wyszkow Group (General Stanislaw Skwarczynski) comprising three infantry divisions. The Polish army's central reserve was provided by the Prusy Army, deployed to the south of Warsaw and backing up the Lodz and Cracow Armies;

commanded by General Stefan Dab-Bìernacki, it was a powerful force of eight infantry divisions, one cavalry brigade and one tank brigade. Facing the Soviet Union in the east, the Polish army stationed a few under-strength units and militia troops to act as a covering screen.

The build-up to war

During the summer of 1939, Hitler increased German pressure on Poland. Göbbels' propaganda machine launched vicious attacks against the Poles, focusing his complaints on Poland's influence over the Free City of Danzig, the anomaly created in 1919 which was populated by Germans but dependent on Poland for the movement of goods in and out of the city. The Polish Government was determined to avoid the fate of Czechoslovakia, and resolutely rebuffed all German demands. The Poles declared that any direct German intervention in the dispute over Danzig would be regarded as an act of war.

BELOW

British tanks on manoeuvres during the inter-war period. Like the French, the British did not understand the necessity of using armour en masse. Underarmed and underarmoured, British and French tanks like these were ill-prepared for combat against the latest models of German panzers.

LEFT
Erich von Manstein (seated, centre) was arguably Germany's finest strategist of World War II. He was one of the chief planners of the Polish campaign and advanced the radical Sichelsschitt plan which lay behind German success in western Europe in 1940. He later played a major role in restoring the German line after the disaster at Stalingrad.

BELOW
One of the consequences of the Nazi–Soviet pact: a Soviet officer returns the salute of a German guard of honour.

Although alerted to the real nature of Hitler's foreign policy, the British and French continued to hope that diplomacy could solve the crisis. Their attempts to mediate only encouraged Hitler in his belief that the 'men of Munich' would once again step back from a full-scale war. Western diplomats had made attempts to bring the Soviet Union onto the Allied side, but Stalin was not impressed by the offers made by Britain and France, and instead turned towards Germany. Although Stalin mistrusted Nazi Germany, the concrete terms offered to him – control of the eastern half of Poland and the Romanian province of Besserabia, and influence over Estonia and Latvia – seemed a better option than those being put forward by the Western powers.

The date for the invasion was set as 26 August. But a day before the attack was due to start, news reached Hitler that Mussolini would not support Germany's war with Poland, and that the Anglo-French alliance with Poland had been formally guaranteed and signed in London. This suggested to Hitler that the West might honour its commitment to go to Poland's aid; shaken, he cancelled the invasion order. Hitler's loss of nerve was only temporary, however, and a new attack date was set for 1 September. The order was confirmed on 31 August: the invasion of Poland would begin at 0445 hours the following day.

CHAPTER TWO

THE DESTRUCTION OF POLAND

Caught by surprise by the Nazi-Soviet pact, the Poles resisted valiantly as the two powers seized their homeland. For Europe, it was the first opportunity to witness the blitzkrieg in full effect.

At 0440 hours on 1 September 1939, German aircraft of the Luftwaffe bombed air bases in Poland. Five minutes later, German ground forces rolled over the border into Poland, while the old German battleship *Schleswig-Holstein* emerged from the early morning mists and started shelling the Polish fortress on Westerplatte. World War II had begun.

The first fatality of the war had, in fact, occurred the previous evening when a German concentration-camp prisoner was murdered by an SS commando unit during a staged attack on a German radio station at Gleiwitz near the Polish border. Organised by the Gestapo chief, Reinhard Heydrich, the raid was a German attempt to provide some kind of justification for Hitler's unprovoked attack on Poland.

A small group of SS men, dressed in Polish army uniforms, attacked the isolated transmitter, fired shots into the air and took over its running. Listeners to the station heard the shots and a voice, speaking in Polish, declare: 'People of Poland! The time has come for war between Poland and Germany. Unite and smash down any Germans, all Germans, who oppose your war!' To complete the charade, the unfortunate concentration camp inmate – who had been forced along by the SS troops and dressed in civilian clothes to look like a radio operator – was shot and his body left at the scene of the attack for later inspection by the world's press. The following day, Hitler proclaimed a state of war between Germany and Poland, citing the Gleiwitz incident as one of the reasons for the invasion.

Although the Polish high command had ordered a general mobilisation on 30 August, the German invasion still came as a surprise. Many Polish reservists had yet to reach their units, and many of these units were in the process of moving to their mobilisation areas when the German maelstrom struck. The invaders soon swept aside the Polish frontier troops, and during the late afternoon of 1 September they began to make contact with forward elements of the Polish army.

The Luftwaffe strikes

Meanwhile, the Luftwaffe had been in action in earnest. The initial task for the German air crews was the destruction of the Polish air force on the ground. All the major bases were heavily bombed, as were air strips in the regions where German advances were expected. Some Polish aircraft did mange to get airborne, but they were either shot down or driven off from the German areas of operation. The old fighter aircraft fielded by the Poles were hopelessly outclassed by the Messerschmitt Bf-109s of the Luftwaffe. Low-

OPPOSITE
A Polish PZL P.37B Lós B medium bomber stands on the runway, alongside a squadron of PZL P.11 fighters. Although successful against the Luftwaffe, many Polish aircraft were caught on the ground by German forces.

flying German aircraft reported that Polish light anti-aircraft and small arms fire was fairly accurate, but at medium and higher altitudes the Luftwaffe could operate with relative impunity.

Despite a belief to the contrary, the Polish air force was not destroyed in the first day of fighting, and it continued to mount operations as best it could. The fighter defences over Warsaw continued to offer resistance for three days, and fighter patrols flew over Silesia and Bohemia-Moravia, while a bombing mission was made against East Prussia. But by 3 September, the Polish air force had ceased to exist as a coherent force, and from then on the German bombers had a virtual free hand over the whole of Poland.

Once the Polish air force had been dealt with, the Luftwaffe could concentrate on ground targets. Particular emphasis was paid to the destruction of road and rail bridges, rail heads and other forms of communication. Subsequent bomber waves attacked administrative and industrial centres, and the masses of Polish troops attempting to fend off the German ground invasion faced near constant bombardment from the air. Attacks on civilian targets were not neglected, and Warsaw was heavily bombed on the first day of war. Central to the German blitzkrieg philosophy was the spread of fear and confusion among the general population, and the long columns of refugees fleeing into central Poland were too easy and tempting a target for the air crews of the Luftwaffe to resist (although, in fairness to the Germans, it was often difficult to distinguish between evacuees and legitimate military targets).

The two armies of Army Group North found their operational areas shrouded in mist

RIGHT

Marshal Edward Smigly-Rydz, Commander-in-Chief of the Polish Army. Although a valiant soldier, he was no strategist. He deployed his forces too far forward along the Polish border line. As a result the bulk of the Polish army was overwhelmed in the opening phase of the offensive.

during the early morning of 1 September, which aided concealment but caused some early confusion with units firing on each other. The German Fourth Army drove directly eastwards from Pomerania to cut off the Polish Corridor, while the Third Army divided its forces between an attack south-westwards (to link up with the Fourth Army in the corridor) and a drive southwards towards the Polish capital. Further north in the corridor, Danzig was secured with little resistance by a brigade of German infantry, although Polish strong points along the Baltic coast continued to offer resistance.

Rapid German success

Spearheaded by General Heinz Guderian's XIX Panzer Corps, the German Fourth Army met only limited resistance during the first day of the invasion. The German command believed the Poles would fall back to the River Brade and there establish a defensive line, but on 2 September German tanks crossed the Brade with minimal opposition. The only problem occurred when tanks of the XIX Corps ran out of fuel and ammunition, and were stranded for a time behind what remained of the Polish front line.

The advance of Army Group North had gone almost like clockwork – a tribute to the excellence of German staff work. For the troops at the cutting edge, however, the experience of combat for the first time could cause problems. F.W. Mellenthin, then an intelligence officer in General Hause's III Corps with the Fourth Army, described one such incident:

Very early in the campaign I learned how 'jumpy' even a well-trained unit can be under war conditions. A low-flying aircraft circled over corps battle headquarters, and everyone let fly with whatever he could grab. An air-liaison officer ran about trying to stop the fusillade and shouting to the excited soldiery that this was a German command plane – one of the good old Fieseler Störke. Soon afterwards the aircraft landed, and out stepped the Luftwaffe general responsible for our close air support. He failed to appreciate the joke.

The surprised troops of the Polish Pomorze Army were only able to mount sporadic resistance against the relentless German assault. In one such engagement (1 September), a unit of German infantry was charged by mounted troops of the Polish 18th Lancer Regiment. During the fighting, the Poles suddenly found themselves outflanked by German armoured cars which inflicted heavy casualties on the Polish cavalrymen, forcing them to retreat in disorder with the loss of their commander, Colonel Mastalerz.

ABOVE
Soldiers of the SS-Heimwehr Danzig round up 'undesirables' in the free city of Danzig. The SS had clandestinely sent troops into Danzig before the invasion, ready to seize key objectives once war was declared.

The Polish campaign
September 1939

Key
German forces

The German invasion of Poland was launched on 1 September 1939. Nine armoured divisions – including the 4th Panzer Division – swept through Poland in just eighteen days, putting the armoured vehicles, and the tactics that became 'blitzkrieg', to the test for the first time.

This incident formed the basis of the legend of Polish lancers attacking German tanks. Later in the campaign, there were a number of actions where mounted Polish troops became involved in fighting with German infantry, and in other instances German tanks attacked Polish cavalry units. Although the Poles had a reputation for reckless courage, their officers were not so foolish as to knowingly commit flesh and blood directly against hard steel. But given the nature of national stereotypes, the story swiftly gained wide credence.

Spirited Polish defence

The German Third Army's advance towards Warsaw was briefly halted by troops of the Modlin Army, holding defensive positions in the Mlawa area. The Poles resisted for three days until a German outflanking movement forced a withdrawal southwards. The troops appointed to the other area of operations assigned to the Third Army – the westwards drive into the Polish Corridor – met fierce resistance around Graudenz, a town on the Vistula, while further north the key bridge

over the river at Dirschau was destroyed by the Poles. Fortunately for the Germans, their armed forces had long experience in the use of pontoon bridges, and the Vistula was promptly bridged at Meve.

On 3 September, Third and Fourth Armies met at Neuenberg, trapping Polish forces in the north of the corridor. At the same time, the Germans began to push back what remained of the disorganised Pomorze Army towards Bromberg. The city of Bromberg had a large German population, and when news of the invasion reached the German community, there was an uprising. Polish troops and other Polish inhabitants put down the uprising with considerable bloodshed, an incident which received wide coverage in the German press and broadcasting services.

The old animosity between Poles and Germans re-emerged in this campaign, and was stoked-up by Hitler and the Nazi propaganda machine. A week before the invasion, Hitler had harangued his senior generals with the details of how he would send SS units into Poland 'to kill without pity or mercy all men, women and children of Polish race or language'. Hitler's hatred of the Slav peoples would ensure that the war in the East would be fought with the utmost severity.

During 4 and 5 September the remnants of General Bortnwoski's Pomorze Army began to retreat back towards Warsaw. For the first time in three days the exhausted Polish troops were not harried by the Germans. The bulk of the German Fourth Army was redeployed eastwards, instead of following the Poles along the plain of the Vistula, and began an advance into East Prussia behind the advancing formations of the Third Army, driving on Warsaw from the north and northwest.

General Rundstedt's Army Group South was responsible for the destruction of the Polish armies across the Silesian border and the seizure of Warsaw from the south. The sky during morning of 1 September was clear over southern Poland, and German reconnaissance aircraft had little difficulty in picking out the long columns of German troops crossing the border. In the centre was General Reichenau's Tenth Army, whose seven mechanised divisions (followed by six infantry divisions) made it the most formidable of the various armies attacking Poland, and reflected its key role in leading the German advance on Warsaw. Protecting the Tenth Army's left flank was the Eighth Army, whose own objective was the capture of Lodz. On the right of the German advance was the Fourteenth Army, which protected the southern flank of the invading forces as well as being assigned the responsibilities of overrunning Cracow and the industrial regions of Galicia.

Continued German success

Advance elements of Army Group South penetrated up to 15 miles into Poland on the first day of hostilities. Among the lead units to cross the border was a reconnaissance com-

BELOW

German troops cross into Poland at the beginning of the invasion. Although the Polish High Command was aware that an attack was imminent, Polish troops on the border were caught by surprise, and German troops were able to advance into Poland with minimal opposition.

Polish cavalry on manoeuvres shortly before the outbreak of war. The Polish Army was undergoing the process of mechanising its cavalry arm when the Germans struck, but the bulk of the cavalry were still mounted on horses.

pany of the 2nd Light Division (Fourteenth Army) led by Hans von Luck. He described the ease with which the Germans advanced into Poland:

We fell in with the armoured reconnaissance regiment. The frontier was manned by a single customs official. As one of our soldiers approached him, the terrified man opened the barrier. Without resistance we marched into Poland. Far and wide there was not a Polish soldier in sight, although they were supposed to have been preparing for an 'invasion' of Germany.

The following day, however, resistance increased and the German advance slowed. The Polish army hoped to form a defensive line along the River Warta and southwards to Tschenstochau, but the confusion caused by the surprise and power of the German attack made such an undertaking impossible. Early on 3 September, Tschenstochau was taken by the Tenth Army, and German mechanised

units secured bridgeheads over the Warta. To the south, the German Fourteenth Army commenced its drive on Cracow, while additional mountain units began to debauch from the high passes in Slovakia's Carpathian mountains, thereby outflanking forward Polish units defending Cracow.

General Polish withdrawal

Aware that both the southern and northern fronts were in danger of total collapse, the Polish high command issued orders on 5 September to begin a general withdrawal towards the Vistula, which was modified the following day to the adoption of a new defensive line running from the Narew river in the northeast, along the Vistula and back along the River San. Marshal Smigly-Rydz had to face the fact that the battle for the frontiers had been a total disaster, and his only hope was to withdraw as many formations as

Sir Nevile Henderson, to deliver an ultimatum to Hitler at 0900 hours the following morning. The ultimatum demanded that if German troops did not cease hostilities and begin a withdrawal of troops from Poland by 1100 hours later that morning, then Britain would declare war on Germany.

When Henderson's statement had been relayed to Hitler, one observer noted that the German Führer sat 'like one turned to stone', before turning angrily to his foreign minister, von Ribbentrop, with the terse, 'What now?' But by now the die had been cast and at 1100 hours Chamberlain broadcast to the British nation the doleful news that Britain was at a state of war with Germany. Later in the day, the French followed the British lead with their own declaration of war against Germany. A local territorial dispute in Central Europe had been transformed into a European war.

In May 1939, General Maurice Gamelin, the French commander-in-chief, had informed the Polish high command that in the event of a German attack on Poland, the French army would undertake an offensive against Germany not later than 15 days after the start of French mobilisation. Unfortunately for the Poles, even this offer would turn out to be too late to be of real help, such was the speed of the German advance into their territory.

The French invade Germany

As a token gesture, French troops advanced into German territory in the Saar region on 7 September. The advance was slow and careful; casualties were avoided and German frontier troops fell back in good order. The French had advanced a mere five miles by the 12th when the Saar 'offensive' was called to a halt. There the French adopted a defensive position until withdrawing all their forces on 4 October. Although the Polish high command held the realistic expectation that help from the Allies would not come in a few days but take several weeks, the inactivity of France and Britain in September 1939 was a bitter pill to swallow.

The declarations of war by Britain and France did, however, have consequences for future German strategy in Poland. The planners at OKH were fearful that the Allies might launch an attack in the west, and consequently were reluctant to send large numbers of troops deep into Polish territory.

BELOW
A Colonel of the 7th Mounted Rifles of the Polish Army wearing the standard officers' khaki service dress with traditional flat-topped, square-shaped czapka. His regiment is identified by the colour of the cap band and the pennant-shaped collar patches. His medal is the Virtuti Militari, a Polish award for gallantry.

BELOW
A Colonel of the 7th Mounted Rifles of the Polish Army wearing the standard officers' khaki service dress with traditional flat-topped, square-shaped czapka. *His regiment is identified by the colour of the cap band and the pennant-shaped collar patches. His medal is the* Virtuti Militari, *a Polish award for gallantry.*

possible to the relative safety of eastern Poland before they were destroyed piecemeal by the marauding panzer columns and Luftwaffe. The first three days of combat had come as a sickening blow to the Polish high command, and help from Poland's allies in the West had become ever more vital if the Polish state was to survive at all.

When news of the German attack on Poland was relayed to the world, the French continued to hope that some forms of mediation could prevent the war from spreading, even calling upon Mussolini to chair an international conference. The British realised that this meant war, and during 1 and 2 September, the British prime minister, Neville Chamberlain, tried to stiffen French resolve to issue a final ultimatum against Germany. On the evening of 2 September, under pressure from his own backbench MPs, Chamberlain instructed the British ambassador in Germany,

ABOVE

A German supply train crossing a river in Poland. The German Army had highly skilled engineer units which were trained in the bridging of wide rivers. Speed was essential to the success of the German plan, and hold-ups were to be eliminated before they occurred.

OKH argued that if the Allied attack did materialise, then Germany's elite formations would have to be transferred westwards as quickly as possible. By contrast, the German commanders on the ground wanted to develop the encirclement of Polish forces well to the west of Warsaw.

In keeping with this idea, General Bock, commander of Army Group North, intended to redeploy the Fourth Army through East Prussia to new positions on the left (eastern) flank of the Third Army to prevent the Polish army from adopting new defensive positions east of Warsaw. It was an imaginative proposal, but OKH considered it to be too risky in the light of the new threat to the Germans' rear in the west, and accordingly vetoed the plan. In the debate that followed, a compromise measure was adopted, and on 5 September

OKH permitted a reinforced XIX Corps, led by Guderian, to make the crossing through East Prussia and attack the Polish forces behind the River Narew. The remainder of the Fourth Army would resume its role of pushing the Poles back towards Warsaw on the right bank of the Vistula.

Guderian's potent army

Guderian now had four mechanised divisions under his direct command: the 3rd and 4th Panzer Divisions and the 2nd and 20th Motorised Divisions. It was an extremely potent force, made more effective because Bock allowed Guderian a free hand both tactically and logistically. As it was not tied down to the slow pace of infantry supply lines, XIX Corps could act as a fully independent mechanised army – the first such force in the

history of warfare. For Guderian, it was the ideal weapon to maintain the German invasion's momentum.

Having smashed through the Polish army's cordon defence during the first two to three days' fighting, Army Group South prepared to exploit its victory. In the centre of the advance, Tenth Army's mechanised divisions began to race ahead of the infantry formations, bypassing strong points and the masses of Polish infantry streaming back towards Warsaw. To the dismay of the Polish high command, Germany's panzer forces were invariably ahead of the retreating Polish infantry, thereby preventing the Polish commanders from having sufficient time to reorganise their battered forces.

Following behind, or sometimes alongside the panzers, were the combat engineer units whose responsibility was to remove obstacles, dismantle booby traps and build bridges. The Poles had anticipated that the German advance would be slowed by the many wide rivers that ran through their country, but German combat engineers were past masters at constructing pontoon bridges. One such engineer was Paul Stresemann. Although a reluctant soldier, his background in construction led him to be posted as an engineer officer, which ensured that he would be in the forefront of the advance when rivers needed to be crossed. Stresemann gives this account of his first bridging operation whilst under enemy fire:

We ran forward with our rubber boats and timbers, with all kinds of shell fire coming at us. It was

kleiner Panzerbefehlswagen
Germany

LEFT

Overall tank shortages ensured the Panzer I was used in large numbers during the Polish campaign. This example is a command model, with a white cross painted on the side for identification purposes (a device only used during the Polish campaign). The tank had a crew of three, and the fixed superstructure contained two radios, a map table and other electrical equipment. They were armed with a single 7.92mm MG34 machine gun.

Polish TP tanks advance in column. The Poles had too few of these tanks to tilt the balance in their favour, and they were not used as effectively as the German panzers on the battlefield.

absolutely terrifying, even though our own people were firing over at the Poles who were concealed in a wood and the ruins of a village. The dust from explosions was flying over us as we ran straight into the river and began assembling the runner rafts and timbers with lashings of rope as a temporary crossing. We had to get our infantry across and then make a stronger bridge for the tanks. But as soon as we floated out into deeper water, we came under terrible fire from a machine gun, and the man nearest me was killed. I saw him fall off into the water and float away, but I could do nothing for him. We jumped into the water and clung to the sides of the rubber boats which in some cases were being holed and becoming useless. I don't know how long this went on, but I was so frightened I could hardly speak, and the noise was tremendous.

I think our Stukas must have dealt with the opposition because the enemy fire became much less, and at last we were able to make some progress and get a bridge across. The infantrymen were splendid and rushed across as soon as we had the last timber in place. It was then that I was able to look around and found that our commander had vanished along with several more men. These assault crossings were always very hard on the engineer units.

The Pilica river was crossed on 5 September, and the Tenth Army began to wheel around in a northeasterly direction towards Warsaw and the Vistula. At this point the Germans received reports that the Polish army was frantically attempting to organise a new army based around Radom (due south of Warsaw). The army was being assembled from various sources, including troops from the

retreating Cracow Army and from the general reserve provided by the Prusy Group.

Encirclement at Radom

Rundstedt instructed the Tenth Army's commander, General Reichenau, to envelop the Polish forces around Radom from the north, south and west. Reichenau's intention was to destroy this last major concentration of Polish forces that lay between the key German objectives of Warsaw and the Vistula. Three army corps (IV, XIV and XV) were assigned to the battle which began late on 8 September. The Poles fought with determination, but the better-armed and better-trained Germans relentlessly ground them down with air support from the Luftwaffe. On 11 September, Radom was captured along with 60,000 Polish prisoners of war (although a few Polish units managed to break out to

nearby forested regions where they continued resistance for several more days).

While the battle for Radom was in progress, panzer units of the Tenth Army reached the Vistula and secured the vital bridgehead at Pulawy on 8 September, and later at Gora Kalwarja. The hopes by the Polish high command of establishing a defensive line on a major river had been dashed once again. When the German infantry had caught up with the tanks (which were temporarily immobile due to fuel shortages), then the panzers would be clear to resume operations east of the Vistula.

The honour of reaching Warsaw fell to General Reinhardt's 4th Panzer Division. Reinhardt's tanks had reached the outskirts of the Polish capital late on 8 September, and an assault was ordered for 0700 hours the following morning. Supported by divisional artillery,

LEFT
A column of German panzers halts briefly amidst the debris of war. The tank in the foreground is a PzKpfw I, armed only with two machine guns; behind are PzKpfw IIs, which had the slightly heavier armament of a turret-mounted 2cm cannon alongside a machine gun. Both tanks were pitifully under-gunned, even for the conditions of 1939–40, but they were able to do great damage to the predominantly infantry armies opposing them.

the German tanks began to drive into the city, but Polish resistance was fierce, and after three hours' fighting – with the advance completely stalled – the order was given to retreat. The Germans had learnt the dangers of using unsupported armoured units in built-up areas the hard way.

Polish countermoves

To the south, the Fourteenth Army captured Cracow on 6 September, and, following a reorganisation of the army's mobile formations, the mechanised XXII Corps advanced eastwards across the River Dunajec to cut off those Polish units escaping to the east of the Vistula. On 9 September, OKH instructed XXII Corps (followed by the rest of the Fourteenth Army) to break through the defences on the River San and wheel northwards towards Chelm with the final aim of making contact with Guderian's XIX Corps advancing southwards from East Prussia. Thus, XXII and XIX Corps would become the two pincers conducting the encirclement of the Polish army east of Warsaw.

The German Eighth Army – on the Tenth Army's northern (left) flank – was also making good progress and closing on Lodz. As a consequence, its own left flank was becoming dangerously exposed, especially from the Polish Poznan Army (directly to the north). German frontier units were assigned to protect the Eighth Army's exposed flank and were later reinforced by two reserve infantry divisions to form Group Gienanth. But the potential threat posed by the Poznan Army was not fully comprehended by either OKH or the advancing Germans.

While the frontier battles were raging along the Polish border, only the Poznan Army, commanded by General Kutrzeba, had not been fully engaged; the German planners at OKH had decided to bypass this force in favour of swift penetration into the heart of Poland. Once the nature of the German advance had become clear to the Poles, Kutrzeba requested the Polish high command for permission to attack the Eighth Army advancing eastwards below his southern flank. The request was refused as Marshal Smigly-Rydz was determined to get as many troops back behind the Vistula as possible, and so the Poznan Army began a long retreat eastwards towards Warsaw, attacked by the Luftwaffe but without interference from German ground forces. Meanwhile, remnants of the Pomorze Army were also retreating towards Warsaw, the two armies meeting up around the road and rail junction at Kutno, roughly half way between Poznan and Warsaw.

On 8 September, Kutrzeba again requested permission to attack the Eighth Army, using both the Poznan and Pomorze Armies. This was a substantial and still largely intact body of troops, consisting of ten infantry divisions and two-and-a-half cavalry divisions. Although any attack would delay the eastward retreat, the Polish high command was in a desperate position, its troops constantly being overrun by the German panzers. They reasoned that a major counter-attack might slow the advance of Army Group South in general, thereby allowing other Polish forces a breathing space, with time to retreat and regroup. Accordingly, permission to attack was finally granted.

RIGHT

The Junkers Ju 87 Stuka (a contraction of Sturzkampf-flugzeug, *or dive bomber) was one of the most effective close-support aircraft of the war. The Stuka was, however, vulnerable to enemy fighters and required air supremacy or fighter support.*

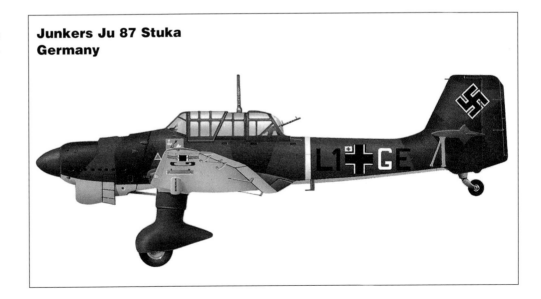

**Junkers Ju 87 Stuka
Germany**

Group Gienanth, originally responsible for the protection of the Eighth Army's flank, had been left behind by the speed of the main German advance. As the Eighth Army neared the River Bzura, its flank guard consisted primarily of the 30th Infantry Division, which was spread out along a front of 20 miles and in no position to mount a coordinated defence. The Polish counter-attack was launched on 9 September, southeast across the Bzura, the only major offensive conducted by the Polish army during the campaign. The next day, the German 30th Infantry Division reported back to Eighth Army Command that it was under attack, suffering heavy casualties and was being forced backwards. Throughout 10/11 September, the Battle of the Bzura raged with great intensity. Although the Poles had managed to force the Germans back, they were short of food, ammunition and other military supplies. One

Polish officer engaged in the fighting explained some of the special problems facing him and his men:

There were dead Germans lying everywhere, on the road and in the ruined buildings. I gave my men orders to go through the Germans' map and trouser pockets in the faint hope of finding the maps which we needed so desperately. At last our search was rewarded: we found a map of the Brochow-Sochaczew area in the pocket of a dead NCO. For us that was the most valuable booty of the entire war.

The Polish counter-attack across the Bzura had come as a surprise to the Eighth Army, but there was no panic and orders were issued to contain the Polish attack. At the headquarters of Army Group South, Rundstedt and his chief of staff, Manstein, saw the Polish attack not so much a problem, but more an opportunity to fulfil the original OKH plan of destroying the Polish army west of the Vistula.

ABOVE

A German 8.8cm anti-aircraft gun in action in Poland. The Germans were quick to realise that their high-velocity anti-aircraft guns were also effective against ground targets, especially armoured vehicles. The western Allies soon came to fear the power of the dreaded '88'.

By now, approximately 170,000 Polish troops were concentrated around Kutno. If they could be encircled, contained and destroyed, then the Polish army would have lost over a third of its ground forces at a stroke.

German redeployment

The redeployment of the German army to deal with the Polish counter-attack was a masterful display of the ability of German general staff officers to move large, complex forces with economy and swiftness. On 11 September, General Blaskowitz was given control over the operation and was assigned formations from both the Tenth Army to his right, and from the Fourth Army advancing from the north. The Eighth Army had dou-

bled in size almost overnight and had six corps working under a single command. One consequence of the coming battle was that the pressure on the Poles in Warsaw was temporarily eased, while German operations on the Vistula were also scaled down.

On 12 September, General Kutrzeba was informed that the remnants of the Lodz Army were retreating towards Modlin, and that any hope of their forces meeting up was no longer feasible. More ominous still were the manoeuvrings of the German forces around Kutno, which threatened the Poles with encirclement. Kutrzeba was in danger of being trapped. On 12 September the Poles attempted to break out of the encirclement with an offensive to the southeast. The

BELOW

German motorcycle teams advance along a muddy track in Poland. The German Army made great use of motorcycles, especially during the early years of the war, finding them useful for reconnaissance and courier tasks.

Germans lost some ground but the ring held firm, and by the 15th the Polish attack had been exhausted. On the same day, the German Tenth Army was ordered to advance northwards to the west of Warsaw to block off any escape route from the Kutno pocket towards the Polish capital.

The Poles made a further attempt to break out on 16 September, to the northeast, in the hope of crossing the Vistula and reaching Modlin. The attempted break-out was once again repulsed, with heavy Polish casualties. The fighting enabled the Eighth Army to further tighten its grip on the Kutno pocket, the Polish troops being compressed into an ever-smaller area, which in turn made them highly vulnerable to aerial attack. On 17 September, the Luftwaffe broke off its bombing operations against Warsaw to concentrate all its efforts against Kutno. The trapped Poles suffered heavy losses as 328 tons of bombs rained down upon them in the pocket.

The Polish defences began to collapse during the 17th: 40,000 men were captured by the Germans on that day, and one last break-out attempt by two Polish divisions was crushed by Tenth Army guarding the approach to Warsaw. The only troops to escape were in small units, most slipping away through the cover provided by the Kampinos forest. Increasingly, the Polish army was breaking down into isolated groups capable, at best, of only guerrilla operations.

German respect for the Poles

Although Hitler had reprimanded his generals when the Poles managed to slow the advance towards Warsaw, for the German high command, the battle of the Bzura was a monumental success, one that even surpassed Hannibal's victory at Cannae – a battle that Prussian staff officers had studied for decades as the benchmark of military triumph. For the ordinary German soldier it had been a tough engagement. Kurt Meyer, later a general in the Waffen-SS but then a junior officer in the *SS Leibstandarte Adolf Hitler*, had fought in the battle attached to the 4th Panzer Division. Despite being a fanatical Nazi, Meyer paid his respects to the Polish soldier: 'It would not be fair on our part to deny the bravery of the Polish forces. The battles along the Bzura were fought with great ferocity and courage.'

While the Poles in the Kutno pocket were still fighting, the Polish high command fell back on a last expedient: the general retreat of

ABOVE
German artillery advances into the Polish heartland. Horses were a vitally important means of transport for the German Army throughout the war.

all forces towards the southeast of Poland to form the 'Romanian bridgehead'. Although the German Fourteenth Army had been pressing directly eastwards along the northern edge of the Carpathians, southeast Poland was the last area where a new line of resistance might be formed, centred around Lwow and the oil-rich region bordering Romania and Hungary.

In the northern theatre of operations, the Polish Modlin Army and the Narew Group began to retreat on the night of 9/10 September, closely followed by the German Third Army. On the Third Army's eastern flank, Guderian's XIX Corps exploited the gap opening up between the two Polish formations. A counter-attack by the Narew Group was repulsed with the Poles suffering heavy casualties. The two panzer and two motorised divisions of XIX Corps were suffering from shortages of fuel and ammunition, and the wear and tear of campaigning was beginning to take its toll of the armoured vehicles, and yet Guderian's miniature 'panzer army' still had the firepower and mobility to overwhelm virtually anything it encountered.

Although Guderian wanted his tanks to operate in a drive east of the River Bug towards Brest-Litovsk, OKH still remained cautious of committing its armoured forces so far east. The original plan was for Guderian to drive south to Siedice, but OKH's realisation that the Poles were attempting to form their 'Romanian bridgehead' forced a change of mind. Guderian was now allowed to

follow his preferred plan to drive southwards along the east bank of the Bug, which would eventually enable him to outflank this last Polish defensive line.

On 14 September, advance units of the 10th Panzer Division reached the edge of Brest-Litovsk, Army Group North's most easterly objective. The following day, the city was captured, although the Polish defenders retired into a fortification known as the Citadel. There they repulsed several more German attacks from the 10th Panzer and 20th Motorised Infantry Divisions. But on the 17th, as the Poles were attempting a break-out, German infantry finally secured the Citadel. The 3rd Panzer Division moved southwards to Wlodova, in the expectation of meeting up with advance panzer units driving northeast from Army Group South.

Although the two great pincers that trapped the Polish forces to the east of Warsaw did not meet physically, they remained only a few kilometres apart, maintaining contact through radio – a fitting tribute to a communication device that had been so important in the success of the German mechanised formations. Actual contact occurred in the original pincer movement towards Warsaw, when elements of the two army groups met at the Vistula bridgehead at Gora Kalwarja, just south of the Polish capital.

The Red Army invades

On 17 September, as the XIX Corps secured Brest-Litovsk, the Soviet army invaded

RIGHT

The Panzer II tank. Although only intended to bridge the gap in service before the arrival of the better-armed and armoured Panzer III and IV tanks, the Mark II was used in large numbers in both Poland and France. It was armed with a 37mm main gun and had a secondary armament of a 7.92mm machine gun.

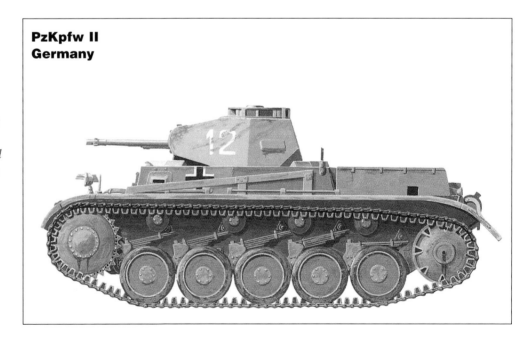

**PzKpfw II
Germany**

Poland. This action came as a complete surprise, not only to the Poles but to the German army, which had been kept in the dark over the secret clause in the Nazi-Soviet Pact of 23 August, which detailed the division of Poland between the two powers in the event of hostilities with Poland.

On 3 September, Foreign Minister von Ribbentrop had cabled Molotov, his Soviet opposite number, suggesting that Soviet forces should invade Poland's eastern regions. The Germans were concerned that Poles might set up some form of administration in the eastern part of Poland which came under Soviet influence and, therefore, outside direct German control. The Soviets had had no knowledge of the date of the German invasion, and were themselves taken by surprise at the astonishing pace of the German attack. Nonetheless, Stalin wanted to ensure that the Soviet Union had control over eastern Poland, if only to build up a buffer zone between German-occupied Poland and the Soviet Union proper. Molotov was instructed to inform Ribbentrop that Soviet forces

would cross the border when sufficient troops could be deployed – 17 September 1939.

Soviet organisation

The Soviet invasion force was divided into two 'fronts' (similar to army groups), totalling more than 20 infantry divisions, 15 cavalry divisions and nine tank brigades. The Byelorussian (White Russian) Front was led by Army Commander Kovalev (consisting of four small armies) and was tasked with the seizure of Polish territory from Brest-Litovsk northwards to the border with Lithuania. The Ukrainian Front of Army Commander Timoshenko (three small armies) was responsible for the invasion of Polish lands south of the Pripet Marshes, with Lwow being its main goal. The southernmost of the Ukrainian Front armies – Twelfth Army – was well equipped with mechanised forces, in order to cut off Polish forces attempting to retreat southwards to the safety of Romania and Hungary.

Polish forces in the east of Poland consisted merely of militia and frontier guards

German infantry take cover behind a PzKpfw I during the bitter fighting in the outskirts of Warsaw. The Panzers were found to be very vulnerable in street-fighting conditions, and were withdrawn from the Polish capital.

ABOVE

A Heinkel He 111 of the Luftwaffe drops its bombload over Warsaw. By this stage, the Poles were unable to defend their capital from aerial attack, and the Germans ruthlessly pounded Warsaw from the air. This was the first example of deliberately targeting civilians during World War II, a precedent that would soon be copied in other theatres of war.

plus a few reserve cavalry squadrons. At first, some Polish troops thought that the Red Army might be coming to their assistance, especially when Soviet troops were seen to avoid combat with the Poles. But as the Red Army marched deeper into Poland – some Soviet mechanised spearheads penetrating as deep as 100km (60 miles) in the first two days – the situation became clearer: Polish units overrun by the Red Army were captured and quickly disarmed, and fighting broke out if the Poles resisted.

The already hopeless position facing the Polish high command was doubly confirmed by the Soviet invasion. The possibility of forming any sort of bridgehead around Lwow was undermined by the imminent arrival of Soviet forces on its right flank. Accordingly, the Polish high command instructed all troops

to retreat back to Hungary and Romania to fight their way past German holding forces; but to try to slip past any Soviet forces unless physically obstructed by them. On 17 September, the Polish president and Government fled to Romania, along with Smigly-Rydz. The previously friendly relations between the two states had encouraged the Poles to seek refuge in Romania, but the following day – as a result of intense German diplomatic pressure on Romania – they were interned and transported deep into the interior of the country.

German withdrawal problems

The sudden arrival of the Red Army marching eastwards caused particular problems for the German army. The Nazi–Soviet Treaty had agreed to divide Poland along the Narew–Vistula–San river line, and German forces were instructed to withdraw slowly to that line. But on 17 September, much of the German army was still engaged in reducing remaining pockets of Polish resistance east of this line, and to withdraw would enable the Poles to retreat to the sanctuaries of Hungary and Romania.

A further problem caused by the sudden arrival of the Red Army was that soldiers had problems distinguishing friend from foe, and on a number of occasions German and Soviet troops shot at each other with loss of life. These incidents were relatively minor, however, and for the most part the German withdrawal was an orderly operation. A certain degree of fraternisation occurred between the German and Soviet forces, and a number of such incidents were recorded by the propaganda units of both sides. At Brest-Litovsk, on 22 September, a combined parade of German and Soviet armoured units was followed by a banquet attended by the two leading commanders from both armies, Generals Guderian and Kriwoschein.

The German withdrawal decision was potentially more difficult for the Fourteenth Army in southern Poland, which had to prevent Polish forces streaming south towards Hungary and Romania. The old fortress city of Przemysl had been invested by the Germans on 10 September (holding out until 15th), while the bulk of the Fourteenth Army pressed on towards Lwow, the last remaining focus of Polish resistance. On the 12th, the German 1st Mountain Division reached the city, but the degree of resistance they encountered forced the Germans to begin a controlled besieging operation. The Zboiska heights dominated Lwow, and on the 13th the Germans fought a hard battle to secure this key position, the city being surrounded on the following day.

The siege was still in progress when, on 20 September, Rundstedt ordered the Fourteenth Army to abandon the reduction of Lwow to the Red Army and retire westwards. Rather than be captured by Soviet forces, however, the Lwow garrison suddenly surrendered to the surprised Germans as they were preparing to leave.

While the Fourteenth Army withdrew westwards, it came into contact with Polish troops crossing its path in a southerly direction. Several engagements resulted, but large numbers of Polish troops were able to bypass the German soldiers and retreat to safety. According to Colonel A.T. Sawczynski (an

artillery officer during the campaign and subsequently a historian of the Polish army), 60,000 Polish troops reached Hungary and 30,000 men crossed over into Romania, while to the north a further 15,000 troops reached Lithuania on the Baltic Sea.

Many of these men travelled to France where a new Polish army was formed. The anguish of these troops, who had not only lost a war but their country, was to remain with them in their long exile. Lieutenant-Colonel Gilewski, a regimental commander in the Podolska Uhlan Brigade described his entry into Hungary on 19 September:

As we rode on this autumn morning through beautiful mountain scenery on our way to a foreign land, the atmosphere was overwhelming. My second-in-command, Major Starnawski, was weeping openly. For hours on end we rode without meeting a soul. Here and there would be the occasional overturned car or bus, and crates of burned-up

BELOW
Polish volunteers stand before a barricade they have constructed as part of the defences of Warsaw. The defenders of Warsaw slowed the German army's plans, but shortages of food, water and other supplies eventually forced a Polish surrender on 27 September 1939.

German soldiers remove Polish street signs, a first stage in destroying the whole Polish state. The Nazis decided to absorb western Poland into the German Reich; the remainder became a colony, designated the Central Government of Poland.

documents as we rode along the gorge leading to the Wyszkowski pass. The regimental adjutant returned by motorcycle with the announcement that the road was empty for some kilometres ahead. We were only a short way from the frontier when we came upon a column of men on the march and hundreds of vehicles. A few hills and valleys further on and we were facing the border. A Hungarian major came towards us with a greeting, asking us to convey to the uhlans that they were to make themselves at home on Hungarian territory.

As German forces in eastern Poland were withdrawing, the remaining areas of Polish resistance were subjected to the full might of the German Third, Tenth and Eighth Armies. Warsaw, reinforced by Polish troops who had escaped from the Kutno pocket, remained defiant. By 15 September, the Tenth Army, from the south, and the Third Army, from the north, had encircled the Polish capital. Both Hitler and his high command were reluctant to conduct a full-scale assault against a well-defended position that would inevitably lead to heavy German casualties. On the 16th, leaflets calling on the Poles to surrender were dropped over Warsaw, and a representative from Third Army headquarters was instructed to demand the surrender of the city. The Poles refused outright; the Germans stepped up their shelling and bombing of the city.

German plans for Warsaw

While the Luftwaffe concentrated on the destruction of water works and power stations, a sustained artillery bombardment from both Third and Tenth Armies was followed by a series of probing attacks by the infantry in the hope of finding and exploiting weaknesses in the Polish defence. Under the leadership of the former commander of the Lodz Army, General J. Rommel, the Poles maintained stiff resistance, and the Germans made little headway. The Poles had sufficient supplies of ammunition, and the ruined areas of the city made good defensive emplacements, which were manned not only by regular soldiers, but by a spirited local militia.

Hitler arrived at Third Army headquarters on 22 September and observed the shelling of Praga, an eastern suburb of Warsaw. Hitler chafed at the delay in the reduction of the city, but opposed any assault on the city east of the Vistula to avoid provoking the Russians. Apart from the problem of potential heavy casualties, according to the terms of the Nazi–Soviet pact this area would come under Soviet jurisdiction. As a consequence, an attack was sanctioned against the western part of Warsaw, which would have the added benefit of driving out civilians towards the east, who would then become the responsibility of the Soviet armed forces.

The attack was assigned to the Eighth Army, whose troops had finished liquidating the Kutno pocket. The Germans made sure that no civilians could escape from the city, thereby increasing the demand for food, which was known to be in short supply. The

BELOW

A young Polish girl weeps over the body of a dead relative. Most sections of the German armed forces and accompanying German administrators acted with great brutality towards the civilian population.

A member of the 1st Panzer Regiment, this corporal wears the special black uniform of the panzer troops. His beret is padded, and serves as a crash helmet. The black collar and silver death's head badge made the uniform very distinctive, and it was popular with German tankcrews for its practicality. Note the lack of equipment or webbing, which would all be stored in the crewmember's vehicle.

Luftwaffe continued to bomb Warsaw's filtration and pumping stations, destroying the regular water supply to the population. As a result, the inhabitants of Warsaw were reduced to drinking directly from the Vistula, with an epidemic of typhoid being a distinct possibility. Most electrical power had been cut off by the Germans, and the city's flour mills were set on fire; the spectre of starvation in the city was beginning to become a reality for its inhabitants and defenders.

Warsaw surrenders

While the Third Army bombarded Warsaw from the north, the Eighth Army opened its assault on the morning of 26 September. The German infantry began to make progress, breaking their way through the outer defences. At the end of the day's fighting, the Poles requested a cease-fire and armistice, which was refused by the Germans who demanded unconditional surrender. For General Rommel and his staff, the situation was hopeless, and rather than prolong the agony of the civilian population, they reluctantly accepted the German terms. Fighting stopped at 1400 hours on 27 September, and the 140,000 Polish soldiers in Warsaw began to lay down their arms and surrender. General Blaskowitz extended the honours of war to the Polish defenders as they prepared to evacuate the capital.

To the north of Warsaw, Modlin continued to resist. German artillery used in the attack on Warsaw was redeployed to shatter the Modlin defences, and a full-scale attack was launched on 27 September, which penetrated the Polish outer defences. Modlin's garrison was now desperately short of water, and food stocks were running low; the garrison commander, General Thommee, arranged for an armistice on the 28th, which was followed by the Polish surrender on the following day.

Apart from a few scattered Polish units continuing guerrilla operations in the country's heavily forested interior, the sole remaining area of resistance came from troops holding defensive positions on the Baltic coast. The Poles fought on with remarkable tenacity, in spite of the dreadful news reaching them of the destruction of the Polish armed forces to the south. Gdynia, the main Polish port on the Baltic, was taken by the Germans on 14 September, although its commander, Colonel Dabek, managed to evacuate much of the garrison to new positions at the

Oxhoefter Flats. The Luftwaffe conducted heavy attacks on the 16th and 17th, followed by a major assault on 18/19 September. The Poles were overrun, although Dabek committed suicide rather than surrender.

The Polish garrison on the Hela peninsula – a thin spit of land stretching out into the Bay of Danzig – came under German fire from air, sea and land before a final infantry attack was launched on 29 September. The Poles were forced back along the peninsula until 1 October, when Rear Admiral Unrug accepted the German offer of surrender. Apart from a few minor skirmishes during the first week of October, the surrender at Hela marked the end of the Polish campaign of 1939 for the Germans.

In 36 days of intense warfare, the Polish army had been destroyed as a fighting force. Fatal casualties amounted to 66,300 men, with 130,000 wounded. The Germans claimed to have captured nearly 700,000 Polish troops, but this figure was almost certainly too high, a total of around 400,000 being more likely. Perhaps as many as 200,000 Poles were taken into captivity by the Soviet Union where many died, but where others managed to get out via the Middle East (and fight with the British). Approximately 100,000 Polish troops had already escaped the German–Soviet net in September 1939 by fleeing to Hungary, Romania and Lithuania.

According to revised German figures, their army suffered 10,600 killed, 30,000 wounded and 3400 missing during the campaign. During September, 217 German tanks had been destroyed, but wear and tear had further reduced the fighting strength of the mechanised divisions. The XIX Corps, which had been withdrawn to East Prussia towards the end of September, was completely immobilised for a while in order to overhaul its battered vehicles, which included tanks, armoured cars and trucks. The Luftwaffe lost 285 aircraft destroyed, with a further 279 damaged beyond repair (Poland lost 284 aircraft in combat and 149 from other causes).

Poland had been partitioned three times by Prussia, Austria and Russia in the late 18th century. In 1939, Poland experienced a fourth partition. To finalise the details, Ribbentrop flew to Moscow, and on 28 September he signed the 'German–Soviet Treaty of Delimitation and Friendship'. In this agreement, Germany accepted the inclusion of Lithuania into the Soviet sphere of influence,

while, by way of compensation, Germany extended its control over Polish territory further east to a new line on the River Bug. Although the Germans wanted access to oil, Stalin refused to surrender the territory east of the River San, which included Lwow and the oil fields of Drohobycz and Boryslaw. Both sides were generally pleased with the new agreement, however, and Stalin was not slow in exercising his 'rights' over the Baltic states, which came under pressure to accept Soviet control. Even before the Baltic states' formal annexation in August 1940, Stalin had turned towards Finland to demand territorial concessions along the Soviet–Finnish border. The Finnish refusal to accept the Soviet demands led to war on 30 November 1939, and while the Red Army suffered heavy losses in the initial stages of the campaign, superior numbers forced the Finns to accept a settlement in March 1940.

Mistreatment of the Poles

The old animosity that both Germans and Russians felt towards the Poles was now given full expression. One of the protocols of the new German–Soviet Treaty declared: 'The two parties will tolerate in their territories no Polish agitation affecting the territory of the other party. They will suppress in their territories all beginnings of such agitation and inform each other concerning suitable measures for this purpose.' In this, if in nothing else, the Germans and Soviets were united.

Over the next six years the people of Poland would suffer terribly. Both the German and Soviet authorities deliberately set about exterminating the political and social elites of Polish society. Following closely in the wake of the German army, SS extermination squads began to carry out summary executions of those declared 'undesirable' – as early as 25 October 1939, 16,376 Poles had already been executed by the German police and armed forces. People living within areas under Soviet control experienced similar treatment. If the Polish campaign had been a triumph for the Wehrmacht, then for the people of Poland it represented the beginning of a living hell.

ABOVE

An example of Nazi barbarism: 64 Poles are summarily shot by German soldiers shortly after the end of the Polish campaign. Despite their claims to the contrary, the German Army was heavily involved in the murder of Polish civilians.

CHAPTER THREE

BEFORE THE STORM

War, for the western Allies, was an anti-climax. The 'Phoney War' saw both sides watching each other from behind their carefully prepared positions, waiting for someone to make the next move.

Even while the German Eighth Army was in the midst of repulsing the Polish counter-attack on the Bzura, Hitler's thoughts were turning towards a showdown with the French and British in the west. He confided to his chief military adjutant, Colonel Schmundt, that immediately operations in Poland had been concluded, then the German armed forces would be redeployed for an offensive. On 27 September, he summoned the commanding officers from the three services of the Wehrmacht to the Chancellery in Berlin. Foremost among the officers gathered at the meeting were General Brauchitsch, the army commander-in-chief, and his chief of staff, General Halder. Hitler announced that he intended to attack France, and that the main thrust of invasion would be conducted through Belgium and Holland's Maastricht 'appendix'. Without waiting to discuss the matter further with his generals, Hitler curtly instructed them to prepare an invasion plan.

This announcement came as a bombshell to Brauchitsch and Halder, cautious generals of the old school who believed that an offensive in the west would have to wait until 1942 to be sure of success. Their reservations were echoed by many other senior generals in the German army, but Hitler was determined that the offensive would go ahead and chose 25

November (less than two months away) as D-Day. The generals continued to procrastinate, but on 19 October the OKH staff produced an invasion plan with the codename Operation Yellow (Fall Gelb).

A new Schlieffen Plan

The Schlieffen Plan of 1914 had been based on a massive outflanking manoeuvre through Belgium, and France's construction of the Maginot Line along the Franco-German border during the 1930s encouraged a renewed assault through the less well-defended Low Countries. Possibly reflecting the reluctance of the German high command for the whole enterprise, the German plan owed little to the great battle of annihilation envisaged by Schlieffen, but instead consisted of a modest advance into Belgium towards Ghent, with the aim of separating the British Expeditionary Force (BEF) from the main French army and securing bases on the Belgian coast to facilitate air and naval operations against Britain.

The bulk of Germany's mechanised forces would be deployed on the northern wing, and airborne troops would be employed to secure key objectives in front of the German advance. General Bock's Army Group B would be responsible for the main attack, supported by a subsidiary force – Army Group A

OPPOSITE

A propaganda illustration from a German magazine intended to convince readers of the strength of the Westwall or 'Siegfried Line'. Although French defences in parts of the Maginot Line were similar to the scene depicted here, the German Westwall was rudimentary and often half-finished.

under General Rundstedt – which would advance into southern Belgium. General Leeb's Army Group C was to be deployed along the length of the Maginot Line in a holding capacity.

This uninspiring plan was received with little enthusiasm by Hitler, who had a natural inclination towards the audacious. During the discussions that followed, Hitler suggested that the weight of the assault might be moved southwards towards an attack across the River Meuse south of Namur. The suggestion was met with incredulity by the OKH planners, but the seed of an idea had been sown in Hitler's mind.

The German plan develops

On 29 October, a revised plan was submitted to Hitler; while allotting more panzer divisions to the south of the attack, it was essentially the same as the original proposal. The next day, Hitler explained to General Jodl at OKW his latest idea, which involved an assault through the Ardennes against Sedan on the River Meuse. Jodl did not, however, pass on the idea to his colleagues in OKH,

who continued with their refinement of the original plan.

Meanwhile, Army Group A had established its headquarters in Koblenz, and Rundstedt's chief of staff, Lieutenant General Manstein, saw the original OKH plan. Manstein was unimpressed: 'I found it humiliating, to say the least, that our generation could do nothing better that repeat an old recipe.' Supported by Rundstedt, Manstein wrote the first of six memorandums to OKH criticising the plan. In his first memo of 31 October he wrote: 'It is conceivable that we will meet with the initial success hoped for against Belgium and the forces that the Allies will rush to her aid. But initial success does not mean total victory. This can only come from the complete destruction of all enemy forces in the field, both in Belgium and north of the Somme.' Manstein concluded his criticism with the suggestion that the centre of gravity of the attack – the *Schwerpunkt* – should be shifted south to Army Group A's southern flank, and consist of a thrust across the Meuse south of Namur, which would push westwards along the Arras–Boulogne axis.

Manstein's suggestions met with a chilly response from OKH, which suspected, not unreasonably, that the motivation behind the plan owed much to an attempt by Army Group A to secure a greater share of the resources (and potential glory) for the coming offensive against France. This was certainly the view of General Bock and his staff at Army Group B, which resented the paring down of its formations for the benefit of Army Group A. Halder ordered that Manstein's memos be filed away and not be brought to the Führer's attention.

Yellow postponed

Hitler had advanced the date for the offensive to 12 November, but the combination of OKH resistance and heavy autumn rains ensured the repeated postponement of Operation Yellow (the offensive would be postponed a total of 29 times before 10 May). The delays had the great advantage for the Germans of providing the planners with time to develop new plans of attack. Unaware of Manstein's proposal, Hitler encouraged his generals to increase Army Group A's forces, and on 11 November he ordered Guderian's XIX Panzer Corps to take up its position with Army Group A opposite Sedan. Guderian knew the area well, and he believed that the hilly and wooded Ardennes region that separated German territory from Sedan was passable to tanks and other armoured vehicles. Thus, bit by bit, the German plan

LEFT
General Fedor von Bock, commander of Army Group B, which was ordered to drive through the Low Countries. Bock was a capable general who played a leading role in the Wehrmacht until his dismissal by Hitler after the failure to capture Moscow in 1941.

moved away from a main attack through central Belgium and Holland, to a wider deployment with the emphasis shifting to southern Belgium.

The cold winter weather of January 1940 provided hard ground for military action, and on 10 January Hitler ordered the offensive for 17 January, as long as the weather remained good and clear. But new forecasts for the 17th suggested foggy weather, which put doubt on

BELOW
German troops amidst the tank traps in the Westwall. Although German propaganda made great play of Germany's defences in the west, Hitler was only concerned with offensive action against France.

the ability of the Luftwaffe to provide the necessary protection for the invasion. Hitler then ordered an indefinite postponement of the attack in the west until the weather improved sufficiently for a successful attack. Before the order was issued, however, a bizarre incident had potentially undermined the entire security of the offensive.

On 9 January, Major Hellmuth Reinberger, a staff officer in the 7th Airborne Division, was instructed to attend a conference in Cologne the following day. Later that evening at a nearby officer's mess, Reinberger accepted an offer from the station commander (a reserve major with a pilot's licence called Hönmanns) to fly him from Münster to Cologne, in order to save a tiresome train journey. The following day, the two men set off in a Messerschmitt Bf-108 reconnaissance aircraft, with Reinberger carrying important documents describing the deployment and operational aims of his division for the coming offensive – in complete contravention of standing orders that secret documents must not be carried in aircraft. At first, conditions were good, but a sudden onset of bad weather forced them off course. Hönmanns believed he was over enemy territory, but before he could find a landmark, the engine cutout and the Bf-108 made a forced landing near the town of Mechelen, which lay just over the Belgian border.

Reinberger desperately attempted to burn the top-secret documents – even enlisting the help of a local Belgian farmer – but he was interrupted by the arrival of a patrol of gendarmes, and the two Germans were arrested. While being held in captivity in a hut, Reinberger made another attempt to burn the papers by thrusting them in a stove, but they were retrieved by one of the Belgian gendarmes. Although badly burned, the documents revealed the broad intention of the Germans to invade through Holland and Belgium. The Allied intelligence services were unsure whether the incident was an elaborate hoax to conceal an attack elsewhere, and they continued to reserve judgement on the veracity or otherwise of the German documents.

The German high command, however, was horrified by the incident. When Hitler was informed of the disaster on 11 January, he

RIGHT
German soldiers manhandle a light infantry gun during winter training prior to the offensive in the west. The winter of 1939-40 was particularly severe, and front-line troops suffered accordingly.

flew into a rage, threatening death to those directly involved and sacking General Felmy as commander of the Second Air Fleet (to which Reinberger belonged). A subsequent report from the German military attaché in Belgium claimed that Reinberger had declared that the papers had been virtually destroyed, with little of importance remaining intact. Nonetheless, doubt remained in the minds of Hitler and the high command as to the precise extent of the Allies' knowledge, which encouraged Hitler to suspend Operation Yellow. In one of the clauses of the postponement order, Hitler insisted that the plan be reworked 'on a new basis, to be founded particularly on secrecy and surprise'.

Manstein's plan adopted

During January, Manstein continued to press for the adoption of the Army Group A plan,

and at a meeting on 25 January with General Brauchitsch, he sharply criticised the OKH plan, going so far as to complain of the 'well-known negative attitude of the OKH'. An exasperated army high command decided to rid themselves of this thorn in their side: on 27 January, Manstein was ordered to take up a corps command far to the east in Stettin. Bitterly disappointed by this 'sideways promo-tion', Manstein found some consolation when OKH announced that it would conduct a series of 'war games' to test the Army Group A plan. On 7 and 14 February the 'war games' revealed that an attack through the Ardennes was in fact a tenable proposition. General Halder, the OKH chief of staff, remained cautious, but he was slowly beginning to accept the idea that only this plan could provide Germany with a battle-winning formula to knock out the Allies in one blow.

ABOVE
An attempt to improve inter-Allied co-operation: a French delegation leaves 10 Downing Street in London, led by Admiral Darlan (left) and General Gamelin (centre).

A fortuitous circumstance of Manstein's posting was an opportunity to meet Hitler. Before taking up senior appointments, it was common for generals to have informal meetings with the Führer, and on 17 January a group of corps commanders, including Manstein, were summoned to the Chancellery. Manstein was invited to discuss his plan, which immediately met with Hitler's approval. The drive through the Ardennes was a risky undertaking, but with the prospect of it destroying the bulk of the Allied armies it appealed to Hitler's gambling instinct. Moreover, it confirmed his own intuitive belief in an attack through southern Belgium. The next morning, Hitler summoned Brauchitsch and Halder to Berlin, where he outlined his new plan (conveniently omitting Manstein's role in its authorship). The OKH leaders had already began to back the idea of a thrust through southern Belgium, and now endorsed Hitler's proposal. They returned to

OKH headquarters at Zossen and began to draw up a new directive incorporating the Army Group A plan.

The new directive was issued on 24 February and reassigned the weight of the attack away from Bock's Army Group B to Rundstedt's Army Group A. Although reduced from 43 to 29 and a half divisions, Army Group B was still vital to the success of the operation, as its advance would draw the best Allied forces into northern Belgium and Holland, and away from the main blow to be struck by Army Group A in the south. Army Group A now had a strength of 45 and a half divisions, which included the bulk of Germany's panzer and motorised formations. Once through the Allied defences, the massed armour of Army Group A would drive to the English Channel, cutting the Allies in two. The plan was called *Sichelsschnitt* (Sickle Cut), reflecting the intended scythe-like nature of the German drive across northern France.

BELOW

Gun apertures in one of the forts of the Maginot Line. The French defences were very powerful, but failed to take into account Germany's willingness to violate Dutch and Belgian neutrality, and thus their ability to outflank the line's defences.

The plan had an added advantage: once the breakthrough had been made, the Allies would be unaware of the direction of the main thrust, which might be directed southwards to outflank the forces guarding the Maginot Line, or might be towards Paris, or even due north onto the Belgian plain.

On the Allied side, France was the senior partner in the alliance and its views dominated Allied strategic thinking. General Maurice Gamelin was the chief of the general staff and, once war was declared, he assumed the post of supreme commander of all French land forces. One of Joffre's most brilliant staff officers during World War I, Gamelin was an intellectual general who lacked the ability to inspire his subordinates and impose his will on the French army. The French politician Paul Reynaud summed up Gamelin's character in these damning words: 'He might be all right as a prefect of a bishop, but he is not a leader of men.'

The almost monastic atmosphere that Gamelin fostered at his headquarters at Vincennes, just outside Paris, was described by Charles de Gaulle, then a maverick colonel in the French mechanised forces: '[He] dwelt in an atmosphere very akin to that of a convent, surrounded by a few officers, working and meditating, completely insulated from current events. General Gamelin gave me the impression of a savant testing the chemical reaction of his strategy in a laboratory.'

French military organisation

Gamelin's isolation from everyday military events was compounded by the overly complex chain of command which acted to shackle military efficiency. As Gamelin was responsible for all French military commitments – which included the colonies – his orders to the armies in northeast France (the key sector) were issued through General Georges, who acted as Gamelin's deputy. Under Georges was General Billotte, the commander of Army Group Number 1, whose line of responsibility stretched from the Channel to the Maginot Line. Although Georges was considered to be an able commander, his effectiveness was undermined by poor health and by his choice of headquarters some 65km (40 miles) away from Paris at La

ABOVE
French artillery fires from armoured cupolas within the Maginot Line. Only a direct hit from heavy artillery would be capable of destroying guns as well-protected as these.

Ferté-sous-Jouarre. But making matters even worse, a new intermediary link in the command chain between Gamelin and Georges was created with the institution of a GHQ Land Forces at Montry – half way between La Ferté-sous-Jouarre and Vincennes – under General Aimé Doumenc.

The French air force, commanded by General Vuillemin, was supposed to cooperate closely with the ground forces, each zone of Air Operations corresponding to an army group. In practice, however, the French air force high command – which reported directly to the minister of national defence – could adopt its own policies. Although the key problem facing the French air force in 1940 was a chronic shortage of suitable aircraft, it also lacked the proper degree of inter-service integration that would protect the ground formations from the attentions of the Luftwaffe.

Whereas the German high command (and subordinate formations) made full use of specialised telephone lines, telexes and encoded radio transmissions, the French high command contented itself with an unreliable telephone network and despatch riders. German commanders were used to receiving information swiftly – and acting on it swiftly. By contrast, the slow and uncertain pace of the French communication system was matched by the leisurely pace of command decision-making, which could take days to complete and implement.

Allied cooperation

The failings evident within the organisation of the French high command were only a part of the overall Allied command weakness. The Germans were able to act as a unified national organisation; the Allies comprised several disparate states with differing national agendas. Anglo–French cooperation was generally good, although the French complained, with some justification, of the slowness of British mobilisation. But while sympathetic towards France and Britain, the attitudes of the Dutch and Belgians caused special problems for the alliance.

French Hotchkiss H-35 light tanks at a parade. They would have made useful reconnaissance vehicles, but instead were too often shackled to infantry formations where they were largely ineffective.

The Netherlands had a long tradition of neutrality, and while fearful of German intentions, it did not want to enter into binding agreements with other powers. Belgium had been part of a defensive pact with France until 1936, when the country returned to the position of strict neutrality it had adopted prior to the German invasion of 1914. Despite the fact that Belgium was almost certain to be invaded by Germany in the event of hostilities, King Leopold III hoped that a public declaration of neutrality would avoid provoking the Germans. The only understanding that existed between France and Belgium was that if Germany attacked then French troops would be allowed to advance into Belgium. While the French wished to develop a full military partnership with the Belgians – if only to agree on mutual dispositions – their requests were repeatedly turned down by the Belgian Government.

The French (and Allied) strategy was almost totally defensive, reflecting the French reaction to World War I. The French were determined to avoid the terrible casualties that had bled the country white during 1914–18 (mainly caused by reckless offensive action), and wished to avoid French soil again becoming the battlefield. In 1939, the number of men available to serve in the French armed forces had been reduced by 300,000 when compared to the 1914 figure, while Nazi Germany could call on far greater numbers than had been possible during World War I. Understandably, this growing discrepancy in numbers encouraged the French to be cautious in husbanding their human resources and avoiding costly attacks.

On a tactical level, the French response to the carnage of the Western Front was to emphasise firepower and downplay mobility, and this doctrine was reflected in the construction of massive fortifications and the deployment of slow-moving armies dependent on the application of heavy artillery. One other consequence of World War I was the complacency the hard-won Allied victory produced in the French high command. The Germans agonised over the reasons for their defeat, but the response of the French generals was simply that they had beaten the Germans in 1918 and would do so again.

The French belief in defence saw its fullest expression in the Maginot Line, begun in

One of the men upon whom the main weight of the German offensive would fall: a private in the French Army. His red collar patches and blue-black kepi identify him as a member of the 182nd Artillery Regiment. The badge on his upper left arm denotes his role as an armourer.

ABOVE

The crew of a French light anti-aircraft gun. The French Army was woefully short of both anti-aircraft and anti-tank weapons, and consequently were unable to counter the attacks by German aircraft and tanks.

1929 and named after the defence minister of the time. The fortifications were a triumph of military engineering: vast, largely subterranean concrete structures complete with artillery of all calibres and underground accommodation for the defenders. Although the French Government claimed that the Line could repel any attack, other observers were less impressed. Lieutenant General Alan Brooke, then a corps commander in the BEF, wrote that the Maginot Line reminded him of a vast battleship, but one which gave him little comfort: 'The most dangerous aspect is the psychological one: a sense of false security

is engendered, a feeling of sitting behind an impregnable iron fence; and should the defence perchance be broken, the French fighting spirit might be well brought crumbling with it.'

The other failing of the Maginot Line lay in the fact that it was uncompleted in 1940. The defences along the Franco–Belgian border were rudimentary and basic compared to those of the Maginot Line, although this did not greatly trouble General Gamelin, the French commander, for it was inside Belgium that he hoped to do battle when the German eventually attacked.

Allied planning

The original Allied plan – issued on 24 October 1939 – called for a limited advance into Belgium by several divisions of the French army (plus BEF) to adopt a defensive position along the River Escaut (or Scheldt), running from Antwerp to Ghent. Once there, they would await the onslaught of the German invasion. Although prudent from a military perspective, the line covered only a small area of Belgium, leaving Brussels and the majority of the country (and the bulk of the Belgian army) to be overrun. Gamelin – ever mindful of his numerical inferiority – was eager to make effective use of the Belgian army's 22 infantry divisions, and consequently suggested a deeper Allied advance to new positions on the River Dyle, which would now stretch from Antwerp to Dinant on the River Meuse.

The Dyle Plan – adopted on 15 November – had the advantages of forming a shorter line, protecting Brussels and improving the chances of a link-up with the main Belgian army when it fell back from its defences along the Albert Canal to the east. Although General Georges expressed reservations about advancing further into Belgium, the British supported the Dyle Plan because it would deny the Belgian coastal area to the German navy and air force, and thus hinder their operations against Britain.

Once the Dyle Plan was in place, Gamelin expressed a wish to increase the numbers of troops employed in the venture, and make provisions to help the Dutch around Breda. This was a fundamental change to the plan – although it was known just as the 'Breda Variant' – and was bitterly opposed by Georges. He pointed out to Gamelin that such a proposal would leave the central sector of the French front line dangerously short of reserves should the Germans attack in that area. In the event, he would be proved right.

Gamelin's belief in the amendment wavered for a time, but the revelations supplied by the documents found on the German staff officer after the Mechelen incident hardened the French supreme commander's resolve that the Netherlands should be defended. On 20 March 1940, the new orders for the Dyle-Breda Plan were authorised and approved by both the French and British Governments.

BELOW

British troops prepare their tanks for combat training. All armoured vehicles demanded a great deal of logistical support, including large quantities of fuel.

French deployment

The original Dyle Plan had called for just 10 French divisions (plus the BEF); the new Dyle-Breda Plan added a further 20 French divisions to the advance into Belgium and Holland. In an army of very variable quality, these divisions represented the cream of the French armed forces, including the bulk of its mechanised formations – all three Light Mechanised Divisions (DLMs), five out of the seven motorised divisions and two of the three armoured divisions. The seven high-quality divisions of the French Seventh Army (General Giraud) were taken out of the general reserve and posted to the extreme left flank of the Allied line, with the aim of racing through Belgium to reach the Dutch around Breda. Giraud complained to his army group commander, General Billotte, of the difficulties he faced, especially in the light of German air superiority. Giraud was joined by other dissenting voices, but the arguments against the plan were not pushed with sufficient conviction and the Dyle–Breda Plan remained in being.

French reserves

Another disturbing feature of the French deployment was the large number of forces deployed to defend the Maginot Line. Besides the garrison, there were a further 30 divisions stationed directly behind the Line. As a consequence, Gamelin's strategic reserve consisted of just 10 divisions, and of these only one was an armoured division with the mobility and firepower to make a significant difference should the invading Germans manage to break through the Allied defences.

The disparity between the German and Allied commanders was demonstrated in their respective reactions to the Polish campaign. Despite having won such a swift and comprehensive victory, the German army conducted thorough evaluations of the performance of their troops, weapons and equipment. The four light divisions were found to be deficient in tanks and were uprated as panzer divisions, while the motorised divisions lost one of their infantry regiments, as an excess of infantry made them unwieldy in action. The panzer divisions had

RIGHT

British troops relax on the beach after an inspection by King George VI. Although the quality of British troops sent to France was generally high, the British Army as a whole was not trained for modern warfare.

ABOVE

General Georges (centre), the French commander-in-chief of the Northeast Front, inspects a unit of British infantrymen, accompanied by the commander of the British Expeditionary Force, Lord Gort (right).

proved themselves to be highly effective, although General Guderian recommended that forward divisional headquarters be made small and more mobile so that they could keep up with the attack. As suspected, the performance of the PzKpfw I and II tanks was found wanting, and production of the heavier PzKpfw III and IV tanks was increased. The flat trajectory of tank guns was found to be useful when firing into the embrasures of bunkers and other concrete fortifications, while the powerful 8.8cm anti-aircraft gun could also smash through any tank armour, and thus perform a dual role.

Although largely confined to the tactical level, the rigour of the German army's self-scrutiny reflected a genuine self-confidence that was manifestly lacking on the Allied side. One of the sad ironies of the French army in 1939-40 was the presence of many intelligent, far-sighted officers in so moribund an organisation. Although they pressed for reform, their voices were largely unheard. French observers present in Poland in September 1939 sent back detailed reports of the German victory, and correctly deduced the reasons for German success.

French analysis of the blitzkrieg

A senior French air force officer, General Armenguad, made a detailed analysis of the new blitzkrieg strategy. He wrote: 'The German system consists essentially of making a breach in the front with armour and aircraft, then to throw mechanised and motorised columns into the breach to beat them down to right and left in order to keep enlarging it, at the same time as armoured detachments, guided, protected and reinforced by aircraft, advance in the front of the supporting divisions in such a way that the defence's manoeuvrability is reduced to impotence.'

Armengaud made his report directly to Gamelin, and presciently informed his commander-in-chief that the Germans would attack in the centre of the French front line, and that such a breach could be made within 48 hours. Gamelin, however, refused to accept

RIGHT

*British tank men swab out
the barrel of a tank while on
manoeuvres. The British
were pitifully short of tanks
in 1939, and were unable to
contribute a single armoured
division to France's defence.
The British armoured
component within the BEF
consisted of a few tank
brigades.*

OPPOSITE

*A scene beloved of British
war photographers: a crowd
of cheering Tommies. These
troops are advancing
through France to take up
positions on the front line.*

the truth of such reasoning, and Armenguad was relegated to a desk job as punishment for his honest assessment. Perhaps the most telling example of the French high command's almost wilful blindness to the realities of war came from General Keller, who, as inspector general of tanks, was France's senior tank officer. Replying to a memorandum sent by Colonel de Gaulle on the danger posed by a German breakthrough, he calmly wrote: 'Even supposing that the present fortified line were breached or outflanked, it does not appear that our opponents will find a combination of circumstances as favourable for blitzkrieg as in Poland. One can see, then, that in future operations the primary role of the tank will be the same as in the past: to assist the infantry in reaching successful objectives.'

Armoured warfare pioneers, such as de Gaulle and Guderian, realised that an integrated armoured force of tanks and motorised infantry and artillery was the key to success on the battlefield. In the west, in 1940,

Germany deployed 10 panzer divisions supported by seven motorised infantry divisions; these formations would act as the cutting edge of the German attack. The Allied armoured formations on mainland Europe consisted of a British tank brigade and the French army's three armoured divisions (with a fourth undergoing formation), plus three light mechanised divisions and seven motorised infantry divisions. In purely numerical terms, the Allies were able to deploy slightly more tanks than the Germans (approximately 3000 French and 300 British against Germany's total of less than 3000) but most of them were distributed amongst the infantry in small penny packets where they could make little impact on the large German armoured formations.

German organisation

As in Poland, the bulk of the German army was provided by the infantry (out of 136 divisions allotted to the campaign in the west, 118

were infantry) who comprised a mix of regular and reserve formations. The 30 well-trained and well-equipped regular infantry divisions of the First Wave would do the bulk of the fighting, supported by the Second and Third Waves, while the 'replacement' and 'territorial reserve' divisions would follow behind to mop up any remaining opposition. The German army of 1940 was not composed of the 'supermen' depicted in the propaganda newsreels; like other armies it was a army of variable quality. A major difference between the Germans and the French lay in the deployment of their formations, so that when the fighting commenced, low-grade French units found themselves overwhelmed by the battle-hardened best of the German army.

In addition to the forces provided by the army, the Germans also deployed two new types of military unit. Organised and controlled by the Luftwaffe was an airborne division, an elite body of troops trained in parachute and glider operations, who would be used with brilliant success in the Low Countries. The SS had sent some of its troops to fight in Poland, and despite protests from the army, the Waffen-SS (Fighting-SS) was expanded to become a sizeable force for the campaign in the west. Dedicated to the Nazi ideal, the Waffen-SS was able to recruit troops of high calibre (and obtain the latest German equipment), although at this early stage of the war the SS units lacked the tactical finesse of the regular army.

The French army committed a total of 94 divisions to the Western Front, which included 63 infantry divisions. Of these, just under half were regular divisions, which were raised from well-trained troops well-equipped with artillery. The others – reserve divisions – were divided into low-grade A and B formations, the latter being particularly poorly armed, equipped and trained. The pacifism that had been such a feature of French society in the inter-war years was reflected in the attitude of many of the reserve divisions; most men had little idea of why they were at war, and even less had much inclination to do any real fighting.

Allied readiness

The months of inactivity between the outbreak of war and the onset of the German offensive had done much to corrode the spirit of the French army. The inactivity, false alarms and bad winter weather took their toll of the already shaky resolve of the ordinary French soldier. Chronic absences of leave by both officers and men, poor discipline and a dangerously high level of drunkenness were some of the symptoms of this malaise. As early as November 1939, General Brooke had been profoundly disturbed at the turn-out of an honour guard of General Corap's Ninth Army (one of the armies that would face the brunt of the German attack through the Ardennes). Brooke later described the march past:

I can still see the troops now. Seldom have I seen anything more slovenly and badly turned-out. Men unshaven, horses ungroomed, clothes and saddlery that did not fit, vehicles dirty, and complete lack of pride in themselves or their units. What shook me most, however, was the look in the men's faces, disgruntled and insubordinate looks, and, although ordered to give 'Eyes left', hardly a man bothered to do so.

The British Expeditionary Force (BEF) was a generally high-grade force, but its total of just 10 infantry divisions (plus an armoured brigade) was a poor numerical response to the gravity of the situation. France had mobilised one man in eight, while Britain had responded with only one man in forty. Under the command of General Lord Gort, the BEF had the distinction of being a fully motorised formation, the first army to be such, which gave it a mobility denied to other armies – even the mighty Wehrmacht relied heavily on horses. German intelligence provided an accurate picture of its strengths and weaknesses, noting that its commanders lacked flexibility but praising the quality of the troops: 'The regular divisions will fight bravely. Their resilience in face of losses and reverses must be rated high.'

Both the Belgian and Dutch armies were made up almost entirely of infantry and lacked the ability to initiate offensive action. The Dutch army had no experience of modern warfare (it had fought its last war as long ago as 1830) and its 11 divisions relied upon defensive fortifications deep within Holland to slow any German advance. The Belgian army had experience from the previous world war, but the quality of its arms and equipment – and its leadership – had progressed little since 1918. Although able to mobilise up to 700,000 men (of which 375,000 were in place in 1940), the Belgians put far too great a reliance on their fortifications along the Albert Canal defence line.

In terms of its land forces, the German superiority over the Allies was not so much a material one, but lay in superior organisation and planning. In the air, however, the Germans had the edge over their opponents in almost every way. The Luftwaffe had at its disposal two air fleets of 1000 fighters, 1550 bombers, 350 dive-bombers and 400 reconnaissance aircraft. The French air force comprised 700 fighters, 150 bombers and 350 reconnaissance aircraft. The RAF in France had 130 fighters and 270 bomber and reconnaissance aircraft (although it did have access to aircraft based in Britain). Thus, the Germans had over 3000 first-line aircraft to pit against an Allied total of approximately 1700. Moreover, the German models were superior to their Allied counterparts, with the exception of the few British-based squadrons of Spitfires which were a match for the German Bf-109 fighters. Organisationally, the Luftwaffe was far superior to the Allied air forces, and the experience of the Polish campaign had only further strengthened a superb fighting machine.

The phoney war

The eight months between the declaration of war and the German offensive in the west was a bizarre period of the war. At sea and in Poland, the war was real enough, but on the Western Front nothing seemed to happen. Commentators of the time began to label this period the Sitzkrieg, the *drôle de guerre*, or, most memorably, the 'phoney war'. Fraternisation between German and Allied soldiers became commonplace, and an aggressive attitude towards the enemy was generally

ABOVE
Although the British Army had introduced the cheap and easy-to-produce battledress in 1937, the old World War I khaki service dress continued to be worn as late as 1940, as shown here by a sergeant in the Welsh Guards.

frowned upon by troops at the front, who wanted to avoid any disruption of their routines. A British war correspondent visited a section of the French front line, and on asking a soldier why he did not fire on German troops making themselves conspicuously visible across no man's land, received the reply: 'If we fire they will fire back.'

One of the salient features of the phoney war was the absence of serious aerial activity. Before the war, the populations of the European nations had been warned of the terrible consequences of the bombing raids that would immediately follow the declaration of war. Fearful of the consequences of initiating a bombing war, the air commanders held back from full-scale action, and con-

tented themselves with dropping vast quantities of propaganda material over enemy cities.

The British were early converts to this painless alternative to genuine conflict, and on 3 September the RAF dropped six million leaflets (weighing over 13 tons) on Germany which informed the people of the 'wickedness' of their rulers. Other similar raids followed in what became known as the 'confetti war'. While these raids proved popular with politicians, the more serious amongst the RAF command openly disparaged them. Air Vice Marshal Harris summed up the whole campaign in a postwar comment: 'My personal view is that the only thing achieved was largely to supply the Continent's supply of toilet paper for the five long years of war.'

LEFT
Bren carriers transport British troops up to the front line in France. Although the British Army was deficient in armour, it was the only force in Europe to be fully mechanised and not rely on horses for transport.

The only effective propaganda came from Germany, where leaflets and radio broadcasts received a sympathetic hearing from many disenchanted French troops in the front line. The main thrust of the German propaganda was to question why the French were at war at all, and to spread distrust of the British, the 'perfidious Albion' which was prepared to sacrifice the last Frenchman for its own purposes. Enemy propaganda generally has little effect on a confident army (or population), but much of the French army of 1940 was open to such persuasion. The idea that British soldiers were making free with French womanhood, while the French soldiers were stranded on the front line, was a popular propaganda theme, although sometimes such schemes went awry. A British officer related how a German propaganda unit erected a vast sign on the front line declaring: 'Soldiers of the Northern Provinces, the British are sleeping with your wives and raping your daughters!' The French troops on the other side quickly hoisted their own hoarding: 'We don't give a bugger, we're from the South!'

While a few thought that the phoney war might go on for ever, as the cold weather of the exceptionally severe 1939–40 winter receded, the prospect of real action began to weigh on the minds of the opposing commanders. For the Allies, it was a question of when and where the long-awaited German onslaught would finally come. Hitler had considered a date in March or April as suitable, but his attention was diverted, and Operation Yellow was postponed again until events in Scandinavia had reached a satisfactory conclusion.

CHAPTER FOUR

HITLER
STRIKES NORTH

While the bulk of the Allies' armed forces waited for a German attack in France, Hitler decided on a bold move north to secure the ports and natural resources of Denmark and Norway.

The spread of the war to Scandinavia came about as a consequence of two separate factors: the export of iron ore from Sweden to Germany via Narvik, and the naval possibilities offered by Norway's geographical position. The bulk of Sweden's iron ore was transhipped from northern Sweden across the Norwegian border to the port of Narvik, which had the advantage of being ice-free all year round (unlike the other iron-ore port of Lulea on the Baltic) but was vulnerable to outside interference. An armed seizure of Norway offered the Germans a means of establishing naval bases which could 'outflank' Britain, whose own position on the western approaches to Europe acted to block Germany's access to the North Atlantic.

But to the conservatively minded Admiral Raeder, commander-in-chief of the German navy, this was a risky option, and on balance he considered it would be better to respect Norway's neutrality. The British, too, were generally in favour of leaving Scandinavia out of the war. If neither side abrogated Norwegian neutrality then all would be well; but if one side acted unilaterally it would steal a march over the other and so improve its strategic position. Thus, there was always the temptation for one side to strike first, if only to forestall the other and secure the Norwegian resources for themselves.

The impetus to interfere in Norwegian affairs came first from Winston Churchill, at that time the First Lord of the Admiralty. He chafed at the inaction of the phoney war and wished to prosecute the conflict as aggressively as possible, regardless of Norwegian neutrality. As early as 29 September 1939, Churchill had proposed that the British Government agree to his suggestion that iron ore shipments via Narvik should be stopped by mining Norwegian coastal waters. Although the Cabinet turned down his request, Churchill continued to press for action. German intelligence became aware of British interest in Norway, and passed on the information to Raeder who in turn warned Hitler on 10 October. Hitler was then preoccupied with plans for the invasion in the west, and had little time to spare for Norway, but over the succeeding months events were to force him to consider armed intervention in northern Europe.

The Finno–Soviet war
The invasion of Finland by the Soviet Union on 30 November 1939 further increased the interest of the major powers in Scandinavian matters. Despite some natural sympathy towards the Finns, the Germans were bound by the terms of the Nazi–Soviet Pact and were unable to act on their behalf. The Allies,

Part of the Finnish capital of Helsinki in flames, following a Soviet bombing raid in the Winter War of 1939–40. As Helsinki was so close to the Finnish-Soviet border, it was vulnerable to air attack, a factor of great strategic importance which helped bring the Finns to the negotiating table.

however, were drawn towards helping Finland. British public sentiment backed the 'gallant Finns', and the French looked favourably on any means of fighting a war outside the confines of France itself after her experiences in 1914–18.

Somewhat cynically, Churchill saw Allied intervention on the Finnish side as a means of cutting off German iron ore supplies from Sweden and, if possible, bringing Norway and Sweden into the Allied fold. He proposed sending a force to Finland via Narvik and northern Sweden, but both Norway and Sweden wisely declined the Allied overtures for military involvement. Other similar plans were in the process of being put forward by the Allies when, on 13 March, the Finns asked the Soviet Union for an armistice. The opportunity gone, any Allied plans for intervention were shelved.

Hitler eyes Norway

Raeder, meanwhile, began to consider the consequences of Allied intervention, and on 11 December 1939 he brokered a meeting between Hitler and Vidkun Quisling, a mentally unbalanced Norwegian right-wing politician. Quisling told Hitler that the Norwegian Government was effectively

under British control, but that as the leader of a national socialist party he could, with German help, take over Norway for the Nazi cause. Although Hitler was sceptical of Quisling's claims, he nonetheless ordered OKW to make a preliminary study of the possibility of mounting a German invasion of Norway in the near future.

During February 1940, the German supply ship *Altmark* was observed sailing through Norwegian coastal waters en route to Germany from the Atlantic. On board the *Altmark* were 299 British prisoners of war who had been taken from ships sunk by the commerce raider *Graf Spee*. On direct orders from Churchill, the British destroyer *Cossack* closed in on the *Altmark*. On 16 February, British sailors boarded the German ship, and in a daring feat of arms successfully released the prisoners. The Norwegians were understandably angry at this flagrant breach of neutrality, but the biggest outcry came from Germany. Hitler was furious at this 'bloody nose' inflicted on him by the Royal Navy, and it was this incident that proved to be the final straw in pushing him towards military action. On 19 February he authorised Operation Weser (*Weserübung*), the code name for the invasion of Norway.

The invasion was to be an exclusive OKW operation, and General Nikolaus von Falkenhorst was assigned responsibility for the planning. Both OKH and the Luftwaffe objected to what they considered to be a strategic sideshow, draining resources from the coming attack in the west, but Hitler was now committed to the plan and insisted that it go through with the utmost speed.

Norway's population comprised just three million people, and its armed forces were small and lacking in modern weapons and equipment. The main problem for the German planners was the country's mountainous terrain and relatively poor overland communications, which could dangerously slow the German advance and thereby allow British naval forces to interfere with the seaborne landings. Speed and surprise were imperative, and for any chance of success, the Germans would need to rely on the close working of the army, navy and air force in combined amphibious and airborne landings throughout Norway.

As Falkenhorst's staff finalised their objectives, it became clear that to provide air cover for the amphibious landings in Norway, Germany would have to take control of the Danish airfields at Aalborg in northern Jutland. Consequently, the operation was extended to include the invasion and conquest of Denmark.

The first stage of the German plan was based on the swift capture of Oslo and the other major urban areas of southern Norway, while other forces would sail further north to capture Trondheim and Narvik. The second stage would comprise a German thrust from central Norway to meet up with the isolated troops in the north, and then repel any landings made by the Allies. Six divisions (one mountain, five infantry) were assigned to the operation, supported by a sizeable air force component (including airborne troops) and virtually the entire German navy (a further two infantry divisions were considered sufficient to overcome Denmark).

German invasion plans

The five-pronged amphibious attack would land around 10,000 German troops in the first phase of the operation. Group 1 (10

BELOW
A soldier of the Red Army frozen to death during fighting in southern Finland. Soviet forces were poorly prepared for the conflict and suffered heavy casualties as a result.

destroyers, plus the battlecruisers *Gneisenau* and *Scharnhorst*) was assigned the most dangerous task: the capture of Narvik, while Group 2 (four destroyers and the heavy cruiser *Hipper*) would sail for Trondheim. Further south, Group 3 (the light cruisers *Köln* and *Königsberg*, plus two naval auxiliary ships and torpedo boats) would attack Bergen. Group 4 (the light cruiser *Karlsruhe* and torpedo boats) was responsible for securing Kristiansand, and Group 5 (the heavy cruiser *Blücher*, pocket battleship *Lützow*, light cruiser *Emden* and other light craft) would sail up the Oslofjord towards the Norwegian capital. The Luftwaffe was to provide air support over southern Norway, as well as securing Stavanger and Oslo airport through airborne landings. On 2 April 1940, Hitler

BELOW
A Danish soldier wearing the obsolete 1915 pattern wool uniform and armed with an 8mm M1889/10 rifle. He is a member of the Jutland Division. The Danish forces were too small and unprepared to offer the Germans any serious resistance, and the country fell quickly after a rapid German advance.

authorised the invasion for a week's time, and early on the 7th the first German warships steamed out of their harbours bound for the Norwegian coast.

On the other side of the North Sea, Churchill had finally convinced the British War Cabinet to allow the mining of the Norwegian coastal waters, known as 'leads'. On 5 April, the British instructed Norway and Sweden of their intentions at the same time as a naval force steamed out from Scapa Flow. Eight destroyers were despatched to mine the approaches to Narvik, while a smaller force would lay a mine field in the leads between Trondheim and Bergen (a third dummy field would be laid outside Trondheim). The battle cruiser *Renown* (and four destroyers) would support the Narvik force. In addition, several battalions of infantry were embarked on transports in readiness for any German attack on Norway that might follow the British mining of the Norwegian leads, but they were instructed to remain in port until the German attack materialised.

The British fleet sails

During 7 April the British made several sightings of German ships steaming northwards but they were unsure of their intentions; the general consensus was that this might be an attempt to break out into the North Atlantic. On the evening of the 7th, the British Home Fleet slipped anchor at Scapa Flow and began to steam towards Norway to intercept the German ships. Commanded by Admiral Sir Charles Forbes, the Home Fleet amounted to

two battleships, one battlecruiser, four cruisers and 21 destroyers – a considerable force in purely naval terms, but one deficient in the anti-aircraft component essential in the 'narrow waters' off Norway.

During the evening the weather deteriorated and severe gales flung the German vessels of Groups 1 and 2 into disarray, the destroyers desperately attempting to keep stationed with the larger escort ships. The heavy seas damaged the speeding destroyers, and the soldiers – who were packed on the decks – began to be washed overboard.

Early on 8 April, German destroyers sighted an unknown vessel which turned out to be the *Glowworm*, one of *Renown*'s escort destroyers. The *Glowworm* gave chase and exchanged fire with a German destroyer. Meanwhile, the *Hipper*, which had turned back to help the German destroyer, opened fire on the *Glowworm*, straddling it with its opening salvo. The *Glowworm* promptly laid a smoke screen and seemed to be about to retreat.

However, the *Glowworm*'s captain, Lieutenant-Commander Roope, realising he would have difficulty escaping from the German battlecruiser, decided to ram the *Hipper*, which had by now followed the *Glowworm* into the smoke. Both ships only glimpsed each other through the smoke and heavy seas for a few seconds at close range, and the *Glowworm* caught the *Hipper* on the starboard side. The *Hipper* suffered heavy damage, but as the destroyer passed by the German ship it caught fire and promptly sank.

German paratroopers land in the snowy wastes of northern Norway. This was the first campaign in which airborne forces were successfully used to seize key objectives behind enemy lines.

The true intention of the Germans became clear later on 8 April when a Polish submarine (attached to the Royal Navy after Poland's surrender in 1939) torpedoed and sank a German troopship. The survivors explained to their Norwegian rescuers that they were on their way to Bergen as part of an invasion force to 'save' Norway from the British. The information was passed to the British by the Norwegian authorities. This confirmed the increasing number of British sightings of a large German maritime force. But the Home Fleet had sailed too far south to intercept the German naval groups, which were now closing in on their respective targets on the Norwegian coast.

The Germans take Narvik

Early on 9 April, as the 10 destroyers of Group 1 entered the Ofotfjord leading to Narvik, its escorts *Gneisenau* and *Scharnhorst* steamed northwest to the relative safety of the open ocean, briefly exchanging fire with *Renown* (which had been protecting the British mine-laying force). The battered German destroyers – their crews and military complement recovering from their ordeal in the North Sea – sailed up the fjord to sight the Norwegian defences at Narvik. The German flotilla commander, Commodore Paul Bonte, and Major General Eduard Dietl (GOC the 3rd Mountain Division), called upon the captain of the ageing Norwegian defence vessel *Eidsvoll* to surrender. The Norwegians refused and the Germans launched three torpedoes into the *Eidsvoll*. The explosions ripped the ship's hull apart, killing all but eight of its 182-man crew.

The German destroyers began to land the infantry, who were forced into action despite the aftereffects of dreadful seasickness. But after a short and sporadic engagement, Dietl managed to persuade the Narvik garrison commander to surrender the port. The Germans had secured their first and potentially most difficult objective with minimum bloodshed, although both Dietl and Bonte realised that British counter-measures would soon follow.

Led by *Hipper*, the destroyers of Group 2 had little difficulty in overwhelming the surprised Norwegian defenders in Trondheim. Further south in Bergen, surprise again came to the aid of the Germans, although the *Königsberg* and an auxiliary ship were damaged by shore batteries before the Germans managed to capture the city.

The airborne landings at Stavanger also proved successful, and the city was soon in German hands. At Kristiansand, the Germans were initially held at bay by coastal defences, but in a sea fog the German ships were confused for Allied vessels coming to the Norwegian's aid, and resistance was soon overcome once the Germans were ashore.

BELOW

German troops disembark in a Norwegian port with the Blücher *in the background. The Norwegian campaign was a triumph for German inter-arms cooperation.*

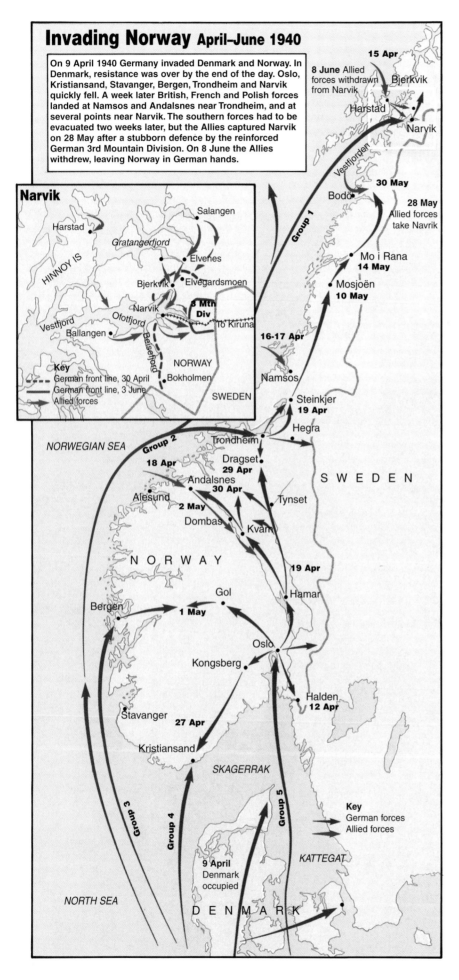

Invading Norway April–June 1940

On 9 April 1940 Germany invaded Denmark and Norway. In Denmark, resistance was over by the end of the day. Oslo, Kristiansand, Stavanger, Bergen, Trondheim and Narvik quickly fell. A week later British, French and Polish forces landed at Namsos and Andalsnes near Trondheim, and at several points near Narvik. The southern forces had to be evacuated two weeks later, but the Allies captured Narvik on 28 May after a stubborn defence by the reinforced German 3rd Mountain Division. On 8 June the Allies withdrew, leaving Norway in German hands.

Oslo resists

The attack by Group 5 on Oslo was to prove the most difficult. The *Blücher* was the lead vessel, spearheading the assault, and contained Vice Admiral Kummetz and a divisional general plus 1000 German infantry. As the ship passed the Oscarborg fortress, it was sunk by Norwegian torpedoes and gunfire. The other ships were forced to retreat. The air assault also ran into problems because of fog, and a recall message was sent out to the German aircraft. One group did not receive the message, however, and managed to land successfully at Oslo airport. Once the airport was in German hands, air reinforcements were rushed in, and by the afternoon of 9 April the Germans prepared to occupy the Norwegian capital.

The attack against Denmark on the other hand went almost like clockwork. Two German motorised brigades broke through the frontier defences early on 9 April and raced up the Jutland peninsula to reinforce the attack on the vital Aalborg airfields being carried out by paratroops and an air-landed battalion. German naval forces were responsible for securing the Danish islands. The ageing battleship *Schleswig–Holstein* (ironically named after former Danish territory taken by Germany in the 19th century) sailed into Copenhagen harbour and landed a battalion of infantry, while overhead the Luftwaffe threatened the Danish capital with air attack.

The Danes lacked the military resources to counter the German invasion, and within the space of just four hours the Danish Government asked the Germans for surrender terms. By the end of 9 April, German aircraft were already operating from Aalborg against targets in Norway.

Norwegian resistance

The Norwegians had rejected the German demand for immediate surrender, declaring: 'We will not submit voluntarily; the struggle is already in progress.' But the Norwegians faced a double-sided problem: not did they lack men and resources, but the sheer speed of the German attack had prevented the orderly mobilisation which was central to the Norwegian defensive strategy. Norway's six military districts were expected to deploy a brigade, which on full mobilisation would be increased to a division. During the first couple of day's fighting, Norwegian resistance was confused and often ineffectual, with some garrisons surrendering to the Germans with hardly a shot fired.

On 11 April, the Norwegian Government appointed Major General Otto Ruge as commander-in-chief. A resolute and capable soldier, Ruge set about organising Norwegian resistance, quelling any calls for capitulation and exhorting his troops to surround and pen-in the Germans holding Oslo and the other coastal enclaves. The new attitude was soon apparent in northern Norway when soldiers of the German 3rd Mountain Division found their way barred by Norwegian troops. In Trondheim, a Major Holterman gathered his forces into the Hegra fortifications and conducted a stiff defence against superior German forces that lasted until early May. Around Oslo, Norwegian troops set about constructing defences to prevent the Germans from breaking out into open country. But despite these positive measures, the only hope for the Norwegians in the long run lay in direct and timely military support from the French and British.

The British response

The British reaction to the German invasion was slow, confused and, too often, contradictory. Having missed the opportunity of catching the German naval forces sailing to Norway, the Admiralty ordered elements of the Home Fleet to attack the Germans off Bergen and Trondheim; but the order was subsequently cancelled and, as a result, time and opportunity were lost. Realising the need for naval aviation, the aircraft carrier *Furious* was despatched across the North Sea, but the order came through so quickly that the ship was unable to embark her fighter group. Even more farcical, the cruisers docked at Rosyth,

BELOW
Ducking away from the heat of the flames, German soldiers advance past a burning building in the Lillehammer region in Norway. After overcoming the shock of the German attack, the Norwegians fought back with determination, and the Germans had to fight hard to gain their objectives.

A lieutenant in the Norwegian Army, depicted here wearing the standard 1912 service dress for officers. Although he wears a grey-green kepi, *the most common head-dress was a soft field cap with matching peak and ear flaps. Various items of winter clothing could also be issued. The Norwegian troops in general fought well, but they were handicapped by the speed of the German attack.*

containing the infantry previously earmarked for service in Norway, were ordered to disembark their troops and rejoin the Home Fleet in the North Sea. During the opening stages of the campaign in Norway, the British prime minister, Neville Chamberlain, facetiously declared that 'Herr Hitler has missed the bus'. Nothing could have been further from the truth: while the Allied commanders prevaricated and debated possible courses of action, their German opposite numbers acted with speed and resolution.

At a tactical level, the British did score a few notable successes. The British submarine *Truant*, operating off Kristiansand, torpedoed the *Karlsruhe* on the night of 9 April and damaged it so badly that the Germans were forced to abandon ship. Other British submarines operating off Danish and Norwegian coastal waters sank several German troop and supply ships, and the *Spearfish* torpedoed and badly damaged the *Lützow*, although it was able to limp back to port. In the air, Fleet Air Arm Skua dive-bombers, flying at extreme range from Scapa Flow, managed to hit and sink the light cruiser *Königsberg*.

At the mouth of the fjord leading to Narvik, the commander of the British 2nd Destroyer Flotilla, Captain B.A.W. Warburton-Lee, wasted no time in taking the initiative. At dawn on 10 April, without waiting for reinforcements, he took his six destroyers to attack the 10 German destroyers further up the fjord. In the ensuing battle, two German destroyers were sunk and three others damaged, although both Warburton-Lee and Commander Bonte were killed. On 13 April, the second naval battle of Narvik took place when British destroyers and the battleship *Warspite* sailed up the fjord and sank the remaining German destroyers.

Moment of crisis

For the Germans in Narvik, the situation looked bleak. Dietl's troops were cut off from their support and a swift Allied landing could have turned the scales in their favour, as the Germans lacked sufficient troops and supplies to resist a properly mounted Allied attack. This was the moment when Hitler temporarily lost his nerve, and on 15 April he ordered Dietl to abandon Narvik and fall back on Trondheim, or, if the situation worsened, to retreat eastwards into Sweden and accept internment. But, fortunately for the Germans, the Allies yet again did not act decisively,

while a prescient German staff officer at OKW declined to send on Hitler's order to Dietl, which was subsequently quickly countermanded when the Führer had regained his nerve.

The British troops who had recently disembarked from their transports at Rosyth were now re-embarked and sent to sea to form the nucleus of a force to take Narvik from the Germans. On the morning of 15 April, the British 24th Guards Brigade landed at Harstad on the island of Hinnöy, but this position was separated from Narvik by a sea channel and a range of snow-covered mountains. Matters were made worse by disagreements between Admiral Lord Cork and Orrey, who were commanding the naval side of the expedition, and Major General P.J. Macksey, responsible for the land forces. Cork pressed for an immediate attack on Narvik,

but Macksey wished to pursue a slow approach which involved a steady build-up of forces to ensure success.

The British troops assigned to the operation also lacked the necessary equipment to fight a war in snow and mountain conditions, and this delay gave Dietl and his Germans valuable time to organise a defence of Narvik. Dietl enlisted the 2600 survivors from Bonte's destroyer flotilla and formed five 'mountain marine' battalions, armed with Norwegian weapons found in Narvik and the surrounding district. This German attitude of imaginative improvisation contrasted markedly with the hidebound decisions and tactics of the Allies in Norway.

The British obsession with Narvik alone was lifted when the strategic importance of Trondheim began to make itself felt. Not only would possession of Trondheim form a defen-sive barrier to any German attack against Narvik and northern Norway, it could form a springboard for a future Allied offensive southwards towards the Norwegian heartland. A new Allied plan was put forward to conduct a landing at Trondheim, supported by other landings at Namsos (to the north of Trondheim) and Andalsnes (to the south). On 19 April, the attack on Trondheim itself was called off because of fears of heavy losses from German air attack. Instead, the Allies would rely on just the two landings at Namsos and Andalsnes to secure Trondheim by a pincer attack.

On 16/17 April, the British 146th Brigade (Major General Adrian Carton de Wiart) and a demi-brigade of the French Chasseurs Alpins were landed at Namsos, while the first part of the 148th Brigade (Major General B.T.C. Paget) arrived at Andalsnes on the

ABOVE

German mountain infantry use inflatable craft to negotiate one of Norway's many fjords. The Germans had a long tradition of mountain warfare, and used their mountain troops to good effect in Norway.

18th. As at Narvik, the Allied forces were not suited to the type of warfare they were being expected to fight. The uncertainties over embarkation had caused the loading of supplies and equipment to be muddled. Even the Chasseurs Alpins, with their training in mountain warfare, lacked the right equipment, as the British commander of the 146th Brigade explained:

The French Chasseurs Alpins were a fine body of troops and would have been ideal for the job in hand, but ironically they lacked one or two essentials, which made them completely useless to us. I had wanted them to move forward, but General Audet [the French commander] regretted they had no means of transport, as their mules had not turned up. Then I suggested that his ski troops might move forward, but it was found that they were lacking some essential straps for their skis, without which they were unable to move.

The Germans consolidated their positions in Norway, and with the arrival of reinforcements began to move over to the attack. The area around Oslo was secured by the Germans between 12 and 15 April, who then began to push northwards towards Lillehammer, where General Ruge's Norwegians had prepared a rough and ready defensive line. The mountainous nature of the region dictated that the main lines of advance were to be focused on two valleys: the Gudbrandsdalen, which ran between Lillehammer and Andalsnes, and the Österdalen, which ran directly northwards towards Trondheim. The German commander in Norway, General Falkenhorst, gave orders for two battle groups to advance up the valleys, while the 2nd Mountain Division in Trondheim, which had been reinforced from the sea by the 181st Division, was to move over from the defensive and instigate offensive operations against Allied troops in the Trondheim region.

German strengths

While the Allies faced all the problems of divided commands and differing national objectives, the Germans were a fully balanced team with a single objective. And the Germans possessed the ace card of the campaign: command of the air in central Norway.

BELOW

French Chasseurs Alpins embark for Norway. High-quality troops, their mountain warfare skills proved very useful in Norwegian conditions.

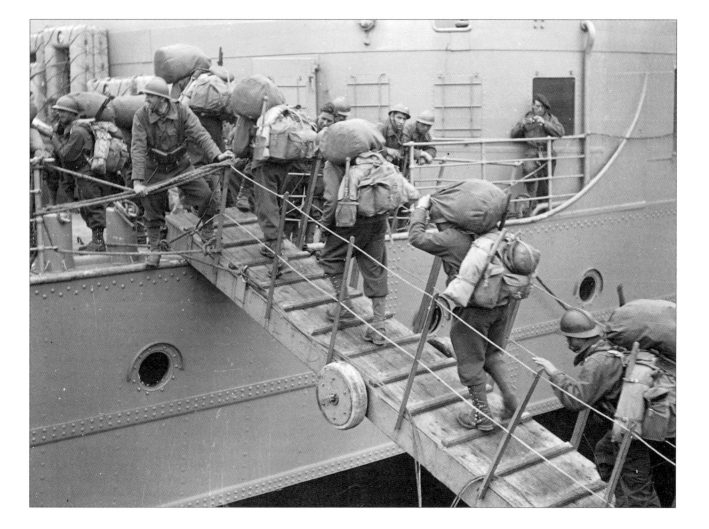

The Luftwaffe bombers harried the movement of the Allied troops, set fire to their depots and attacked their positions. Above all, the Luftwaffe kept up a non-stop offensive against British and French warships which, lacking sufficient anti-aircraft guns and ammunition, proved highly vulnerable in the narrow coastal waters around Norway, as they were unable to manoeuvre. German air superiority eventually made the ports of Namsos and Andalsnes virtually unusable, thereby preventing further Allied reinforcements from coming to the aid of the hard-pressed Norwegians.

Besides the conduct of offensive operations, the Luftwaffe had been indispensable in its logistical role, ferrying men, ammunition and equipment throughout Norway. The Junkers Ju-52 – the reliable workhorse of the Luftwaffe – flew over 3000 sorties in an airlift that transported 3000 troops, along with 2370 tons of supplies and 250,000 gallons of fuel, the largest ever aerial transport of men and material to date.

The Allies attempted to redress the aerial imbalance by the despatch of the aircraft carriers *Ark Royal* and *Glorious* (from the Mediterranean), and the despatch of a squadron of Gladiator aircraft. But they were too few in number and were dispersed over too wide a front to be an effective counter to the massed aircraft of Luftflotten 5.

Although the Germans met some determined Allied resistance during the offensive in central Norway, there could be little doubt of the overall outcome. On 21 April, Group Fischer launched its attack up the Österdalen, and by the 28th it had met up with German forces advancing south from Trondheim. Meanwhile, Group Pellengahr fought its way up the Gudbrandsdalen, forcing the combined Norwegian–British force to retreat back towards Andalsnes. On 28 April, in the light of these events, the Inter-Allied Supreme War Council decided to abandon central Norway to the Germans and concentrate all available forces against Narvik.

General Ruge took the Allied decision with good grace, although he was determined to carry on the fight against the Germans, even if Norway were overrun. King Haakon and the Norwegian Government (together with the nation's gold reserves) were evacuated to Tromsö in the far north. Also removed for safekeeping was the supply of 'heavy water' from the Rjukan factory, which had been bought by the French Government as a preliminary stage towards constructing a 'high-power bomb'.

The Allies land at Narvik

With the Allied evacuation of central Norway complete by 3 May, the Norwegian campaign entered its last act: the battle for Narvik.

Allied objectives had been narrowed down from 'saving' the whole of Norway to securing Narvik and blocking the iron-route from Sweden. Allied reinforcements, which included a substantial French presence, sailed northwards, while the command structure was finally overhauled: Admiral Cork was appointed overall Allied commander in the Narvik sector, and Macksey was replaced by Lieutenant General Claude Auchinleck.

The French 1st Chasseur Light Division (General Marie Emile Béthouart) was landed in the Narvik sector between 28 April and 7 May. The division comprised a demi-brigade of Chasseurs Alpins, a demi-brigade of the French Foreign legion and a demi-brigade of Carpathian Chasseurs (from Polish troops who had escaped to the West), plus a small allotment of artillery and light tanks.

On 13 May, General Béthouart ordered his troops to capture Bjerkvik, just outside Narvik. A battalion of the Foreign Legion and three French tanks were landed by British landing craft, supported by naval gunfire from British warships in position just off Narvik. This was the first time that specialised tank and infantry landing craft had been used in a combined amphibious operation (although over the next few years such operations would become commonplace in warfare across the world). The French tanks overran the German machine-gun positions, while

the legionnaires secured Bjerkvik and met up with local Norwegian soldiers.

German resistance

Dietl's position was looking increasingly desperate, although on 22 April he was reinforced by an air-dropped parachute battalion, and three days later a hastily-trained unit of mountain troops was also parachuted into the Narvik perimeter. Although useful and good for morale, these troops were insufficient in themselves to beat off the impending Allied attack; Dietl would have to await the arrival of ground troops from the south. The Germans had, in fact, made good progress in their northward march, Group Feuerstein capturing Mosjöen on 10 May and pressing on towards Bodö, the last important town before Narvik. There they were met by elements of the British 24th Brigade and Norwegian troops. While this force slowed the German advance, the experienced German mountain troops continued to force their way towards Narvik.

On 28 May, the Allies launched their attack on Narvik itself. Following a preliminary naval bombardment, troops from the Foreign Legion landed on the northern side of the Narvik peninsula in landing craft, followed by a combined Norwegian–French force in fishing boats. A German counter-attack on the landing zone was repulsed. The Allied troops fought their way along the peninsula, before expelling the Germans from the town of Narvik. General Béthouart prepared to exploit his advantage by pushing the Germans back towards the Swedish frontier and towards Norwegian forces, who would break up and disperse the retreating Germans. The Germans in Narvik faced almost total destruction by the Allies, but events outside this narrow sector were to rescue them.

The long-awaited German offensive in France and the Low Countries was proving disastrous for the Allies, and on 31 May the British Cabinet ordered Admiral Cork to withdraw from Narvik. On 1 June, Cork informed the Norwegian monarch of the Allied decision, and over the next few days the 25,000 men of the Allied expeditionary force to Norway were withdrawn to Scotland. King Haakon and his government also embarked for Britain and exile, leaving General Ruge, at his own request, to face the Germans. On 8 June, the last French and British troops left Norway; the following day armistice negotiations were instigated. On 10 June, Ruge signed the instrument of surrender, which allowed the Norwegian troops to disperse to their homes. Professional officers were given the same favour if they undertook not to take up arms against the Germans. Ruge refused and was imprisoned in Königstein castle.

Compared with other theatres of war, losses in the Norwegian campaign were light. German casualties totalled 5660 killed, wounded and missing, with 1317 killed on land and 2375 lost at sea. Norwegian casualties in killed and wounded totalled 1335; British killed and wounded and missing on land amounted to 1869 men, while the corresponding number for the Franco–Polish force came to 530 casualties.

The loss of the *Glorious*

The Allied withdrawal from Norwegian territory was not the end of the campaign,

BELOW
French Chasseurs Alpins look on as a British Blackburn Skua is prepared for takeoff on a frozen Norwegian lake. The arrival of these aircraft came too late to prevent Allied defeat in Norway.

BELOW

A French Chasseur Alpin, complete with full kit which includes a pair of skis (although they had little opportunity to use them in Norway). This over-burdened infantryman is armed with a pistol and a 7.5mm MAS carbine. He wears the blue chasseur beret whilst carrying his helmet in his hand.

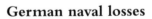

however. On 4 June, Admiral Raeder had ordered a naval sweep to attack Allied positions and shipping in and around Narvik. The German squadron consisted of the battle cruisers *Scharnhorst* and *Gneisenau*, the heavy cruiser *Hipper* and an escort of four destroyers under the command of Vice Admiral Wilhelm Marschall. After reaching the Narvik area, Marschall disregarded his original orders and decided to sail into deeper waters and destroy the Allied vessels making their withdrawal from Norway.

On the morning of 8 June, the German force surprised and sank a tanker and the empty liner *Orama*, although it spared the hospital ship *Atlantis* (which in turn observed the conventions of war by not reporting the Germans' position on its radio). Later on in the day, Marschall came upon British aircraft carrier *Glorious*, which inexplicably had no aircraft on patrol and was trapped by the rapidly advancing German ships. Opening fire at 28,000 yards, the *Scharnhorst* and *Gneisenau* scored hits with their opening salvoes and set the *Glorious* ablaze. The two destroyers escorting *Glorious, Acasta* and *Ardent* attempted to hold off the German battle cruisers, but were overwhelmed and sunk in turn. Before the *Acasta* went under, however, it launched a torpedo against Scharnhorst which killed 48 crewmen and caused severe damage. Despite the heroic efforts of the British destroyers, they were unable to prevent the *Glorious* from sinking, with British losses from this action amounting to 1515 men killed, with only 43 survivors.

German naval losses

The crippling of the *Scharnhorst* ended the German venture. *Hipper* had already been sent off to Trondheim to refuel, and *Scharnhorst* limped back to port. Marschall's display of initiative earned him a rebuke from Raeder, who had him replaced by Vice Admiral Lütjens. *Gneisenau* was detached to escort *Scharnhorst*, but on 23 June it was hit by a torpedo from the British submarine *Clyde*. Both battlecruisers were laid up in dock for several months. The heavy losses inflicted on the German navy were the one real consolation the Allies could take from this otherwise disastrous campaign. Ten destroyers and three cruisers had been sunk, while three other cruisers and two battlecruisers were laid up in dock for several months. These losses meant that the German navy would be able to play little part in the subsequent OKW plan to invade England after the fall of France.

Naval losses apart, the German invasion of Norway had been an almost complete success. In both the plan and its execution, the Germans had demonstrated their mastery of warfare in the three elements of land, sea and air, in marked contrast to the British, who had failed to look beyond their traditional single-service boundaries. Ominously, the campaign revealed to the Germans the shortcomings of

both the French and British armed forces. As German morale soared, so the Allied politicians bickered, the French being particularly insistent that the blame for the fiasco in Norway be laid at Britain's door.

One important political casualty of the Norwegian campaign was the British prime minister, Neville Chamberlain. The growing disquiet in Parliament over Chamberlain's handling of the war reached a head after the British withdrawal from Andalsnes and Namsos in early May. Although he survived a motion of censure on 8 May, it was obvious to Chamberlain that he had lost the confidence of Parliament, and accordingly he agreed to step down as premier.

By a strange irony, his successor was the man most responsible for British involvement in Norway. But Winston Churchill managed to avoid the fallout caused by the Norwegian failure, and on 10 May he walked into 10 Downing Street as the new prime minister. On the very same day, the Wehrmacht launched its offensive in the west.

ABOVE

Their discarded helmets lying around them, captured British soldiers queue up for a midday meal at a camp near Trondheim. Although relatively few Allied soldiers were captured during the campaign, news of their imprisonment was broadcast to the world by the German propaganda machine.

CHAPTER FIVE

THE FALL OF THE LOW COUNTRIES

The Dutch and Belgian armies were ill-prepared for the sudden German attack in May 1940. Under sustained aerial assault, the Low Countries were battered into submission within weeks.

owards the end of the first week in May 1940, Allied intelligence sources began to report the likelihood of an imminent German invasion in the west. Similar reports had been made over the past few months, thus these new sources of information were not taken too seriously by the Allied commanders (although better aerial reconnaissance would have revealed an enormous build-up of military activity just behind the German border). In fact, a French bomber pilot flying back from a night mission – a leaflet-dropping exercise over Düsseldorf – reported seeing the headlights from a column of vehicles 100km (60 miles) long approaching the Ardennes region. And information supplied by Swiss intelligence pointed out that eight military bridges had recently been laid across the Rhine, which should have strongly suggested the probability of German military activity to the Allied commanders.

For Hitler and the generals at OKW, the main factor in deciding when to strike was the weather, which had to be sufficiently good to permit air operations, as much of the German plan depended on the Luftwaffe's air support. On 7 May, after the campaign had been delayed several times, an increasingly impatient Hitler warned Göring that he would allow him just one more postponement. Two days later the Luftwaffe's chief

meteorologist informed Hitler that the weather would be good enough for combat operations the next day.

Although most German troops knew the great offensive would not be long in coming, it was not until 2100 hours on 9 May 1940 that the code word 'Danzig' was sent to all military units, which was the signal to attack on the following morning. The high levels of secrecy that Hitler had insisted upon after the Mechelen incident earlier in the year ensured that the exact date and time had been concealed from his own troops until the very evening of the invasion. Late on 9 May, Hitler boarded a special train at a station in Berlin, and travelled to his battle HQ at Münstereifel in western Germany.

German invasion preparations
Both the Dutch and Belgian intelligence agencies had good sources of military information, and on the evening of the 9th they too became aware that war was inevitable; all along the Dutch and Belgian borders there were signs of massive German troop movements and other preparations. In Brussels, after some delay, the Belgian Government ordered a general alert at 2315 hours and transmitted news of this decision to their British and French allies. The Dutch, who had received signals of German intentions from

OPPOSITE
General Heinz Guderian, architect of Germany's armoured forces and a panzer corps commander in France 1940. His breakthrough in the Ardennes sealed the fate of the French and Allied armies.

ABOVE

Fortresses such as the Dutch example above betray the mindset of the Allied authorities: they hoped that physical obstacles would deter the Germans from invading, but if an attack came, the fortifications would be sufficient to repel the invaders.

their military attaché in Berlin, prepared to blow up their frontier bridges to delay the German advance, although failures in communication ensured that many Dutch front line troops were unaware of the situation.

The invasion came at a particularly difficult time for the Allies politically. In Britain, Neville Chamberlain's government was on the verge of collapse, and MPs were in the process of selecting a new prime minister after Chamberlain's resignation. In France, the government headed by Paul Reynaud was also undergoing a crisis, which almost led to the premier's resignation and that of General Gamelin, the French commander-in-chief. The emergency in Britain was resolved by the selection of Winston Churchill, but in France, in the light of news of the imminent German attack, Reynaud decided to stay in office and not ask for the dismissal of Gamelin – although he had little faith in his commander's military ability, which was to be shown as lacking by the events of the next few weeks.

Army Group B

The German Army Group B (Colonel General Fedor von Bock) was assigned responsibility for the invasion of Holland and central Belgium. Although Bock's forces had been pared down (much to his chagrin) in favour of the main thrust from Army Group A to the south, their contribution was essential to overall German success. Bock was assigned two armies which had gained valuable combat experience from the Polish campaign: the Eighteenth Army (General Georg von Küchler) and the old Tenth Army, now renumerated as the Sixth Army (General Walther von Reichenau) – the same army that would be annihilated two years later at Stalingrad under the command of General von Paulus.

The Eighteenth Army was ordered to invade Holland and destroy the Dutch armed forces as swiftly as possible. Küchler had the smallest allotment of armoured forces of any of the German armies, just the under-strength 9th Panzer Division, which was largely equipped with the almost obsolete PzKpfw I and II light tanks (only 38 of the division's tanks were heavier models). But the Eighteenth Army had a trump card: the bulk of Germany's airborne forces. General Kurt Student's 7th Airborne Division – later to see action in Crete – was an élite body of para-troops, originally an army formation but subsequently transferred to the Luftwaffe. The division was highly trained and motivated, and its lack of heavy weapons would be com-pensated by the aggression and combat expertise of its soldiers. The other component of the German airborne spearhead was the 22nd Air Landing Division, an infantry for-mation whose soldiers had been trained to carry themselves and their equipment in transport aircraft or gliders.

Troops from these two divisions would be used to seize key strategic points within Holland – bridges, airfields and government buildings – and await the arrival of the ground forces. Airborne soldiers had been used to good effect in the recent Norwegian campaign, but this was the first time that they formed the cornerstone of the attack, the conquest of a state from the air.

The Sixth Army was allotted the two panzer divisions of General Erich Höpner's XVI Panzer Corps; they would drive across the Maastricht appendix – the narrow strip of Dutch territory 'hanging' between Germany and Belgium – and break into the main Belgian defences along the Albert Canal. Once the panzers had broken through this defensive line, the infantry divisions would follow them into central Belgium, and there engage head on the advancing armies of France and Britain.

The 28 and a half divisions of Army Group B would be supported by the aircraft of Luftflotte II, commanded by General Albert Kesselring, a former senior artillery officer who had been transferred into the Luftwaffe to provide Germany's newest armed service with greater command experience.

The Germans invade

In the early hours of 10 May, the Luftwaffe set off from its airfields to begin the invasion. Mines were laid along the British and Dutch coasts; airfields in Holland, Belgium and France were attacked, as were road and rail centres deep behind the lines. The main weight of this initial aerial attack was reserved for Holland, as Heinkel and Dornier bombers

flew out into the North Sea before turning landwards towards the Netherlands coast to attack the Dutch seat of government in The Hague, and the airfields at Schipol (Amsterdam), Bergen-op-Zoom and Waal-haven (Rotterdam). Despite intelligence warnings, the Dutch were caught by surprise, and within minutes much of their air force had been destroyed on the ground by the Luftwaffe's attacks.

The key objective of the 22nd Air Landing Division was The Hague, and the capture of the Dutch Government and royal family. In case he would need to request an audience with Queen Wilhelmina to discuss surrender terms, the division's aristocratic commander, Graf von Sponeck, packed a full-dress uni-form. The German plan was to secure the airfields at Valkenburg, Ypenburg and Ockenburg – which ringed The Hague –

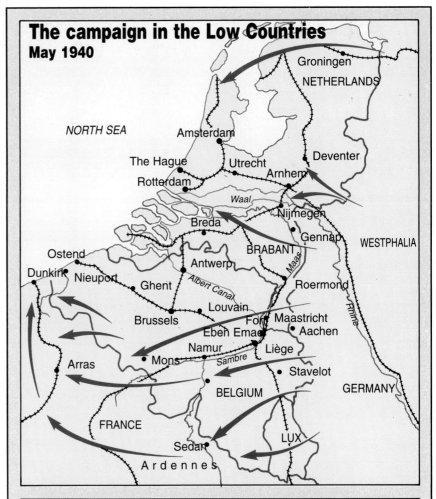

The campaign in the Low Countries
May 1940

Only hours before the German offensive in the Low Countries was due to begin, on the night of 9/10 May 1940, German special forces were deployed to secure the invasion routes by seizing bridges and holding them until the arrival of the main invading army. They took the key bridges at Stavelot, Roermond and Gennap; and as the German armoured divisions drove on to the North Sea the clandestine work of the special forces continued.

The commanding officer of a battalion of Dutch cycle mounted infantry. The collar insignia of two stars and a bar denote his rank as a lieutenant colonel. His arm of service is indicated by the blue piping on the collar and the bicycle wheel. The bicycle was an effective substitute for proper mechanisation in the predominately flat terrain of the Netherlands.

before closing in on the capital. But the airfields were difficult to find in the morning light and many paratroops, who were to hold open the airfields for the main body of troops being transported in Ju-52s, were dropped too far from their targets. As the German Ju-52 transports closed on the airfields, the Dutch were now on the alert and sent up a withering hail of fire. At Ypenburg, out of one flight of 13 aircraft, only two survived. At the other airfields, obstacles placed there by the Dutch, and the flaming wrecks of shot-down Ju-52s, made it impossible for succeeding waves of German aircraft to land. Sponeck was wounded and large numbers of his men were either killed or captured. After discussing the situation with the headquarters of Luftflotte II, Sponeck abandoned the idea of capturing The Hague and instead ordered his battered units to support the attack on Rotterdam to the southeast.

The 7th Airborne Division experienced much better fortunes during this initial stage of the invasion. Paratroop drops secured the key Waalhaven airfield south of Rotterdam, the bridges over the River Maas at Moerdijk and the town of Dordrecht. Equally important, the lightly-armed German paratroops were able to hold these positions in the face of Dutch counter-attacks.

The most audacious manoeuvre of the first day's fighting was the attempt to seize the Willems bridge in Rotterdam itself. At first light, 12 Heinkel float planes landed on the Maas in the heart of Rotterdam's port area, carrying 150 infantry and combat engineers. The float planes taxied towards the bridge, before disgorging the troops in rubber boats. The Germans managed to capture both ends of the bridge, although they soon came under fierce Dutch fire, which would have dislodged them had they not been reinforced by German paratroops. Throughout 10 May, both sides fought bitterly for the bridge, with the hard-pressed Germans just managing to hold their ground. Eventually, the arrival of reinforcements from Waalhaven ensured that the balance of forces at the bridge turned in the Germans' favour.

But until German ground troops arrived, the paratroops and air-landed infantry could only act in a holding role. The main force would have to smash its way through central Holland, which involved crossing the River Mass near the German border. Securing the bridges over the Maas had been a major pre-

occupation of the German planners, with Hitler taking a personal interest in the whole programme. Cloak and dagger operations appealed to Hitler, and as early as November 1939 he had suggested using soldiers dressed in Dutch uniforms for the operation. Admiral Canaris, the head of the Abwehr (German military intelligence), was instructed to organise the deception, and after stealing Dutch uniforms he began training the special undercover unit in this mission. The unit was known as the Brandenburger Company (later greatly expanded in size) and comprised volunteers with special language skills who could operate behind enemy lines.

The Brandenburgers made elaborate plans to capture intact the three main bridges over the Maas, at Nijmegen, Roermand and Gennap. Only the Gennap operation proved to be successful, however. At dawn on 10 May, the Dutch soldiers guarding the Gennap bridge saw men dressed in Dutch police uniforms (who were, in fact, either Dutch fascists or Dutch-speaking Germans) escorting a group of German 'prisoners' (armed with concealed grenades and sub-machine guns) towards the bridge. The Dutch guards were overpowered in the ensuing melee, and a German armoured train crashed through the defences on the bridge.

Lieutenant Walther, the commander of the Brandenburger detachment, was one of the first men to receive a Knight's Cross from a delighted Hitler, for now the plain of Holland lay open to the German army. The tanks of the 9th Panzer Division – supported by a formation of motorised Waffen-SS – rolled across the bridge and began to race along the banks of the Maas towards Rotterdam. Although the 9th Panzer Division was poorly supplied with medium PzKpfw III and IV tanks (the best tanks then available to the German army), it was expected to face little effective opposition because the Dutch were deficient in anti-tank weapons and had no tanks of their own.

First French contact

As the Germans drove towards Rotterdam, the armoured vanguard of the French Seventh Army (General Giraud) advanced along the Belgian coastline and into Holland, as part of the prearranged Breda Variant to the overall Dyle Plan. But when Giraud reached Breda he found no Dutch forces to link up with, as they had all been withdrawn north-

LEFT
The German attack on Rotterdam: a Ju 52 disgorges its load of paratroops over the Dutch port in the early hours of the invasion.

LEFT
German Ju 52 transport aircraft drop paratroopers over a target in Holland. German mastery of 'war in three dimensions' came as a profound shock to the Dutch and Belgians, who were ill-prepared to cope with the disruption that the paratroops could cause behind the front line.

A German parachutist waiting to board his aircraft. He wears the standard equipment for a paratrooper in 1940, and has a parachute strapped to his back. Note the large thick leather gloves he wears to protect his hands. The German paratroops were extremely well-trained, and their expertise and daring helped speed the downfall of both the Netherlands and Belgium.

wards to defend Rotterdam from the German airborne attack. Giraud divided his forces, but around midday on 11 May, French troops encountered advance elements of the 9th Panzer Division around Tilburg, just south of Rotterdam. Disconcerted by this unexpected encounter with the enemy so soon in the campaign, the French recoiled, and under attack from the Luftwaffe they withdrew away from Rotterdam and the Dutch forces fighting the Germans. After just two days of actual combat, Gamelin's much-vaunted Breda Variant had been abandoned.

On 12 May, German armour and Waffen-SS troops met up with the hard-pressed airborne soldiers defending their positions to the south of Rotterdam. The way was now clear for German ground troops to mount the second stage of the offensive against the Dutch – the attack on Vesting Holland

(Fortress Holland), which contained the major cities of Rotterdam, The Hague, Utrecht and Amsterdam. And with complete command of the air, this second phase of operations was considered to be little more than a formality.

Eben Emael

As the River Maas had been a key obstacle for the Germans in Holland, so it was for the German Sixth Army's offensive into Belgium. The main Belgian defensive line was built along the Maas and the Albert Canal. In order to drive deep into Belgium, the Germans had to capture the bridges on the far side of Maastricht, where the Maas and the Albert Canal joined each other in a complex series of waterways. The whole area was heavily fortified and defended by no less than three regiments of the Belgian 7th Infantry Division. The key to the defences was the fortress of Eben Emael, considered by professional observers at the time to be the strongest emplacement of its kind in Europe.

The Belgians were confident that Eben Emael was sufficient enough to hold out against any attack for days, if not weeks. Sited on the west bank of the Albert Canal, roughly triangular in shape, and protected by deep ditches and the near sheer slope of the Albert Canal, it was armed with two 120mm guns and 16 75mm guns in armoured turrets and casemates. But the defenders were thinking along 1914-18 lines, and the fort suffered from two vital flaws: firstly, it did not effectively dominate the area and could not provide covering fire over the whole Maastricht sector, and, secondly, its own defences were vulnerable to aerial attack. And it was from the air that the Germans would make their attack.

Hitler had taken a close and direct interest in the proposed assault on Eben Emael, and despite scepticism from OKH – and even from the more compliant OKW – he accepted a daring and radical solution to capturing the fort (and adjacent bridges) with a gliderborne landing. Paratroops would not have been able to land on such a small target with sufficient accuracy, and the time needed to redeploy them after their drop would have given the defenders more time to organise a coherent defence. Above all, gliders possessed the advantage of silence, as they could be released from the tow aircraft at a distance of 20km (12 miles) from the fort and bridges.

Junkers Ju 52 transport
Germany

The German Junkers Ju 52 transport aircraft was capable of carrying up to 18 fully-equipped soldiers. Reliable and robust, the Ju 52 was the workhorse of the Luftwaffe and served in all theatres throughout the war. It was known affectionately by German soldiers as 'Iron Annie' or 'Tante Ju' [Auntie Ju].

His ripcord trailing behind him, a Geman paratrooper dives out of the side of a Ju 52 at low altitude. German parachutes had a relatively high terminal velocity and were hard to control, and as a result minor accidents, such as sprained and broken ankles, were fairly common.

Gliding had been a popular pastime in prewar Germany, and the Luftwaffe had begun basic pilot training in gliders because of the Versailles restrictions on the use of conventional aircraft. As a consequence, the Germans could draw upon a large pool of the very best glider pilots capable of the precision flying needed at Eben Emael.

The timing of the operation was critical because the glider pilots would need good visibility to see their targets. As a consequence, Hitler overrode army objections and put forward the invasion plan from 0300 to 0530 hours, when there would be sufficient light for the gliders to land safely at the fort and ensure that enough troops would be available to complete the operation.

Under the command of Captain Walther Koch, a force of 424 paratroops (who would fly to their targets in 42 gliders) began to train for the operation in conditions of utmost secrecy. The men were isolated, denied leave and forbidden to talk to men of other units. They were frequently moved and used false unit designations. They practised attacks on old Czech fortifications in the Sudentenland and later against demolished Polish forts near Gleiwicz.

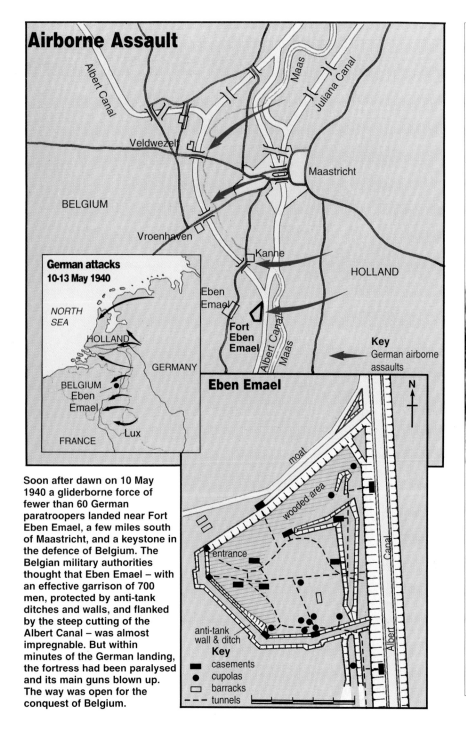

Soon after dawn on 10 May 1940 a gliderborne force of fewer than 60 German paratroopers landed near Fort Eben Emael, a few miles south of Maastricht, and a keystone in the defence of Belgium. The Belgian military authorities thought that Eben Emael – with an effective garrison of 700 men, protected by anti-tank ditches and walls, and flanked by the steep cutting of the Albert Canal – was almost impregnable. But within minutes of the German landing, the fortress had been paralysed and its main guns blown up. The way was open for the conquest of Belgium.

Hollow charges

Leap-frogging the Belgian defences to land troops on the top of Eben Emael was only the first step; once there, the Germans would be confronted by hardened steel cupolas and doors, capable of resisting the sort of equipment an ordinary soldier could carry in a glider. The solution to this problem was as novel as the mode of transport used to get the men to the fort. Shortly after the end of World War I, German scientists developed the hollow-charge explosive into a military weapon. For years it had been known by mining engineers that if a hollowed-out lump of explosive were placed against a piece of steel plate, then the resulting explosion would produce a similar hollow in the steel plate. The German scientists – and later those from other nations – discovered that if the cavity was formed into a cone and lined with thin metal, the charge would actually blow a hole into the steel plate. The German hollow charges were light enough to be carried by glider troops, but they could do as much damage to steel plate as a conventional weapon many times their weight.

The German paratroops assigned to Eben Emael were equipped with 50kg (110 pound)

BELOW
A Ju 52 that has been shot down somewhere between the Hague and Rotterdam. German airborne losses were heavy during this phase of the fighting.

Exhausted but triumphant, German paratroopers relax after their brilliant success in capturing the supposedly impregnable fortress of Eben Emael. Their distinctive helmets and camouflage smocks can clearly be seen.

Equipped with bicycles, a unit of German infantry advances into the Low Countries to secure positions captured by the airborne forces.

shaped charges which could be placed on top of a steel gun cupola, and when detonated would blast through as much as 30cm (12 inches) of armour plate. The hole itself would not be very wide, but splinters of hot metal driven from the target plate, and the blast of hot explosive gases, would do extensive damage to any installation protected by the armour plate, especially to human beings sheltering inside. The attack of 10 May would be the first time that hollow-charge explosives were used in warfare.

The task of capturing Eben Emael was the responsibility of Lieutenant Rudlof Witzig and his company of paratroop engineers. Witzig describes the final training that prepared them for this feat of arms:

We had been thoroughly drilled in out tasks, and in the strict orders which our small number – 85 men, including pilots and allowing for no losses during the flight – made it imperative to observe.

Our earlier study of aerial photographs and a relief model, made to scale on a sand table, had convinced us that our initial assault had to be restricted to the central installations. First, we had to destroy all infantry weapons and anti-aircraft guns firing in the open, and after that the artillery, particularly where directed to the north [towards the bridges]. Speed was essential, since anything not accompanied in the first 60 minutes would be made practically impossible later by the increasing strength of the enemy defence.

Glider attacks

Early on the morning of 10 May, the gliders of the Koch Detachment began to land among the defences covering the bridges at Veldwezelt and Vroenhoven which crossed the Albert Canal to the west of Maastricht. Using the confusion caused by the sudden appearance of these unfamiliar aircraft – which seemed to many Belgians to be con-

ventional aircraft in trouble – the Germans cut the cables to the bridge demolition charges, as well as to nearby telephone lines. At the Kanne bridge, which ran south from Maastricht, the landings went less well, however, and there the defenders were able to blow the bridge and inflict heavy casualties on the Germans.

At Eben Emael, 11 gliders swooped out of the early morning mist where they were met by machine-gun fire from the defenders. But the suddenness of the attack caused sufficient confusion to allow the German paratroop engineers to get out of their gliders and overcome the Belgian machine gunners with few casualties. The paratroops then dragged their hollow-charge explosives to the gun cupolas and detonated them. Five of the cupolas were silenced immediately, the explosive jet blasting through the armour and wrecking the guns beneath (and killing or injuring the gunners). The cupolas holding the heavy 120mm guns were too thick to use hollow-charge weapons, and so specially-designed cylindrical charges were pushed into the gun muzzles, where they detonated and jammed the gun breeches.

The struggle for Eben Emael continued throughout the day. Although the defenders, who outnumbered the attackers, failed to come out of the fortification, they refused to surrender. The paratroops dropped explosives down the ventilation shafts and used portable flame-throwers to silence machine-gun posts. The original plan was for the paratroops to clear the roof, and then enter the fort and keep up pressure on the garrison until ground troops arrived, but Belgian artillery in the surrounding area began to shell the fort, while

nearby Belgian infantry also joined the fray. German ground troops had expected to use the Kanne bridge to reinforce the paratroops on Eben Emael, but its destruction meant that the battle continued throughout the night of 10/11 May. On the morning of the 11th, however, a party of German army engineers managed to cross the Albert Canal using inflatable boats, and with the arrival on the scene of more German reinforcements via the other bridges, the Belgian garrison felt compelled to surrender.

German success

Hitler's delight in the capture of Eben Emael produced a rash of medals for the paratroops, Witzig and Koch both receiving Germany's highest award, the Knight's Cross. The penetration of the Albert Canal defences was the vital first step which would allow the panzers of Reichenau's Sixth Army to drive into the hinterland of Belgium. The Allies had hoped that the Belgians could hold their line for four to five days, thereby giving time for the Franco-British armies to move up and occupy the Dyle Line. The Germans had broken through in just 36 hours.

The second advantage accruing to the Germans was psychological. The gliders were hastily removed from Eben Emael and details of the employment of hollow-charge explosives were kept secret. How such a powerful fortress had fallen so easily disturbed many in the Allied camp, especially the French, who now began to have doubts about the impregnability of their all-important Maginot Line. Göbbels stoked the fire of uncertainty by talking of a 'new method of attack', which was interpreted to mean the use of

RIGHT

One of the most powerful tanks in service in 1940, the Char B1 was heavily armoured and equipped with tow main guns, a 47mm anti-tank gun and a 75mm low-velocity gun for firing high explosive charges. Fortunately for the Germans, the tanks were hard to operate effectively, were unreliable and were distributed among the infantry in small penny packets.

Char B1-bis heavy tank France

FLANDRES

poisonous gas. As a result, unease among the civilian population of the Low Countries increased dramatically.

The Allied response to news of the German invasion on the morning of 10 May had been to instigate the Dyle Plan. At 0700 hours General Gamelin issued orders for the advance of Army Group Number 1 into Belgium. To the north, on the Allied left flank, General Giraud's Seventh Army moved swiftly through Flanders to the mouths of the Schelde and Zeeland in his albeit unsuccessful attempt to link up with the Dutch at Breda. The British Expeditionary Force (BEF), commanded by General Lord Gort, began to move up to its position along the Dyle Line between Louvain and Wavre, just to the south of the Belgian army.

On the BEF's right was General Blanchard's First Army, which had been ordered to take over the Line between Wavre and Namur. General Corap's Ninth Army was to pivot on its centre, and its left-hand wing would hold the Line along the River Meuse (the French name for the Dutch Maas) up to Namur, while its right wing remained in position. The Second Army, under General

Huntziger, would remain in place, holding the sector between Donchery and Longuyon. The Dyle Plan utilised the bulk of the Allied forces, some 41 divisions and 600,000 men, to fill the gap between the Channel and the Maginot Line. Many of the best troops available to the Allies were used in its implementation. If it failed, then the consequences would almost certainly be disastrous for the Allied cause.

After the months of inaction during the phoney war, the Allied troops felt a sense of relief as they marched forward to battle, although Lieutenant General Alan Brooke, commanding the BEF's II Corps, expressed a sense of disbelief that combat was imminent: 'It was hard to believe on a glorious spring day, with all nature looking its best, that we were on the first step towards one of the greatest battles in history.' The advance was made in good order, a reflection of the hard work put in by the Allied staff planners during the previous months. But Gamelin's armies moved and thought like those of World War I: while they could conduct a preordained movement with considerable efficiency, they were slow to react to events, which by the end

ABOVE
A swastika sign marked out on a road junction in Holland serves as a signal to the Luftwaffe that the position was under German control. In such a fast-paced advance, it was easy for German aircaraft to confuse its own troops for those of the enemy.

A column of German tanks advances up a road in Holland. Although only one panzer division had been allocated to the conquest of the Netherlands, it played an important part in eliminating enemy strong points and providing necessary 'muscle' for the lightly-armed airborne troops.

of 11 May included repeated breakthroughs along the Dutch and Belgian borders by the German army.

French weakness

Leading the advance of Blanchard's French First Army was the Cavalry Corps, a high-grade formation of two light armoured divisions (DLMs) under the command of General René Prioux. Making good progress, the tanks of the Cavalry Corps had reached their section of the Dyle Line at Gembloux by 11 May, but Prioux was shocked at the poor state of the defences awaiting his troops. The Belgians had been responsible for the construction of the Line which, because of prewar neutrality restrictions and a desire not

to provoke the Germans, the Allies had been prevented from inspecting. At the same time Prioux received news that the Germans had breached the Albert Canal defences. Open country lay between him and the advancing Germans, ideal terrain for panzers. Prioux reported his concerns to his superiors, even suggesting that the Dyle Plan be abandoned in favour of the original manoeuvre to the Escaut Line. Prioux was overruled, but General Blanchard was instructed to press forward faster towards the Dyle Line to ensure his arrival a day earlier than the previously stipulated date of 15 May.

The German staff at army high command (OKH) were pleased when they received news of the Allied advance into Belgium. The prime object of Army Group B's invasion of the Low Countries was, in the words of British military writer Sir Basil Liddell-Hart, to 'wave the matador's cloak' to attract the attention of the Allies, and in so doing distract attention from the main thrust through the Ardennes. Hitler exclaimed: 'I could have wept for joy; they'd fallen into my trap!' While it was expected that the German Eighteenth Army should have little trouble in removing Holland from the military equation, it was impressed upon General von Reichenau that his Sixth Army must engage and pin down the Allied forces in central Belgium, thereby preventing them from being redeployed to the Ardennes region once the Allies discovered the true German intentions. But the Allies remained blissfully unaware of the German strategy, their attention focused on events in central Belgium.

Allied air support lacking

In light of the fact that the Germans had managed to secure enough bridges over the River Maas/Meuse, then it was essential that Allied aircraft be employed in their destruction. But the whole Allied air response was remarkably slow and ineffective. The French, fearful of Luftwaffe reprisals against Paris and other cities in northeast France, refused to sanction bombing raids in German territory, at a time when the long columns of panzers waiting to break through the Allied defences were at their most vulnerable, backed up on roads awaiting the chance to move. On 11 May, a squadron of Belgian Fairey Battle light bombers attacked the bridges at Maastricht, but their puny bomb loads were inadequate

to the task, while the slow speed of the Battle made it vulnerable to the German anti-aircraft defences that now ringed these crucial bridges. Of the 15 aircraft that went into action, only five returned.

On the 12th, the RAF, and later the French air force, were instructed to attack the bridges at Maastricht, which were now enabling Höpner's panzers to move onto the Belgian plain. RAF Blenheim bombers launched their attack early in the morning, but of the nine aircraft sent on the mission, seven were shot down by German fighters. At midday, French Bréguet bombers flew towards the bridges at tree-top height, but intense and accurate anti-aircraft fire caused heavy losses for little gain. The final attack of the day was by part of a squadron of Fairey Battles of the RAF, which pressed home their attack with the greatest bravery, resulting in the loss of all but one aircraft, which managed to limp home.

The net result of this attack was the smashing of a single truss on the Veldwezelt bridge. A survivor of the raid was told by his German captors: 'You British are mad. We capture the bridge early Friday morning. You give us all Friday and Saturday to get our flak guns up in circles all round the bridge, and then on Sunday, when all is ready, you come along and try to blow the whole thing up.' The German soldier's comment summed up much of what was wrong in the whole Allied response to the German invasion.

Casteau conference

As the Allies had failed to construct an effective command organisation in the period before the invasion, on 12 May a conference

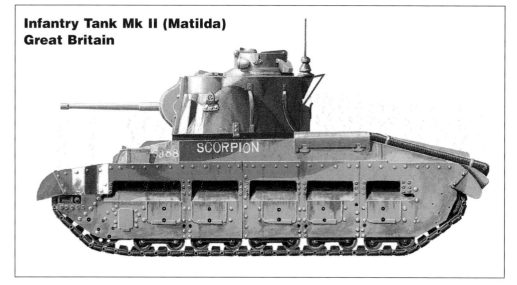

**Infantry Tank Mk II (Matilda)
Great Britain**

SCORPION

LEFT
The British Infantry Tank Mk II was commonly known as the Matilda, so named because the Mk I variant had a passing resemblance to a cartoon character, Matilda the duck. Although slow and armed with a light two pounder gun, the tank's heavy armour was sufficient to withstand German tank guns of this period.

The Germans were quick to advertise the exploits of their airborne troops to a wider audience, if only to help demoralise the Allied soldiers. Here, German paratroopers are interviewed by members of the neutral foreign press, alongside a captured enemy soldier.

was hastily convened at a château at Casteau, near the old World War I battlefield of Mons, to attempt to remedy the situation. Attended by the Belgian monarch King Leopold and his military advisor, the French foreign minister Daladier and Generals Georges and Billotte, and Lord Gort's chief of staff, Sir Henry Pownall, the meeting failed to find the necessary command solution, giving Billotte vague responsibility to act as Georges' 'delegate' in coordinating policy. In effect, the Belgian and British commands were left to operate on their own. The failure by the French high command to provide their junior allies with effective command and guidance, and coordinate an effective response to the German attack would have serious consequences in the days ahead.

While the Casteau conference was still in session, the military situation in Holland was deteriorating swiftly. To the north of the country, German troops had marched through Groningen and reached the eastern shore of the Zuyder Sea. In central Holland, German

ground forces had pushed forward to Deventer and Arnhem (which had been captured by paratroops the previous day), and would soon be in striking distance of Utrecht and Amsterdam. Further south, the 9th Panzer Division had linked up with the airborne forces holding the Moerdijk bridge on the evening of the 12th; Holland was now effectively cut in half, and with the retirement of Giraud's French Seventh Army westwards it had to face the Germans on its own.

During 13 May, the Germans pressed hard against the Dutch holding Rotterdam and the defences of Vesting Holland. To the consternation of General Küchler, commanding the German Eighteenth Army, the Dutch maintained a determined resistance and progress was slow. OKH applied pressure on Küchler to finish off the Dutch quickly, in order to release troops from his command for the major battles being fought elsewhere. At the end of the 13th, he issued orders for the men under his command to 'break resistance in Rotterdam with all means'.

Dutch surrender

On 14 May, the Dutch army accepted that resistance could not be continued indefinitely, and negotiations for a cease-fire began. The Luftwaffe now had complete air supremacy, and to ensure Dutch compliance, a force of 60 Heinkel He-III bombers was despatched to attack the centre of Rotterdam. While negotiations between the Germans and Dutch were continuing, the bombers closed on the city. Attempts were apparently made to call back the German bombers, but were not registered. For 20 minutes the Heinkels bombed the defenceless city causing huge fires and massive damage to property – it was estimated that 78,000 people were made homeless by the raid. In the terror and confusion of the moment, Dutch officials claimed that a total of 30,000 people had been killed, although the actual figure was closer to 900. The exaggerated figure immediately worked to the German's advantage psychologically, however, sending shock waves of fear throughout the major cities of western Europe. Civilian morale in Belgium and France had suffered yet another blow.

Later in the day, the Dutch commander-in-chief, General Winkelman, accepted the German terms for unconditional surrender, and Dutch troops were ordered to lay down their arms on the morning of the 15th (although resistance in Zeeland continued until 17 May). Holland had been knocked out of the war after just five days of combat. Ships of the Dutch navy, together with Queen Wilhelmina and her government, crossed to Britain to carry on the struggle in exile. They were joined by the Dutch merchant marines, whose three million tons of shipping was placed at the disposal of the Allies.

During the early stages of the invasion of the Low Countries, the Luftwaffe had concentrated its might against Holland to help speed its reduction, but now its aircraft were progressively redirected towards the battle for Belgium. From as early as 12 May, the Allies began to report increasingly heavy attacks, especially by Stuka dive-bombers who were covering the advance of the 3rd and 4th Panzer Divisions of Höpner's XVI Panzer Corps. As Belgian troops fell back from their positions on the Albert Canal (and from the

BELOW

A German PzKpfw II stands guard on a road near Drontheim; enemy casualties lie nearby. Although only armed with a light 2cm main gun, the Mk II was swift and reliable.

Ardennes) towards their allotted sectors on Dyle Line, the only substantial force facing the charging German panzers was Prioux's Cavalry Corps.

The two divisions of the Cavalry Corps – 2nd and 3rd DLM – were equipped with Somua and Hotchkiss H-35 light tanks, roughly 175 per division, which made them slightly inferior in numbers to the divisional allotment of the panzer formations facing them. The quality of the armour of both sides was roughly equal, the main difference separating the two sides was the superior tactical awareness of the Germans when using tanks on the battlefield.

The first tank battle

Around the town of Hannut, the lead German and French tanks began to engage each other on 12 May – the first tank battle of the campaign. Although the fighting was indecisive, the German panzers did not have things their own way, and the Cavalry Corps held its positions. The following day the battle was rejoined, with the armour of both corps engaged in a full-scale tank-versus-tank battle. The main fighting took place around the village of Merdorp, to the west of Hannut. The Germans were impressed by the thick armour of the Somua tanks (which was capable of deflecting the German shot from longer ranges), but through the superior manoeuvrability of their panzers they were able to find weak spots in the French tanks. One German officer criticised French tactics at Merdop, describing 'the fact that they fight single and

in loose formation, not all together under one command. They cannot take advantage of strength and number.'

By the end of the day's fighting both sides had suffered heavy casualties, but it was Prioux, whose headquarters faced being over-

RIGHT

The main anti-tank weapon of the British expeditionary force, the 2-pounder was heavy and lacked the ability to penetrate heavy frontal armour. Effectively obsolete by the time of the German offensive, most of those in service were lost in the evacuation at Dunkirk.

**QF 2-pounder Anti-tank gun
Great Britain**

run, who was forced to retreat. Using the cover of darkness, the French withdrew their tanks behind Belgian anti-tank defences at Perwez. Although Prioux had slowed the advance of the German XVI Panzer Corps – the spearhead of the Sixth Army – his corps was not in a fit state to initiate the independent operations that would so soon be required of it.

Ardennes threat

During 13 May, the reports reaching General Georges, commander-in-chief of the Northeast Front, of a German invasion through the Ardennes and over the upper Meuse began to suggest that this might be a major offensive. The French Ninth and Second Armies, directly facing the attack, were in danger of buckling, and by the evening of the 13th, Georges, whose health was poor, was reported to be on the verge of a breakdown. But because of poor Allied lines of communication, General Gamelin and the Governments of France and Britain remained unaware of the gravity of the situation in the southern sector of the front.

On 14 May, the German Sixth Army closed on the Dyle Line, and its commander, General Reichenau, was given the instruction: 'Attack the enemy positions between Louvain and Namur on the 15th, so as to prevent consolidation of Allied forces in this position.' In other words, the Allies on the Dyle Line were to be attacked and held in this position by an aggressive assault by the Sixth Army to prevent any orderly withdrawal. German panzer and infantry divisions attacked the French First Army in the Gembloux region, and pushed in the French line, but fierce counter-attacks by General Aymes' IV Corps and Prioux's battered Cavalry Corps repulsed the Germans. Reichenau was reluctantly forced to call off the attack at 1630 hours, with the intention of resuming the battle the following day using a more orthodox set-piece attack.

Further north, the German XI Corps made an attack against British positions around Louvain. The Germans succeeded in breaking into the city, but were expelled in a counter-attack by the British 3rd Division (commanded by Major General Bernard Law

ABOVE

German anti-aircraft artillery in action. The German armed forces employed their 8.8cm guns with great versatility, using them against ground targets when necessary. They were found to be particularly effective against tanks, whose armour was too thick for conventional anti-tank guns.

A member of an RAF Whitley bomber crew prepares for takeoff in May 1940. He is wearing an Irvin 'Harnisuit' which contains an inflatable life-belt and parachute attachment points. The Whitley bomber, like much of the British equipment, was effectively obsolete by the outbreak of war, although they were used in front line service until 1942. On 19 March 1940, Whitleys were the first RAF aircraft to bomb Germany since 1918.

Montgomery) which was supported by a heavy artillery barrage from the division's old but still effective 60-pounders. By the end of 15 May, all German attacks on the Dyle Line had been repulsed, and despite continuing attacks by the dominant Luftwaffe, the Allies in this part of the front could take some satisfaction from their day's work.

During 14 and 15 May, the German panzers of Army Group A crossed the Meuse and broke through into open country. The Allied positions on the Dyle Line had now been outflanked, and on the evening of the 15th General Billotte made the momentous decision to order the abandonment of the Dyle Line. The Allies would withdraw to the line of the River Escaut (Schelde) and adopt the original defensive position that had preceded Gamelin's Dyle Plan. In the circumstances, this was probably the only decision open to the French high command, but again the poor Allied chain of command meant that the British and Belgian commanders only heard of the decision to withdraw the following morning, and then only through the initiative of their own liaison officers.

The consequences of retreat

The decision to retreat was greeted with understandable bitterness by the Belgians, who now would have to surrender the vast majority of their country to the invaders. The Belgian Deputy chief of staff, General Derousseaux, subsequently commented: 'It came like a shot out of the blue, and with the subsequent surrender, it is my worst memory of the campaign. The general staff was stunned by it. We had to shake ourselves back into action and make the necessary preparations for execution of this order.'

The disengagement of the Allied armies from the Dyle Line was a potentially difficult manoeuvre, as they were still being engaged along the front by the German Sixth Army. That the Allies were able to withdraw towards the Escaut Line in generally good order was a consequence of the, by now, relatively slow advance of the Germans. The XVI Panzer Corps had been withdrawn south and placed under the command of Army Group A, which now had nine of the 10 panzer divisions available in the west. The loss of the Höpner's tanks not only took away much of the Sixth Army's mobile cutting edge, but as the Panzer Corps had most of the bridging equipment, the infantry found their progress

thwarted when faced by the many canals and rivers that crossed the region.

The problems faced by the retreating troops were the incessant air attacks from the Luftwaffe and the growing refugee problem. Constant bombing attacks took their toll on the morale of the Allied armies. One French NCO summed up the feelings of hopelessness experienced by the ordinary soldier, who had no means of fighting back against his aerial foe: 'Not to see the enemy face to face, to have no means of defence, not to see the shadow of a French or Allied plane during hours of bombing, this was one of the prime reasons for the loss of our faith in victory.'

For the civilian populations of Holland, Belgium and France, the news of the German airborne attacks, combined with the Luftwaffe's bombing raids, produced a climate of panic, which was unwittingly encouraged by the attitudes of the authorities who issued warnings of the danger of 'Fifth Columnists'. The more suggestible people began to see 'paratroops' in the most unlikely situations, and on occasions even nuns and priests found themselves arrested as Nazi spies.

The fear of German conquest – the threat of which was real enough – produced a mass exodus as people sought safety from the invaders. Long columns of civilians clogged the road, as literally millions of people fled westwards (two million Dutch and Belgian refugees, and possibly as many as five million French). Such numbers became a nightmare for the Allies, who were either withdrawing to new positions or desperately attempting to reinforce existing ones. Although the British Expeditionary Force had drawn up precautionary schemes for an organised evacuation, British troops found themselves overwhelmed by this exodus. General Brooke provided this account of the problem:

Many women were in the last state of exhaustion, many of them with their feet tied up with string and brown paper where their shoes had given out. I was informed by the prefect that these were the 800,000 people whom we had evacuated westwards. They had run into the German armoured forces, and into rumours of these forces where they did not exist. Like one big wave, the whole of

One of the many traffic jams caused by the swift advance of the Germans into Belgium in May 1940. Military police were used at major junctions to assign priority to combat units.

humanity, short of food and sleep and terrified to the core, was now surging back again and congesting all roads at a moment when mobility was a vital element.

By the end of 19 May, despite such problems, the Allies had completed their withdrawal to the Escaut Line. The Belgian army held the sector from Terneuzen to Oudenarde (the site of one of the Duke of Marlborough's victories) with 11 divisions, plus a further seven in reserve. The BEF was deployed along the River Escaut (Schelde) from Oudenarde south to the Franco–Belgian border, with seven divisions in the line and one in reserve, although Gort subsequently began to redeploy units along his right flank as an insurance against the threat of a German attack from the south.

Despite being tired from their march to the Dyle Line and back again under heavy aerial attack, the men of the BEF remained in good shape. The French First Army had experienced a harder time than the British, having borne the brunt of the German Sixth Army's assault, but it too remained in line, although its right flank was unsupported, having lost contact with the French Ninth Army. Much of Prioux's Cavalry Corps, to the

BELOW

Belgian officials walk past destroyed rail track, the result of a German bombing raid. The Luftwaffe played a key role in interdiction bombing, preventing the movement of Allied reinforcements.

dismay of its commander, had been parcelled out to provide armoured support to the infantry divisions.

French paralysis

The inability of the French high command properly to assess the situation and to issue coherent orders to counter the German threat had undermined the confidence of both French commanders in the field and the British. General Sir Edmund Ironside, the British CIGS, jotted down his feelings about the French in a diary entry for 17 May: 'We have lived in a fool's paradise. Largely depending upon the strength of the French army. And this army has crashed or very nearly crashed. At this moment it looks like the greatest military disaster in history.'

The BEF's commander, Lord Gort, had been given no orders from his nominal superior, General Billotte, for several days, and the British were unsure of what the French intended to do to stem the German advance into France. From 19 May onwards, Gort's concern for the security of his forces deepened, especially when in conversation with Billotte he realised that the French had no

adequate strategic reserves to counter the continued German advance. On the 19th, he warned the War Office that he might have to consider evacuating the BEF from the continent, although in genuine loyalty to his French comrades, he regarded such an action as a last step only.

Also on 19 May, General Gamelin was dismissed from his post as commander-in-chief. The patience of his political master had finally snapped, and Reynaud had him replaced by General Maxime Weygand, who had to be flown to France from Syria. The timing of the command change could not have come at a worse moment, as Weygand would take time to comprehend the situation, and for the Allies time was in short supply.

The Channel reached

On the evening of 20 May, German tanks of Guderian's Panzer Corps reached the Channel Coast. In just ten days the Germans had divided the Allied armies, cutting off the Belgians, the British and large numbers of French troops from the main French armies to the south. As Ironside had feared, the Allies were staring at total disaster.

ABOVE

An exhausted unit of Belgian artillery retreats back from the city of Louvain, 22 May 1940. After less than two weeks' fighting, the Belgian army was at the point of collapse.

CHAPTER SIX

PANZER BREAKTHROUGH

The German armoured thrust through the Ardennes was swift and devastating; the Allies, reeling in the face of so quick an onslaught, were almost powerless to resist the German advance.

On the evening of 9 May 1940, the commanders and troops of Army Group A received their orders to attack in the west. Colonel General von Rundstedt's Army Group A comprised 45 and a half divisions divided into three armies: Fourth Army (General Kluge), Twelfth Army (General List) and Sixteenth Army (General Busch). The spearhead of Army Group A's attack was provided by its three panzer corps and supporting motorised infantry; not only would they smash through the enemy front line, they would also exploit the breakthrough by charging deep into enemy territory. If they failed in this mission, however, then the whole German offensive would collapse in ruin.

Panzer Group Kleist was the main strike force and comprised General Heinz Guderian's XIX Panzer Corps (1st, 2nd and 10th Panzer Divisions, plus a reinforced Grossdeutschland Regiment) and Reinhardt's XLI Corps (6th and 8th Panzer Divisions), both corps supported by General von Wietershiem's XIV Motorised Corps. Although Guderian was acknowledged as Germany's premier tank expert, his fiery nature led to him being subordinated under the more cautious General Ewald Kleist.

Providing a northern flank guard to Panzer Group Kleist was Hoth's XV Panzer Corps (5th and 7th Panzer Divisions). The comman-

der of the 7th Panzer Division was the then unknown Major General Erwin Rommel, who had commanded Hitler's army escort guard during the Polish campaign. Although an infantryman, Rommel had been so impressed by the performance of the panzers in Poland, that he asked and received from Hitler the command of the one of the newly-uprated Light Divisions. Within the space of a few months Rommel mastered the complexities of leading an armoured formation, and during the forthcoming campaign would make a reputation for himself that more than rivalled the other established panzer generals.

The French defenders

Facing the German invasion force were two understrength and under-equipped French armies. The Ninth Army (General Corap) comprised four infantry divisions, two light mechanised divisions and two cavalry divisions. The Second Army (General Huntziger) comprised five infantry divisions and two cavalry divisions. There were few regular formations within either army, most being poor-quality reserve or fortress divisions, which were fatefully deficient in anti-tank and anti-aircraft guns. Both the Ninth and Second Army came under General Billotte's Army Group Number 1, but from the moment hostilities began the overworked

OPPOSITE

One of the consequences of the German breakthrough in the Ardennes – the total defeat of the Allied armies and the evacuation from Dunkirk. Here, officers and men of the Royal Ulster Rifles wait on an improvised pier at Dunkirk.

Part of Rommel's 7th Panzer Division advances deep into France in an armoured column, as a German reconnaissance aircraft flies overhead.

Billotte was more concerned with operations further north on the Belgian plain.

During the early hours of 10 May, long columns of armour wound their way through the Ardennes and over the German border into Belgium and Luxembourg. The panzer divisions amounted to well over 2000 tanks and thousands more other vehicles, creating the biggest traffic jam in military history. Rundstedt's chief of staff estimated that the armoured columns stretched back as much as 160km (100 miles), a fact which caused deep anxiety to the German high command, fearful that the Allies would be able to discern their plan for an invasion through the Ardennes. And the long, often stationary columns presented a perfect target for aerial attack. The Luftwaffe maintained an enormous protective barrier over the tank formations, but Allied air activity was surprisingly light, the French showing little interest in aerial reconnaissance.

German planning

The superb staff planning which was a hallmark of German operations ensured that what could have been a logistic nightmare, worked as smoothly as possible. All road junctions were manned by military police, who directed the traffic following carefully laid down procedures. Vehicles that broke down were ruthlessly pushed off the road. One tank driver in the 1st Panzer Division described the advance over the frontier:

With every hour that goes by, it becomes more lively on the approach roads, more and more troops quartered here in the Eifel are getting under way. We overtake marching, riding and driving columns.

The noise of the motors gets on one's nerves in this night of uncertainty. The drivers must exert the utmost powers of vision, so as not to end up in the roadside ditches. It's pitch dark.

Once news of the German offensive had filtered through to the Allied high command, General Gamelin, the French commander-in-chief, instituted the Dyle Plan. In accordance with Gamelin's directive, the left wing of Corap's Ninth Army advanced forward to the Meuse. Meanwhile, the cavalry formations from both Ninth and Second Armies were ordered to meet any German troops that might come through the Ardennes. As the Allies were convinced that the main thrust would come through central Belgium, the cavalry advance was intended to be a reconnaissance action to discover German deployment in the region. On 10 May, the French cavalry of the Ninth Army encountered a strong force of German tanks and retired. The following day, several more engagements between the French cavalry and German armour took place. The 2nd and 5th Light Cavalry Divisions of the French Second Army were thrown back with heavy losses, while the cavalry formations of the Ninth Army were forced back across the Meuse.

By 11 May, the Allies were aware that German forces were pressing through the Ardennes, but were unaware of the numbers involved and what the Germans' intentions were. (Received wisdom was that this was a feint designed to take away Allied attention from the main battle in central Belgium – the exact reverse of what was actually happening!) General d'Astier, commander of the air forces attached to the Army Group Number 1, described the attack as merely an 'energetic thrust'. The Allied high command was not unduly worried by events and adopted a position of 'monitoring the situation'.

Guderian's attack

While the XV (Hoth) and XLI (Reinhardt) Panzer Corps had a relatively unimpeded drive towards their first serious barrier, the River Meuse, Guderian's XIX Panzer Corps had to cross the wooded and steeply-banked valley of the River Semois. Although his forces were now under aerial attack and being shelled at long-range by French 155mm guns near Sedan on the Meuse, the attack across the Semois went well, largely because the French retired in a poorly coordinated fashion, and allowed the German infantry to

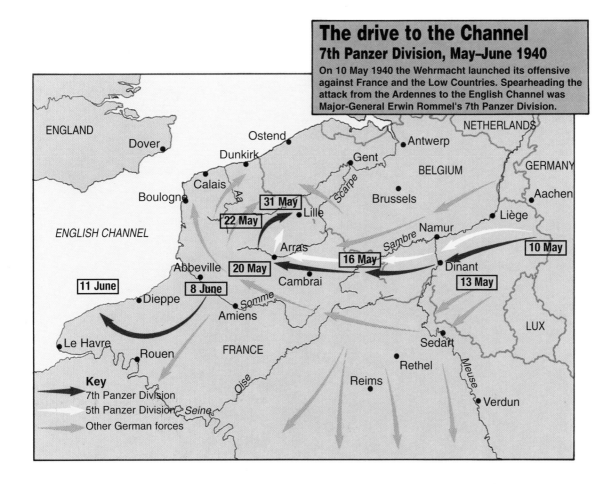

The drive to the Channel
7th Panzer Division, May–June 1940
On 10 May 1940 the Wehrmacht launched its offensive against France and the Low Countries. Spearheading the attack from the Ardennes to the English Channel was Major-General Erwin Rommel's 7th Panzer Division.

Key
7th Panzer Division
5th Panzer Division
Other German forces

infiltrate and bypass French strongpoints. On
12 May, Guderian had a narrow escape while
planning the advance on Sedan at a hotel on
the banks of the Semois:

*Suddenly there was a series of explosions in
rapid succession; another air attack. As though that
were not enough, an engineer supply column, carrying fuses, explosives, mines and hand grenades,
caught fire and there was one detonation after
another. A boar's head, attached to the wall immediately above my desk, broke loose and missed me
by a hair's breadth; the other trophies came tum-
bling down and the fine window in front of which I
was seated was smashed to smithereens and splinters of glass whistled about my ears.*

The Meuse reached

During the 12th, the leading elements of the
1st and 10th Panzer Divisions emerged from
the Ardennes and reached the Meuse on
either side of the old fortress city of Sedan
(also the site of the decisive Prussian victory
over the French in 1870). During the
evening, the French retired from Sedan (on
the east bank of the river), blowing the
bridges over the Meuse, which at this point
was unfordable. Guderian was short of
artillery, and the 2nd Panzer Division was

some way behind the other two formations.
Guderian was unsure whether to attack
immediately the following day, but his superior, Kleist, had been informed that the
seemingly powerful defences on the French
side of the river were only partially complete,
and he encouraged an immediate attack.
Guderian was promised the full might of the
Luftwaffe on the following day, which would
lessen the need for artillery support.

At midday on 13 May, the French defenders were subjected to the most ferocious aerial
bombardment yet seen in the war. Wave after
wave of dive-bombers, light and heavy
bombers and fighters swarmed over the
French positions which consisted of the 55th
and 71st Infantry Divisions, 'B-Class' reserve
formations who mostly contained 'fat and
flabby men in their 30s'. The Luftwaffe's
pounding was crucial to German success, and
was watched eagerly by the troops who
would soon make the assault over the Meuse.
An NCO in the 1st Panzer Division watched
the dive-bombers:

*Simultaneously, like some bird of prey, they fall
upon their victim and then release their load of
bombs on the target. We can see the bombs very
clearly. It becomes a regular rain of bombs, that*

whistle down on Sedan and the bunker positions. Each time the explosion is overwhelming, the noise deafening. Everything becomes blended together; along with the howling sirens of the Stukas in their dives, the bombs whistle and crack and burst. A huge blow of annihilation strikes the enemy, and still more squadrons arrive, rise to a great height, and then come down on the same target. We stand and watch what is happening as if hypnotised; down below all hell is let loose!

The main effect of the Stuka dive-bombers was psychological; in reality they caused relatively few casualties in the hilly and wooded west bank of the Meuse, but for the frightened troops undergoing this bombardment it seemed that each aircraft was directed personally at him. A French officer describes the effect on his men:

The gunners stopped firing and went to ground, and the infantry cowered in their trenches, dazed by the crash of the bombs and the shriek of the dive-bombers; they had not developed the instinctive reaction of running to their anti-aircraft guns and firing back. Their only concern was to keep their heads well down. Five hours of this nightmare was enough to shatter their nerves, and they became incapable of reacting against the enemy infantry.

The infamous '88'

During the bombardment, German 8.8cm anti-aircraft guns were used to knock out enemy emplacements near the water line. Although designed for shooting down aircraft, the high-velocity flat trajectory of these guns proved ideal in this role – and in knocking out enemy tanks.

At 1600 hours, the German aircraft returned to base, the French artillery silenced. At this moment the first wave of attackers began to cross the Meuse. The Grossdeutschland Regiment and the 1st Rifle Regiment (from 1st Panzer Division) began to cross the river on inflatable assault boats. Some boats sank but enough made it to the other side to construct the first stages of a bridgehead. The elite German infantry fought their way up the slopes of the river bank, knocking out bunkers and other emplacements on the way. Grossdeutschland soldiers noticed that the French would retreat from defensive positions such as pillboxes without much of fight, as they believed that they would be killed if caught in pillboxes. An officer in the Grossdeutschland reveals the speed and self-reliance demanded of soldiers in this operation:

LEFT
A German 15cm field artillery piece fires against French positions. Before firing, each shell was removed from the wicker cases (bottom right), which were used to protect the shells in transit.

Well-camouflaged German troops paddle along a river in inflatable boats. The Germans had planned extensively for the river crossings they would encounter in the invasion of France and the Low Countries, and German attack infantry made good use of these lightweight craft.

There can be no pause; the objective must be taken in daylight. Then the road will be clear for the panzers. The enemy must be given no rest. The second pill box is taken and we can make out the anti-tank gun position. New assault troops are brought forward, the machine-gun group fights down the riflemen's positions on the left and enables the company to move forward. One again the grenadiers move out. They climb the slope, through deeply cratered countryside, cross deep barbed-wire barriers until the French open defensive fire from behind a ridge. Machine guns and machine-pistols send out their death-bringing bullets. Hand grenades explode; nobody pays attention

to the enemy fire. There is not time to stop. The leading troops are already in the enemy's position. Close combat fighting, hand to hand, with a wild swing the attack is driven forward.

French disarray

The French defensive line began to collapse, and survivors fled to the rear spreading alarm. At 2000 hours in the village of Bulson, 8km (five miles) from Sedan, panic spread to French heavy artillery batteries, who destroyed their guns and ammunition, and fled to the rear. At this point only a few German infantry units were clinging onto the west bank of the Meuse; all the tanks and heavy equipment had yet to cross the river. But such was the shock of the German attack that the French were in disarray.

By midnight the German penetration south of Sedan was sufficient for Guderian to bring up his engineers to lay their pontoon bridges over the river, to allow the passage of tanks and artillery. The 1st Panzer Division had pushed forward to occupy the tactically important Mafée heights, and the 1st Rifle Regiment had penetrated to a distance of 10km (six miles) in only a few hours of combat. By the early hours of 14 May, XIX Corps had secured itself a bridgehead which would allow it to build up forces for a subsequent break-out.

The 6th and 8th Panzer Divisions of Reinhardt's XLI Panzer Corps launched their attack across the Meuse at Monthermé on the afternoon of 13 May. They lacked the air support that proved so vital to Guderian's attack, and they encountered stiff resistance from the French 102nd Infantry Division, one of the few regular formations in the French Ninth Army. The German infantry were supported by the guns of their tanks, which were able to fire directly into the slits and embrasures of the French defences. The Germans managed to secure a foothold on the far bank but were held there, the awkward terrain and stiff resistance preventing any further progress.

Further north, the XV Panzer Corps of General Hoth reached the Meuse at Dinant on the night of 12/13 May, the advance led by the 7th Panzer Division's Major General Rommel. The Germans were unable to get across the river as a result of sustained fire from the French defenders, and Rommel worked hard to sustain the morale of his clearly shaken troops. As the early morning mist began to clear, the Germans came under renewed fire, and in an attempt to conceal his men, Rommel pushed forward to the front line and ordered some nearby houses to be set alight to provide a smoke screen. Despite this measure Rommel was forced to admit: 'The situation when I arrived was none too pleasant. Our boats were being destroyed one after the other by the French flanking fire, and the crossing eventually came to a standstill.'

Although the main attack was stalled, on the previous evening reconnaissance troops of the 7th Motorcycle Battalion discovered a weir over the Meuse just south of Dinant which was not only undamaged but unguarded. Although the French corps commander covering this stretch of the river was aware of the weir, the battalion he sent to defend this position had failed to carry out his orders. Encouraged by Rommel, the soldiers crossed over the weir's footbridge and established a precarious foothold on the far bank. During the 13th, the German motorcyclists hung on grimly as the French attempted to

snuff out this tiny pocket, but under repeated Stuka attacks the defending infantry failed to coordinate with the tanks of the 4th Light Cavalry Division and were repulsed.

Increased German pressure

By the afternoon of the 13th, Rommel's troops on the river had received reinforcements of tanks and artillery, which began to whittle down the resolve of the defenders. Again the tanks proved highly effective in a bunker-busting role, according to an account by Captain König of the 25th Panzer Regiment: 'The fire of the panzer guns, the 75mm shells as well as the well-scattered 20mm quick-firing cannon, soon show an effect. The companies shoot almost as if they were in training, and no unrecognised target, no suspicious movement of the enemy, remains unnoticed.' By the day's end, engineers from the 7th Panzer Division had built a pontoon bridge, and by the morning of 14 May, 15 German tanks had crossed the river.

ABOVE

The Fiesler Storch was used by the German troops as a reconnaissance and light utility aircraft. Here, an example overflies a column of German tanks during a brief lull in the fighting in France. The tanks are Czech-manufactured PzKpfw 38(t) tanks obtained from Czechoslovakia after the German takeover in 1939.

Outdated Allied tactics

The 13th had been a crucial day for the German armoured formations: they had crossed the main defensive obstacle that lay between them and open country, and although their three bridgeheads were small, they were sufficient to allow them to build up their forces for the next phase of the battle.

The Allied reaction to the German offensive was based on the old World War I concept of containment. French reinforcements were directed to the front line, but instead of being thrown into battle immediately to crush the German bridgeheads, they halted and waited for the next German move. This allowed the Germans to carry on with their consolidation phase, so that throughout 14 May tanks and other vehicles were able to cross the Meuse. The only real threat came from the sky, as the air forces of France and Britain made renewed attacks on the Meuse bridges. During the 14th, nearly 200 Allied bombers attacked the pontoon bridges around Sedan with almost suicidal determina-

tion. But in the same way that the German defences had been built up around their bridges further down the river at Maastricht in Holland, so it was around Sedan: the Allies suffered terrible losses from anti-aircraft fire and roving German fighters. By the end of the day, 85 Allied aircraft had been shot down; the panzers continued to cross the river.

On the ground, the French high command committed their strategic reserves which, although whittled down because of 'Breda Variant' plan, still included two powerful armoured divisions. On 14 May, the 3rd Armoured Division, assigned to Huntziger's Second Army, was instructed to attack the bridgehead at Sedan. The drive towards Sedan was slow due to refuelling problems, and when the division neared its target the order was countermanded. Instead, it was instructed to adopt a defensive position and disperse its tanks along an 18km (12 mile) front.

Further north, the 1st Armoured Division had been given orders to advance on Dinant, but its progress was also fatefully slow, as recorded by one French observer: 'It took them a long time to reach their positions, for the roads were cluttered with fleeing troops and civilians; it took the armoured division seven hours to cover 32km (20 miles). It was short of petrol. It would be unable to fight that day. Its commander halted it.' While XV Panzer Corps was building up its position in the Dinant bridgehead, General Corap of the French Ninth Army confirmed the halt order for the 1st Armoured Division, which was instructed to await the arrival of the 4th North African Infantry Division before launching a counter-attack.

The success of the German incursions across the Meuse had come as a profound shock to Corap, and by the evening of 14 May he began to contemplate a withdrawal to a new 'stop-line' back from the Meuse. Further south along the French line, General Huntziger, commander of the Second Army, ordered the formations on his left wing, which had been battered by the attack at Sedan, to withdraw in a southerly direction. As a consequence, a substantial gap began to open up between the two French armies, at exactly the place where Guderian's XIX Panzer Corps was preparing to break out from the Sedan bridgehead.

Guderian's plan was for the 1st and 2nd Panzer Divisions to attack due west against and around the right flank of the French Ninth Army, while the 10th Panzer Division and the Grossdeutschland Regiment adopted a more defensive strategy by pushing back the left wing of the French Second Army. The tanks of the 10th Panzer Division were not properly in position when the battle against the French Army's XXI Corps began on 15 May. As a result, most of the fighting was carried out by the infantry, with the Grossdeutschland to the fore. The French XXI Corps comprised the 3rd Motorised Division, supported by the tanks of the 3rd Armoured Division. In theory, this powerful force could have inflicted serious damage on Guderian's left wing, but the dispersal of the French tanks and their subordination to the requirements of the 'infantry battle' prevented any such success.

The French counter-attack

On the 15th, the XXI Corps cautiously went over to the offensive, their advance simultaneously countered by an attack from the Grossdeutschland. During the day, the fighting swirled around the hill-top village of Stonne, much of it a straight fight between German anti-tank guns and French tanks. The 32-ton 'B' tanks of the French 3rd Armoured Division were formidable weapons, whose heavy frontal armour was impenetrable to the 3.7cm anti-tank guns of the German troops. And yet, to prevent the French breaking the German line at Stonne, the Grossdeutschland managed to fight off repeated French tank attacks through their superior battle skills. Lieutenant Beck-Broichsitter, the commander of the 14th Anti-Tank Company, was awarded the Knight's Cross for his defence of Stonne. He describes the French assault from a position by the village's water tower:

About 10 French tanks roll in on a wide front. At some 40km/h (25 mph), the drivers swing their vehicles about, and then fire. They are firing from the water tower, the three guns are hit in the middle of the road; immediately three are wounded, but the section holds! The duel begins! In an hour-long running battle, Hindelang's section stops with its fire the attacking infantry, as well as the flank fire from the water tower and also from the wooded hill. The fight for the village slackens. Against the tough French attacks some of our rifle companies gradually crumple away. Self-propelled guns help again and again …four heavy infantry guns are brought into open positions, and fire with 15cm shells on the water tower. But it does not budge. The losses are getting greater. Some of the anti-tank guns are shot full of holes. They carry on shooting.

At the very height of the 10-hour battle, a two-gun section from Beck-Broichsitter's company came under attack from three French 'B' Tanks:

The fire of the three heavy tanks threatens to wipe out the anti-tank section. But it remains in position. One moment, one of the colosseses crosses the front. The left gun commander, Senior Corporal Giesemann, discovers in the middle of its right side a small-ribbed surface; apparently it is the radiator! It is not much bigger than an ammunition box. He aims at it. A tongue of flame shoots out from the tank. Both gun commanders now fire at this small square in the side of the 32-tonners. The left gun is shortly afterwards wiped out by a direct hit. Now Hindelang retreats with the one remaining gun into the village. The three 32-tonners are knocked out!

Although the Grossdeutschland Regiment represented the cream of the German army at the time, the determination of the defence was in marked contrast to the French reluctance to hold their ground during the battles on the Meuse.

A French gun crew prepares a 155mm howitzer for action on the Second Army's front. Although the French had long experience in the use of artillery, they failed to stop the Germans from crossing the Meuse river and breaking out into open French countryside.

Last gasp defence

Towards the end of the 15th, the French tank attacks, although spread out widely along the XXI Corps front, began to cause the Germans some concern. At around 1700 hours, the Grossdeutschland commander, Colonel Graf von Schwerin, reported to General Schaal of the 10th Panzer Division that his troops had been expelled from Stonne and were 'in a state of complete physical exhaustion and hardly fit for combat'. Fortunately for the Germans, reinforcements from the XIV Motorised Infantry Corps began to arrive, just as the French commander called off his attack. The Germans reoccupied Stonne the following day.

The 1st and 2nd Panzer Divisions, their open left flank protected by the Grossdeutschland Regiment and the 10th Panzer Division, smashed into the right flank of the French Ninth Army. Corap attempted to block their path with the elite 3rd Brigade of Spahis, the 152nd Regiment (from the crack 14th Infantry Division) and the 53rd Infantry Division. While the 2nd Panzer Division had little difficulty in carving a way through the down-at-heel reserve 53rd Division, the 1st Panzer Division was virtually fought to a standstill by the Spahis and the 152nd Regiment. But at the end of the day, the exhausted French were forced to retire from the battlefield. The last line of French resistance in front of Guderian's XIX Panzer Corps had been broken.

Further down the River Meuse, Reinhardt's XLI Panzer Corps had been confined within its bridgehead around Monthermé by the French XLI Corps. The

French troops held their ground well, but suffered heavily from Luftwaffe attacks. When Corap ordered them to retire to his stop line, the XLI Corps began to fall apart. On the morning of 15 May, the tanks of the 6th and 8th Panzer Divisions broke out from Monthermé and trampled through the retreating French XLI Corps, dismembering it in the process.

By the end of the day, the leading German tanks had advanced as far as Montcornet – nearly 60km (38 miles) from the Meuse – and only 17km (11 miles) from Corap's headquarters at Vervins. During the advance to Montcornet, Reinhardt's panzers overran elements of the French 2nd Armoured Division, which was in the process of redeployment. As a consequence, most of the divisional artillery was lost, and the tanks and their transporters were dispersed over a wide area, and thus incapable of acting as a division. The 2nd Armoured Division (the last of France's three fully formed armoured divisions) had been destroyed before it had even been committed to battle.

Unfortunate timing

The blow landed by the right fist of the German offensive – Hoth's XV Panzer Corps – was equally dramatic, with Rommel's 7th Panzer Division in the forefront. Again the

Germans were able to exploit Corap's withdrawal order to their advantage. As the French prepared to retire, they were hit by the panzers. The French 1st Armoured Division, which had already withdrawn its artillery to the rear in anticipation of the retirement order, was caught in a pincer movement by the 7th and 5th Panzer Divisions during refuelling. While the Germans employed the handy 'jerrican' to carry their fuel, French tanks were laboriously refuelled using motorised tankers, which were vulnerable to attack. Although the French tankmen fought back, they were only able to offer spasmodic resistance, and by the end of 15 May the 1st Armoured Division had been destroyed as a fighting formation. The infantry of the French 11th Corps were overrun in the process. By nightfall Rommel's tanks had advanced through Philippville, and well beyond Corap's increasingly notional 'stop-line'.

French defeatism grows

In five days of battle, Kleist's Panzer Group and XV Panzer Corps had destroyed eight divisions of the French Ninth and Second Armies, and prized open a gap 70km (44 miles) wide in the French line. The Ninth Army was on the verge of disintegration, and its broken commander, Corap, was relieved of his command on the night of 15/16 May. His

LEFT
A German staff car comes under enemy fire. German casualties were remarkably light for the territory gained in the opening phase of the campaign.

replacement, General Giraud (transferred from the Seventh Army in Flanders), could do little to restore the situation, and was captured by a German patrol on 19 May. The defeatist spirit that ran through much of the French army began to gain momentum after the first shock of battle. Increasingly, large numbers of French troops were either throwing away their arms and fleeing the battlefield, or surrendering without a fight.

A German soldier in the 6th Panzer Division wrote a report for the division's war diary, in which he described seeing a column of French prisoners marching into captivity in good order and led by their officers:

They had, however, no weapons and did not keep their heads up. They were marching willingly without any guard into imprisonment. There were finally 20,000 men, who here in the sector of our [XLI Panzer] Corps, on this one day, were heading backwards as prisoners. How was it possible, these soldiers French soldiers with their officers, so completely demoralised, would allow themselves to go more or less voluntarily into imprisonment?

The ease with which the French surrendered surprised the German soldiers, who had been expecting them to have fought more like their forefathers in World War I. After driving the French back through Philippville, Rommel noticed how 'hundreds of French motorcyclists came out of the bushes and,

together with their officers, slowly laid down their arms. Among them were several officers, from whom I received a number of requests, including, among other things, permission to keep their batmen and to have their kit picked up from Philippville.'

The reaction of the French high command to the German offensive through the Ardennes was slow and muddled, in large part a consequence of the cumbersome chain of command which prevented a swift response to any new event. As ever, the French generals operated along the lines adopted during the previous war. They based their assumptions on the fact that German attacks in World War I – such as the great 1918 offensive – might make deep inroads into the Allied line, but they were always brought to a halt. Using the logic of 1918, the French generals of 1940 argued that this latest German offensive would eventually lose momentum and so be contained. But, of course, the German offensive through the Ardennes was actually gaining rather than losing momentum.

General Gamelin, the French commander-in-chief, had little idea of the seriousness of the German attack through the Ardennes until the evening of 13 May, by which time the panzers had crossed the Meuse. Even then he believed the situation could be 'patched up' by sending in reserves, but the French

RIGHT

Using a pontoon bridge section, SS troops ferry an infantry gun across a river. This was the first time that the SS forces were extensively used in combat, and for the most part they fought well.

strategic reserve had been fatally weakened by the deployment of most of its best troops to conduct the Breda Variant of the Dyle Plan. Over the next couple of days, Gamelin continued to exude an aura of confidence. The turning point came late on the evening of 15 May, when reports reached Gamelin that the Ninth Army had effectively fallen apart and that German troops had reached Montcornet.

A shocked Gamelin then telephoned Daladier, his old political ally and now the minister of national defence. The US Ambassador to France, William Bullitt, was with Daladier when Gamelin's call came through, and he noted down the desperate conversation between the two men. When Gamelin explained that he had no reserves to counter the German thrust, Daladier

ABOVE

British troops rest by the roadside, awaiting contact with the German Army.

**SOMUA S-35 medium tank
France**

LEFT

The French SOMUA S-35 medium tank was the best armoured fighting vehicle available to the Allies in 1940: it was swift and manoeuvrable, adequately armoured and equipped with a 47mm gun capable of firing both solid shot and high explosive shells.

exclaimed, 'So, it means the destruction of the French army?' Gamelin replied, 'Yes, it means the destruction of the French army!'

A desperate French appeal

That evening, the French Government appealed directly to Winston Churchill for more troops and aircraft. Churchill flew to Paris on 16 May and was 'dumbfounded' to be told by Gamelin of the gravity of the situation. The complacency that had permeated through the French Government and military circles was replaced by succeeding emotions of despondency, despair and, at times, panic. Fearful that the German breakthrough was aimed at Paris, the French Government was preparing to flee to Tours. Churchill noticed that as Gamelin was explaining the French army's predicament, 'outside in the garden of the Quai d'Orsay clouds of smoke arose from large bonfires, and I saw from the window venerable officials pushing wheelbarrows of archives on to them.' Although Churchill was reluctant to release aircraft from the defence of Britain, he nonetheless promised the French a further six squadrons.

Paradoxically, the unease experienced by the Allies was shared by Hitler. Although the German front-line commanders were confident that victory lay in their grasp, Hitler had been taken aback by the deployment of the French armoured divisions. Although the French attacks had been poorly coordinated and achieved little (except perhaps their own destruction), they suggested to Hitler that they might be just the first stage of a great counter-attack. The usual role of Hitler the gambler being held back by the more conservative generals of OKH was reversed. During 16–17 May, the OKH chief of staff, General Halder, argued that the Allies were not strong enough to launch a counter-attack towards Sedan, and that the panzers should be allowed to thrust forward without delay. But Hitler remained paralysed by anxiety, and demanded that the armoured divisions halt and await the arrival of the infantry.

On the night of 15/16 May, Guderian had received a telephone order from Kleist to postpone any advance until the infantry came up in support. Guderian protested strongly and was allowed to continue the advance for up to 48 hours. On the morning of 17 May, Guderian was summoned by Kleist and curtly told to obey the stop order. A furious Guderian offered his resignation, and was only mollified by the direct intervention of General List, the commander of the Twelfth Army. A compromise order was instituted in which Guderian formally accepted Kleist's authority (and that of the German high command), but was allowed to continue the advance with a 'reconnaissance in force'. Guderian exploited this loophole to the full, and conducted the 'reconnaissance' with the entire 1st and 2nd Panzer Divisions!

LEFT
German panzers – PzKpfw 38(t) light tanks – advance across open territory. The 38(t) equipped the 7th and 8th Panzer Divisions and was well-regarded by the German panzer arm.

OPPOSITE
The face of defeat: a demoralised French soldier stares into the camera before being led away into captivity.

de Gaulle counter-attacks

On 17 May, as Guderian surged forward into France, Colonel Charles de Gaulle launched an attack along the German's southern flank. Given command of the 4th Armoured Division, de Gaulle found it was a division in name only, as it consisted of a few inadequately trained tanks units and some motorised infantry. At first light on the 17th, de Gaulle attacked towards Montcornet and penetrated the enemy some 32km (20 miles) before being forced to halt in the face of German air and ground superiority. In his memoirs, de Gaulle wrote: 'All the afternoon the Stukas, swooping out of the sky and returning ceaselessly, attacked our tanks and lorries. We had nothing with which to reply. Finally German mechanised detachments, more and more numerous and active, began skirmishing in our rear.' By nightfall, the French had withdrawn, having taken 130 Germans prisoner.

Two days later, the 4th Armoured Division attacked again, its objective the bridges over the Serre, vital to the panzers advancing westwards between the River Oise and Amiens. The French tanks nearly overran Guderian's headquarters, but in the face of repeated bombardment from marauding dive-bombers they were forced to retreat. Ordered by General Georges to conserve his tanks, and threatened by an encircling movement from German troops, de Gaulle withdrew his battered forces to temporary safety behind the River Aisne.

The German panzer divisions, having broken through the French defences, now proceeded to reap their reward. On 16 May, Rommel's division had taken roughly 10,000 prisoners and 100 tanks, and suffered only minimal casualties. On the 17th, the panzers reached the Sambre-Oise Canal and Leon. The Allies were in full retreat on all fronts, and the Germans were noticing how French

BELOW

German troops swarm up a hillside ready to attack French defensive positions. The German infantry proved as aggressive as their panzer counterparts.

resistance was declining. Although the Guderian and his fellow tank commanders had been forced to pause on the 17th, as a result of the uncertainty felt by Hitler and Kleist, the pursuit was resumed the following day. The Germans were crossing the old battlefields of World War I; by the evening of 18 May, Guderian had reached St Quentin and Rommel secured Cambrai (the site of the British tank offensive of 1917).

German reinforcements

By now, the Allied armies to the north of the 'panzer corridor' were retreating westwards, and to prevent any Allied interference from that direction, Hoth's XV Panzer Corps was ordered to consolidate its position around Cambrai, although Rommel managed to persuade his corps commander to allow him to advance forward and occupy the heights around Arras on 20 May. The previous day, Höpner's XVI Panzer Corps had been switched from Army Group B to join the main panzer assault in the south, taking up a position on the left of the XV Panzer Corps. Army Group A could now dispose of a total of nine panzer divisions, followed by six motorised divisions.

During 19 May, the divisions of Guderian and Reinhardt spent much of their time bringing up supplies and making minor repairs in preparation for the final push to Amiens and the Channel coast. The panzers had been driving and fighting almost continuously for 10 days, their tiredness kept at bay by the prospect of inflicting a crushing defeat on the French. The extraordinary swiftness of the German advance owed much to the skill and determination of the panzer generals. The command style of men such as Guderian or Rommel was a world away from the slow and methodical approach adopted by their enemies. Walther Nehring, Guderian's chief of staff, explained how his commander led his men from the front:

Guderian's method of working was interesting. He would set off in the morning with his small skeleton staff in an armoured command car containing his adjutant and a signals officer with his radio equipment. He was accompanied by a small semi-tracked vehicle for rough ground, and two despatch riders, so that he could direct operations from the front. He was in constant radio contact with me while travelling, and on his return in the evenings there was always a thorough discussion to assess the situation. These methods proved

efficient and were introduced throughout the tanks corps. Corps HQ was always at pains to follow its divisions as closely as possible in the interests of short lines of communication.

Early on 20 May, the German tanks were once again on the move, and at 0900 hours the 1st Panzer Division drove into Amiens, while the 2nd Panzer Division leap-frogged towards Abbeville. The speed of the advance once again caught the Allies by surprise: a British artillery battery was captured on a parade ground armed only with blanks because the gunners were conducting firing practice, while an RAF squadron only avoided the same fate by flying off its aircraft in the nick of time. At 2000 hours on 20 May, a battalion from the 2nd Panzer Division drove into the coastal town of Noyelles; the exhausted but delighted tank crews could now gaze out over the sea. During that day alone they had advanced an incredible 100km (63 miles). Over the last 11 days, the German panzers had fought their way through the French defences and advanced nearly 400km

ABOVE
A French tankman surrenders to German infantry, his knocked-out Char B tank behind him. Despite its heavy armour, large numbers of Char Bs were put out of action by German ground troops.

ABOVE

Despite being too slow to fight against high performance single-engined fighters, like the Spitfire and Hurricane, the Messerschmitt Bf 110 was a useful ground attack plane, and was later to be successful as a nightfighter.

(250 miles). They had also inflicted a devastating blow against the French army from which it would never recover.

Hitler's delight

Hitler and OKW were astonished at the speed and ease of the German victory. General Jodl recorded in his diary: 'The Führer is wild with joy. He sees victory and peace within his grasp.' Indeed, the whole operation caught the German military planners off guard. They had not developed a new set of orders to take into account the panzer victory, as Guderian observed: 'On the evening of this remarkable day we did not know in what direction our advance should continue; nor had Panzer Group Kleist received any instructions concerning the future prosecution of the offensive.'

For the next two days, the German armoured forces on the Channel did virtually nothing apart from recuperate from their wild charge across France, and it was not until 22 May that orders were drawn up to commit Guderian's panzers to advance northwards and close the trap holding the French First Army and the BEF. Guderian prophetically remarked: 'We have wasted two days. We shall need them at Dunkirk.'

On 18 May, General Gamelin had at last realised the intention of the German thrust through the Ardennes; it was not directed at Paris, as so many had feared, but was aimed at reaching the Channel to divide the Allied armies in two. The long flanks on either side of the 'panzer corridor' left the Germans open to counter-attack, and on the morning of the 19th Gamelin issued his 'Personal and Secret Instruction No. 12', a coordinated attack against the 'corridor' from both north and south. Unfortunately for the Allies, the plan was several days too late and now there were not sufficient mobile forces available to carry out the plan.

Before Gamelin's orders could be put into effect, he was sacked by Paul Reynaud, the French prime minister, and replaced on the morning of 20 May by General Maurice Weygand, a 73-year-old veteran who had been recalled from Syria in a last-ditch attempt to reverse the disaster facing France. Despite his advanced years, Weygand was a soldier of some energy, and although he refused to 'guarantee success' he introduced a much-needed sense of resolve into the French high command. But Weygand was concerned about the practicality of Gamelin's plan, and decided to rescind the order until he had conducted his own reconnaissance of the front line. Consequently, more time was lost – when France had no time to spare.

A new Allied plan

On 20 May, General Ironside, the British chief of the Imperial general staff, conferred with the BEF's commander, Lord Gort, and then with General Billotte, the commander of the French Army Group Number 1. Ironside was as ignorant of the true state of the battle as Weygand was, and ordered Gort to use the BEF to fight its way through to Amiens and restore the Allied front line. Gort was forced to point out that the bulk of his forces were already engaged with the German Sixth Army in the east, and that he lacked the resources to cut through the 'panzer corridor', especially now that it was being reinforced by hard-marching German infantry divisions.

Gort informed Ironside that he was already planning to mount a limited attack of his own, against the Germans around Arras, employing the two divisions that were not engaged in the fighting along the Escaut Line. Ironside then met Billotte and Blanchard (the

First Army commander), where he was dismayed by their lack of resolve. He noted that they 'were in a state of complete depression. No plan, no thought of a plan. Ready to be slaughtered. Defeated at the head without casualties.' Although Ironside's comment was not entirely fair, it at least brought home to him the gravity of the situation. During a heated conversation with Billotte, it was agreed that the French would support the British attack on the 21st. Gort, however, did not pin much hope on the French promise, stating 'they would never attack'.

The British forces available for the operation consisted of the under-strength 5th and 50th Divisions and the 1st Army Tank Brigade, under the command of General Franklyn. The force was further depleted by demand for units to hold positions along the Escaut Line, so that the attack would be conducted by just two tank battalions and two infantry battalions, with limited artillery and anti-tank support. The tank contingent consisted of 58 Mark I and 16 Mark II (Matilda) tanks. Both tanks were well armoured, but the Mark I was only armed with a machine gun,

BELOW
Two RAF fighter pilots discuss tactics in France, 1940. Fearful of an attack against Britain, RAF Fighter Command held back the bulk of its squadrons for home defence; this was, in retrospect, wise, as the aircraft were thus available for the Battle of Britain.

so that the only effective offensive capability was confined to the Mark Is with their 2-pounder guns. Although some aerial cover was promised, none came on the day, leaving the skies open for the Luftwaffe.

In retrospect, the attack at Arras came to take on a greater significance than has ever been intended by Franklyn and Major General Martel, the officer who would lead the force unto battle. Their orders were simply to, 'support the garrison in Arras and to block the roads south of Arras, thus cutting off the German communications (via Arras) from the east'.

The French component of the attack was due to be provided by General Altmayer's V Corps, but when Blanchard's liaison officer, Major Vautrin, informed Altmayer of the proposed operation, he was told that the V Corps was not in a fit state to launch such an attack. Vautrin reported back to Blanchard the disturbing news that, 'General Altmayer, who seemed tired-out and thoroughly disheartened, wept silently on his bed.' On the evening of the 20th, Blanchard informed Gort that Altmayer's troops would not be able to move until 22 May, but said that Prioux's Cavalry Corps would be able to provide flanking cover.

Although Prioux was one of the few capable and resolute commanders in the French army, his forces had already been depleted by previous heavy fighting, as well as being dis-

BELOW

Refugees flee their homes in the face of the German advance. During May and June 1940 millions of civilians packed the roads of northern France, severely hampering the movement of Allied forces.

persed amongst the infantry formations. As a result, his contribution to the following day's action would necessarily be limited. Nonetheless, Gort decided to go ahead with the attack.

Poor Allied intelligence

The Allies knowledge of German strength south of Arras was poor. It in fact consisted of Rommel's 7th Panzer Division and the Waffen SS Totenkopf Motorised Division, with the 5th Panzer Division in support. Rommel was leading his troops in a flanking manoeuvre around Arras when the British struck. The British had been slow to organise their forces, and it was not until the afternoon of the 21st that the tanks got under way. The advance consisted of two columns – a tank and infantry battalion in each – which drove in a south-easterly movement around Arras, with elements of the French 3rd Light Mechanised Division on their right flank.

Almost immediately they came upon the lead troops of the 7th Panzer Division.

The right-hand British column surprised a German force in the village of Duisans, and then drove onto Wailly, where they overwhelmed units of the Totenkopf; many of the Waffen SS troops fled in panic at the arrival of the lumbering but powerful British tanks. Rommel and his staff were advancing in the middle of the division when the British struck, and with his customary zeal he set about rectifying the situation in Wailly:

The enemy tank fire had created chaos and confusion among our troops in the village and they were jamming up the roads and yards with their vehicles, instead of going into action with every available weapon to fight off the oncoming enemy. We tried to create order. After notifying the divisional staff of the critical situation in and around Wailly we drove off to a hill 1000 yards west of the village, where we found a light AA troop and several anti-tank guns located in hollows and a small

ABOVE
German infantry advance across the open ground of northern France, having broken through the French defences. For these men, hard marching was the order of the day if they were to keep up with the fast-moving panzers and consolidate their gains.

wood, most of them totally under cover. About 1200 yards west of our position, the leading enemy tanks, among them one heavy, has already crossed the Arras-Beaumetz railway and shot up one of our Panzer IIIs. It was an extremely tight spot, for there were also several enemy tanks very close to Wailly on its northern side. The crew of a howitzer battery, some distance away, now left their guns, swept along by retreating infantry. I brought every available gun into action at top speed against the tanks. With the enemy tanks so perilously close, only rapid fire from every gun could save the situation. Soon we succeeded in putting the leading enemy tanks out of action. About 150 yards west of our small wood a British captain climbed out of a heavy tank and walked unsteadily towards us with his hands up. We had killed his driver. Over by the howitzer battery – despite a range of 1200 to 1500 yards – the rapid fire of our anti-tank and anti-aircraft guns succeeded in bringing the enemy to halt and forcing them to turn away.

Rommel's account described the end of the British right-hand column's advance, but the left-hand column made even better progress, capturing several villages and overrunning German positions. An advance party of British troops even reached Wancourt on the River Cojeul – the final objective of the advance – but lack of support and the intervention of the Luftwaffe forced the British to turn back. The British had advanced 16km (10 miles), destroyed a large number of German tanks, guns and transport, and captured over 400 prisoners. As in previous engagements against Allied armour, the German 8.8cm anti-aircraft guns had proved highly effective, knocking out many of the British tanks. In fact, they were the only guns within the panzer division capable of penetrating the frontal armour of the British Mark II tanks. At the end of the day's fighting only 26 Mark I and two Mark II tanks were fit for action. For the British, the attack was over.

The consequences of Arras

The importance of the British attack at Arras lay not in its physical action – for in numerical terms it was little more than a raid – but in its psychological effect upon the Germans. The level of German surprise can be gauged from Rommel's signal of the evening of the 21st: 'Very heavy fighting took place between 1530 and 1900 hours with hundreds of tanks and their supporting infantry.' In fact, Rommel assessed the very modest British force as numbering five divisions. Hitler was sufficiently worried by the situation that he sent Keitel to Arras in person, where he completely revised the German dispositions. The 7th and 5th Panzer Divisions (plus Totenkopf)

A French B-1 tank that has been knocked out in the Somme region of northern France. The hull-mounted 75mm gun is clearly visible. French tanks, unlike their German counterparts, were not used together in large numbers, and so they made much less impact on the battlefield.

was placed on the defensive, while the 6th and 8th Panzer Divisions were turned around and sent eastwards to support the Germans around Arras.

From this point onwards, the German conduct of operations became increasingly cautious. Rundstedt admitted that it was only this attack that had caused him any real concern during the campaign, and the attention of OKH turned away from the exploitation of Guderian's dash to the Channel to defensive matter around Arras. This, of course, bought the Allies valuable time, which ultimately helped make the evacuation at Dunkirk a realistic option.

The Allies were unaware of this moderation in the German attitude towards armoured operations. Paradoxically, the strength of the German positions around Arras – and the inability of the Allies to launch a coordinated operation – convinced

Gort that the survival of the BEF depended on a retreat to the Channel ports and evacuation to Britain.

While the British were fighting around Arras, General Weygand was in the process of meeting the Allied commanders in Belgium. He had flown northwards over the 'panzer corridor' the previous day, and had wasted much time in tracking down the senior Allied generals. On 21 May, Weygand called a conference in Ypres of the commanders-in-chief of the French, British and Belgian armies. When he arrived only King Leopold was there; Billotte arrived later in the afternoon, but Gort was delayed and only got to Ypres when Weygand had been forced to leave (considerably to the latter's annoyance).

Pinching the panzer corridor

Weygand's plan was for simultaneous counter-attacks against the 'panzer corridor' from

ABOVE

German mechanised forces pass a column of French prisoners. Despite lacking sufficient troops to supervise their prisoners properly, the Germans found the French surprisingly compliant as POWs, as the speed of the German advance had broken their morale.

ABOVE
With sirens howling, a Stuka drops its bombload – a demoralising sight for the enemy infantry below.

RIGHT
Newly-surrendered French colonial soldiers come under the guard of German Luftwaffe ground troops. Like the British, the French had a number of soldiers from their overseas colonies fighting for them.

were too committed already to be redeployed for such a major operation. Consequently it was decided that the BEF must provide the bulk of the troops. It remained to persuade Gort to agree to the plan. When Gort arrived at Ypres he informed the conference that German troops had already crossed the River Scheldt – the mainstay of the Escaut Line – and were threatening to cut off his forces to the south. In addition, Gort maintained that the Allies in the north were not strong enough to mount a counter-offensive. At the end of the conference it was agreed that the Belgians and the French would relieve British positions to allow Gort to muster up to five divisions for the counter-attack, which was to be launched on 23 May.

The misfortune that had dogged the Allies throughout the campaign continued. Driving back to his headquarters, Billotte was involved in a car accident and mortally injured. At a stroke, this removed the man with the clearest picture of the proposed counter-attack. Blanchard succeeded Billotte as commander of Army Group Number 1, while Prioux assumed command of the First Army. The confusion caused by these changes served to further undermine the already shaky Allied command structure, and for the remainder of the campaign the three Allied armies acted independently of each other.

On 22 May, Panzer Group Kleist had been given the order to resume the offensive. Guderian's three panzer divisions were to fight their way north-east along the Channel coast, with each division being allotted one of the three major ports – Calais, Boulogne and

north and south. Initially, he asked for a major contribution from the Belgians and the French First Army for the northern counter-attack, but King Leopold and Billotte managed to convince him that their forces

Dunkirk – their capture would cut off the Allies from any chance of a mass evacuation of troops to Britain.

For the first time in the campaign, the Germans began to encounter increased air activity from the Allies; the Luftwaffe were operating increasingly far from their bases, the RAF correspondingly closer. This made the advance slower, although by the end of the 22nd, the 2nd Panzer Division was at the gates of Boulogne and the 10th Panzer Division was closing on Calais. The Franco-British garrisons of both ports refused to surrender, and conducted valiant defences, which bought valuable time to the Allies retreating towards Dunkirk, the last available evacuation port.

Boulogne held out until 25 May, and Calais was not captured until the evening of the 26th. When given the opportunity to surrender, the British commanding officer at Calais, Brigadier Nicholson, replied: 'The answer is no. It is as much the British army's duty to fight as it is the German army's.'

The 1st Panzer Division was ordered to drive eastwards and capture Dunkirk. By the evening of 23 May the division's vanguard had reached the River Aa, south of Gravelines, where it was stopped by determined French resistance. While Guderian prepared to attack the next day, renewed doubts affected some of the senior German commanders. Rundstedt had become uneasy about the French armies to the south of the 'panzer corridor', and he had not overcome the shock of the attack at Arras. Thus on the evening of the 23rd he ordered Kleist to halt and reorganise his panzer forces in case they were needed to repel any possible French attacks from the south.

Hitler halts the panzers

The following day, Hitler visited Rundstedt's headquarters at Charlesville. There, Rundstedt

BELOW
A mixed group of British and French prisoners are led away into captivity after helping defend Dunkirk.

explained his worries over the possible threat from the south, arguing that the marshy Flanders plain was not suitable for tank operations, and that, anyway, it would only be a matter of time before the Allies in the northern pocket capitulated. Hitler agreed completely, as he too wished to husband his armoured forces for the forthcoming battle with the remaining French formations south of the River Somme. While Brauchitsch and Halder at OKH argued to continue the tank attack against the Allies defending Dunkirk to prevent any Allied escape, Hitler was adamant and issued a 'Führer Order' on 24 May calling a halt to the panzers.

Guderian was marshalling his troops for a last attack to secure the port of Dunkirk, and the arrival of the 'Fuhrer Order' – which had to be obeyed on pain of death – came as a dreadful shock. 'Hitler ordered the left wing to stop on the Aa,' wrote Guderian. 'It was forbidden to cross the stream. We were not informed of the reason for this. The order contained the words: "Dunkirk is to be left to the Luftwaffe." We were utterly speechless.' The 'Halt Order' was the single great mistake made by the Germans during the 1940 cam-

paign in the west. If the panzers had been given their head, then the Allies would have been trapped and forced to surrender, and over 200,000 of Britain's best soldiers would have been permanently lost, with all the consequent implications for her war effort.

Despite the problems caused by the death of Billotte, the Allies attempted to carry out the plan agreed at the Ypres Conference of 21 May. But yet again, outside events were to prevent any fulfilment. General Küchler's Eighteenth Army – which had earlier conquered the Netherlands – was redeployed to fight on the right flank of the Reichenau's Sixth Army. On the night of 23/24 May, a heavy bombardment heralded an offensive against the Allied line by both German armies. The Belgians, who held the majority of the line, began to waver in the face of such a powerful attack, well-supported by the Luftwaffe. The direction of this new German assault was well-chosen, being made on both sides of the town of Courtrai on the River Lys, the junction between the forces of the Belgian army and the BEF. The Belgians rushed up their last reserves to plug the gap in the line.

The British commander, Lord Gort, was only too well aware of the danger presented by the German attack; if the Germans broke through then they would sever the BEF's communications with the Channel and Britain. To make matters worse, the BEF's supplies of ammunition were running dangerously low, and with the roads clogged with panic-stricken refugees and retreating soldiers it was possible that the BEF would be unable to operate as a fighting force if the supply system broke down.

Gort's decision

On 25 May, Gort took it upon himself to ignore his orders to provide troops for the forthcoming 'Weygand Offensive' – which had already been postponed – and sent them to occupy a barrier position against the German attack from the east. By so doing, Gort had tacitly decided to abandon the campaign in northern France and Belgium. It was a momentous decision which would leave Britain's allies to their fate, but Gort reasoned that his first priority as a British commander was to save the BEF to fight another day. In order to avoid being outflanked by advancing German troops, General Franklyn's mechanised units had already withdrawn from Arras, which had already caused some bitterness among French units who now faced being outflanked in turn by the Germans. Gort began to marshal his troops for a fighting withdrawal to Dunkirk.

As early as 19 May, the British War Office and the Admiralty had begun discussions to consider the 'possible but unlikely evacuation of a very large force in hazardous circumstances'. Code-named Operation Dynamo, the planning was put under the charge of Vice Admiral Sir Bertram Ramsay, the energetic and capable Flag Officer, Dover. As a precautionary measure, Ramsay commandeered every boat and small ship he could find to assemble a fleet of trawlers, ferry boats, motor yachts and even some flat-bottomed Dutch *schuyts* which had recently taken refuge in England. As well as these 850 or so commercial craft, Ramsay was also able to deploy an impressive fleet of 39 destroyers plus other light naval craft. The planning went ahead in great secrecy. The French were not consulted, an action which not only caused bad blood, but meant that French naval forces were only able to play a relatively minor role once the evacuation began.

As plans for Operation Dynamo got under way, the British and Belgian forces were desperately fighting to hold off the combined might of the German Eighteenth and Sixth Armies. On 25 May the German attack pierced the Belgian line in several places, and on the next day German infantry began to push deep into Belgian positions. During the afternoon of 26 May, King Leopold signalled Generals Blanchard and Gort that Belgium could not continue to resist for long. Also on 26 May – at 1857 hours – the British Ad-

BELOW
A heavy British anti-aircraft gun abandoned on the beaches of Dunkirk. Although such equipment was left behind due to a lack of space, anti-aircraft weapons were vital to deter the Luftwaffe from attacking the ships in the harbour.

The situation at Dunkirk required men on the ground to be adaptable. Here British trucks have been used to improvise a pier, allowing men to get out to the waiting evacuation boats without having to wade or swim long distances.

miralty activated Operation Dynamo, the evacuation of troops from the Belgian and French coasts. But at that stage the bulk of the BEF was still engaged with the Germans, and some distance from the beaches.

The Belgians capitulate

During the morning of 27 May, the Belgian high command accepted that they must begin the process of surrendering, even though its would place the British and French troops in Flanders in a terrible position, and release yet more German troops against them. At 1230 hours, King Leopold signalled to Gort: 'The army is very discouraged. It has been fighting continuously for four days under intensive bombardment, and the moment is approaching when it will be unable to continue the fight. In these circumstances, the King will find himself forced to surrender to avoid collapse.' The French received a similar message later in the afternoon.

In order to provide the Allies with a little more time to withdraw their troops to more advantageous positions, the Belgian's strung out the armistice negotiations with the Germans for several hours during the evening of 27 May, but at 0400 on 28 May the Belgian armed forces were ordered to lay down their arms as Belgium had accepted the German offer of unconditional surrender. The Belgian surrender was condemned by the British and especially by the French, whose forces were left in a particularly vulnerable position by the decision of the Belgians to stop fighting.

To make matters worse, Hitler now rescinded his Halt Order, so that the motorised units of the panzer division were thrown into the fray from 27 May onwards. The armour of Hoth's XV Panzer Corps, led by Rommel, advanced towards Armentières as one arm of a pincer movement, the other being provided by the infantry of the Sixth Army advancing from the east.

When the pincers met on the evening of the 27th, two corps of the French First Army under the command of General Molinié were encircled around Lille. Molinié's troops – predominantly North African – fought with great determination and courage in what was a hopeless position, and in so doing they helped the BEF and the remnants of the First Army to fall back to the Dunkirk bridgehead in comparative safety. So impressed were the Germans by the determination of the French defence of Lille, that when the garrison eventually surrendered, they were allowed to march out of Lille with full battle honours, with a guard of honour provided by General Wäger's XXVIII Corps.

The encirclement and loss of the Lille garrison further strained relations between the French and British, when it was claimed by French commanders, including General Blanchard, that the BEF's withdrawal to Dunkirk had left the defenders of Lille in an impossible position. From a French view, the British withdrawal seemed particularly self-serving, but from a wider perspective there was little else that the British could do, and, it should be remembered, the prime cause of the whole catastrophe had been French military incompetence.

BELOW
RAF fighter pilots wait in their dispersal huts, ready for action over the skies of northern France. Although the men on the ground were often unaware of British aircraft fighting overhead, the RAF played a key role in limiting the activities of the Luftwaffe over Dunkirk.

Further north, Guderian's troops fought their way across the River Aa, and on 28 May captured Wormhoudt and Bourbourville. On the 29th, Gravelines was captured, the last town before Dunkirk. But by now the Germans were facing the well-defended Dunkirk bridgehead and found their progress slowed. Eventually, most of the German tanks were withdrawn from the cluttered battlefield to prepare for Operation Red, the coming offensive against the rest of France. Guderian's final comment on this phase of the campaign reflected the frustration felt by the panzer commanders: 'What the future course of the war would have been if we had succeeded at the time in taking the British Expeditionary Force prisoner at Dunkirk, it is now impossible to guess.'

The RAF was faced with the difficult task of forming an air umbrella over the Dunkirk perimeter and keeping the Luftwaffe at bay. A total of 2739 sorties were flown by the RAF and 177 aircraft were lost during the evacuation period. Marshal Göring had boasted to Hitler that the 'National Socialist' Luftwaffe should be given the job of eliminating the Allied pocket at Dunkirk rather than the 'reactionary' army. Although Hitler remained sceptical, he gave the Luftwaffe priority in this mission. A combination of poor weather and the RAF prevented Göring from fulfilling his

boast, and only on 27 May and 1 June did the Luftwaffe have the upper hand, although to the men on the beaches the constant bombing attacks by Stukas and other German bombers were psychologically punishing.

Discipline was often poor during the early stages of the evacuation, with scenes of drunkenness and panic being far from rare. Officers and naval ratings had to use physical force to keep some of the men under control. But the arrival of front line troops installed greater order, and the vast bulk of the Allied troops waited patiently in long lines for their turn to embark.

The evacuation gains pace

On the 27th, the total number of men evacuated was only 7669, and reflected Ironside's private comment that the BEF would be fortunate if they got 30,000 men back to Britain. But on 28 May better use was made of the port's facilities, and the day's figure rose to 17,804. During the succeeding days, evacuation totals rose, reaching a peak of 68,104 on 31 May. A growing problem was the disparity in British troops being evacuated over their French comrades, in part due to a lack of orders from the French high command to allow their men to be evacuated. When Churchill was reproached for this by Weygand, the British prime minister ordered

RIGHT
*Exhausted and battle-weary
British troops disembark at
a British port after their
ordeal at Dunkirk. To
rescue over a third of a
million men from under the
noses of the German Army
was a major feat of arms.*

that both British and French troops should be taken off the beaches on equal terms.

By 3 June the last British troops had been evacuated, but a French rearguard continued to man the defences around Dunkirk, with the Germans little more than a mile from the beaches. The following morning, Ramsay risked sending in his ships for the last time to pick up as many French as possible. There were, in fact, far more French troops than expected, and although some 27,000 got away from Dunkirk, as many as 30,000 French were left behind to face the final German advance alone (an event exploited by the Germans to encourage anti-British sentiment amongst the French). On 4 June the Germans marched into Dunkirk; less than a month after the first German attack, the war in northern France was over.

Dunkirk: defeat or victory?

A remarkable total of approximately 338,000 men were evacuated from Dunkirk (of which around 110,000 were French) for the loss of six British and two French destroyers and numerous other smaller craft. It had a been triumph of improvisation, a case where

victory was snatched from the jaws of defeat. And at a time when the British had encountered a succession of calamities, it was a great boost to morale. But, as Prime Minister Churchill warned the House of Commons on 4 June: 'Wars are not won by evacuations.' The vast bulk of the BEF's arms and equipment had been left behind in France (which included 2473 guns, 63,879 vehicles, 20,548 motorcycles, and 500,000 tons of stores and ammunition). It would take time to re-equip the evacuees. British casualties were 68,111 killed, wounded and taken prisoner. The Dutch had lost 2890 killed and 6889 wounded. Belgian casualties amounted to 7500 killed and 15,850 wounded.

German losses at this point in the French campaign were put at 10,252 killed with around 50,000 wounded and missing. According to German sources, over a million Allied prisoners had been taken by their forces. But the campaign was not over yet, and as the last Allied troops to escape the Germans in the north were being ferried from Dunkirk, the panzer divisions were driving south to destroy what remained of the French army and capture Paris.

ABOVE

Allied prisoners of war begin a new life behind the wire, an ordeal most would continue to endure for a further five years. The men in the foreground are engaged in the age-old military task of spud-bashing, otherwise known as potato-peeling.

CHAPTER SEVEN

THE FALL OF FRANCE

After the Belgian surrender and British evacuation at Dunkirk, only the shell-shocked remnants of the French army stood against the exultant Germans: the end was not long in coming.

On 5 June – the day after the capture of Dunkirk – the German high command commenced Operation Red, the destruction of the French armed forces south of the Somme-Aisne line. Immediately after Guderian's dash to the sea and the formation of the 'panzer corridor', the Germans had captured bridgeheads over the Somme and Aisne rivers. They would act as springboards for the coming offensive, and all attempts by the French to eliminate them were fiercely resisted.

As the panzer divisions travelled south from the Dunkirk perimeter, they were reinforced and reorganised for Operation Red. They were divided into five separate corps, each of two panzer divisions and one motorised infantry division. The XV Panzer Corps operated on the German right flank, closest to the Channel. The XIV and XVI Corps were combined into Panzer Group Kleist, and were assigned to Bock's Army Group B and deployed between Amiens and Péronne. The other two corps – XXXIX and XLI – were combined into Panzer Group Guderian, and were deployed on the left of the German line along the River Aisne as part of Rundstedt's Army Group A. The arrival of new formations from Germany brought the combined German strength in France at this stage of the campaign to 104 divisions.

The German plan was simply to break through the French defensive line and then use their mechanised formations to advance as swiftly as possible into France to isolate and surround the various major groupings of the French army. The XV Corps would race along the Channel towards Brittany. Panzer Group Kleist would drive into central France, bypassing Paris (which would be left to the infantry to capture). Panzer Group Guderian would advance due south through eastern France, with the aim of cutting off the mass of French troops stationed in and behind the Maginot Line. General Leeb's Army Group C, stationed opposite the Maginot Line, would finally see action by pinning down the defenders in the Line and so preventing any possible escape to southern France.

French weakness

The French losses in the opening phases of the campaign could not be replaced, and even by withdrawing reserves from the Alpine front with Italy, Weygand was only able to deploy around 60 divisions along the 360km (225 mile) front between the Channel and the French right flank on the Meuse. Among these forces were two Polish divisions and the British 51st Division and 1st Armoured Division, the latter formation still woefully short of tanks, artillery and anti-tank guns.

OPPOSITE

The swastika flies over a street in Paris, a symbol of German domination. The French government declared the capital an 'open city', and the Germans entered Paris on 14 June without opposition.

German troops relax on the shore line, following their breakthrough on the western sector of the French line on 8 June.

Two further British divisions were in the process of being shipped over to France, but the British numerical commitment to the final battle for France was slight.

Weygand's defensive plan abandoned the continuous front idea that had so conspicuously failed at Sedan, and was based on a chequer-board system of defensive points called 'hedgehogs'. Each hedgehog would be built around a defensible feature, such as a hill or village, and be packed with infantry and guns. The defenders would maintain their positions, even if the Germans pushed forward beyond them to leave them isolated. Behind the hedgehogs would be mobile reserves which, it was hoped, would counterattack any German thrust. The French, however, lacked sufficient mechanised formations to counter the strength of the five German panzer corps. And once the defensive crust had been penetrated, the Germans would have a free hand.

The French air force had made good their earlier losses, and with greater support from the RAF, they were able to deploy greater numbers of aircraft. Nonetheless, the Luftwaffe still had the numerical edge and, crucially, was far better organised and led.

Operation Red

The start of Operation Red was to be staggered, with Army Group B launching the attack on 5 June, while Army Group A waited until the 9th. The French army now demonstrated far greater resolve than it had shown on the Meuse a few weeks earlier. The German tanks were unable to break out of their bridgeheads, and the German infantry was caught by heavy fire from the French strong points. 'In these ruined villages,' wrote a German soldier, 'the French resisted to the last man. Some hedgehogs carried on when our infantry was 20 miles behind them.' All along the Weygand Line, the French fought with a new-found desperation, old World War I '75s' blasted the German tanks, while the infantry stood their ground.

The German XXIII Corps received a drubbing from the redoubtable 14th Infantry Division, one of the few French formations that had distinguished itself during the battles around Sedan. Commanded by General de

Lattre de Tassigny, the 14th Division counter-attacked the German corps and retook the German bridgeheads over the Aisne, capturing some 1000 prisoners in the process. The German corps commander, General Schubert, praised the far-improved performance of his opponents:

The attack ran up against an enemy whose morale was unshaken and who, in a well-arranged position, stood up to our preparatory artillery bombardment with minimal losses. The bearing and tactical skill of the enemy were totally different to those of earlier battles. The units of the 14th Division let the German infantry approach to within point-blank range in order to make certain of them. In many places the French marksmen posted in trees kept up their fire until they had exhausted their last cartridge, without heeding the advance of the German forces.

The morale of the French 14th Division was extraordinary. The French went out to look for their wounded, when their comrades had no chance of evacuating them, and cared for them. They left provisions with the wounded who could not be taken along when they fell back. The 14th Division

fought on 9 and 10 June in a manner that recalls the attitude of the best French troops of 1914–18 at Verdun.

Costly defence

The defence of the Weygand Line progressively used up the best troops in the French

ABOVE
From his vantage point, a German soldier looks down on a French town that is either burning or in ruins.

LEFT
Confident and well-armed, a section of German infantry marches through a town badly damaged in recent fighting. Although they met some early reverses, German assault troops finally overwhelmed the French defenders on the Somme line.

army, and inevitably the superior numbers and firepower of the German formations began to make their presence felt. The first German breakthrough came on the right of the German attack, spearheaded by Rommel's 7th Panzer Division. After being pinned down by the French during the first day's fighting, Rommel was able to exploit a weakness in their defences by sending his panzers forward across some low-lying ground and over two undamaged railway bridges, which the French had failed to destroy. Once the French line had been penetrated, the panzers drove straight for the River Seine. On 8 June, the vanguard reached Elbeuf on the Seine, isolating the city of Rouen, before swinging north-west to reach the Channel at Fécamp.

St Valery surrender

This action trapped the French IX Corps, which included the British 51st Division and elements of the French 2nd and 5th Light Cavalry Divisions. Although the French and British troops put up resistance, they were in an impossible position, unable to mount an effective defence as they waited to disembark. On 12 June approximately 45,000 Allied troops (including 12 generals) surrendered to Rommel at St Valéry, although about 3000 succeeded in breaking though the German cordon. Rommel had been impressed by the tenacious defence of the British troops, and so was especially pleased to capture the GOC of the 51st Division, Major General Victor Fortune. For the captured British troops,

however, this was a despairing moment, despite Rommel's description of the event:

Particularly surprising to us was the sang froid with which the British officers accepted their fate. The General, and even more, his staff officers, stalked round laughing in the street in front of the house. The only thing that seemed to disturb them was the frequent photographing and filming they had to endure by our Propaganda Company and some other photographers. The captured generals were now invited to an open air lunch at a German field kitchen, but they refused with thanks, saying they still had supplies of their own. So we ate alone.

After securing Le Havre on 14 June, the 7th Panzer Division was ordered forward towards Cherbourg, while its sister formation, 5th Panzer Division, raced westwards into Brittany. Resistance was minimal, and Cherbourg was captured on 19 June, the last act of the 7th Panzer Division in this extraordinary campaign.

In contrast to the success of Hoth's XV Panzer Corps, the two corps of Panzer Group Kleist were unable to effect a breakthrough across the Somme. In order that the attack not get bogged down, Bock diverted the panzer group eastwards, to cross the Aisne next to Panzer Group Guderian. After two days of hard fighting, which included a flank attack on the XXXIX Panzer Corps by General Buisson's armoured group, the exhausted and outnumbered French Fourth Army began to waver. On 11 May, Guderian broke through the Weygand Line, soon to be followed by

Kleist's panzers. By nightfall on the 11th, Reims was captured, and on the following evening Guderian reached Châlons-sur-Marne. Kleist's Panzer Group began to advance to the east of Paris, while German infantry formations marched directly towards the French capital from the north.

Weygand's pessimism

For the French, the situation was desperate. Although Weygand was an energetic soldier who had done much to put some spirit back into the French army, he had always been pessimistic about France's ability to hold the German onslaught. Increasingly, he began to voice his doubts, much to the consternation of the French prime minister, Reynaud, who was determined to carry on the fight. On 9 May, Weygand informed the government that a German breakthrough could come at any time. He concluded the message with the gloomy pronouncement: 'If this should happen our armies will fight on until exhausted, to the last round, but their dispersion will only be a matter of time.' A few days later – as the Germans were breaking through the French defences – Weygand's pessimism was such that he informed the government: 'I will continue to resist, if the Council orders me to do so. But at this moment I have to make this clear: the ending of hostilities must be considered soon.'

France's dire situation was made even worse on 10 May, when Mussolini declared war on France. The Italian dictator, resentful of German military success against France, was determined to get a share of the spoils, and he announced to the world that Italy was to 'liberate' Savoy, Nice and Corsica from French rule. The cynical nature of the declaration – when France was on the verge of defeat – brought widespread condemnation from world leaders; President Roosevelt of the United States angrily declared, 'the hand that held the dagger has stuck it into the back of his neighbour'.

The Italian force assigned for the attack on France consisted of two armies, 24 divisions strong, with a further eight divisions in reserve. Defending the Alpine passes that separated the two countries were just three French reserve divisions and three fortress divisions, commanded by General Orly. The attack began on 20 May, but Orly had deployed his troops with considerable skill, and he bottled up the attacking Italians into the long mountainous valleys, while his own troops held the high ground. As a consequence, the Italian numerical superiority was largely negated. The attack soon ground to a standstill, and only on the Côte d'Azur did the Italians make any headway. When the armistice came into effect the French troops still held their positions along the Alpine defence line. While the French could take some satisfaction from the military conduct of their troops, the invasion painfully exposed the shortcomings of the Italian army.

As the Germans neared Paris, so long columns of refugees fled the capital for the south. The government had already left for Tours and then subsequently Bordeaux. The decision whether to defend the city or leave it to the Germans was undecided until 11 June, when Weygand declared Paris an 'open city'.

BELOW
A German howitzer team crosses a pontoon bridge. The main artillery piece available to the German infantry division was the 10.5cm howitzer, capable of firing a 14.81kg (32.65lb) shell to a range in excess of 12,000 metres (13,123 yards).

A French fort on the Italian border. Although the Italian army avoided these strongpoints, they were also unsuccessful when attacking the French in more open battlefield conditions.

The decision was a sound one on practical grounds, as the Germans intended to bypass Paris if defended, and then only bomb and bombard it into submission when the campaign was over. Thus, a defence would serve no military purpose, especially when set against dreadful destruction and great loss of life that such a defence would entail. But the

abandonment of the capital was nonetheless a profound psychological blow to the French people. On hearing of the order not to defend Paris, the writer André Maurois declared: 'At that moment I knew everything was over. France deprived of Paris, would become a body without a head. The war had been lost.'

Exhausted German troops rest on the limber of a gun carriage, shortly after the entry into Paris. The loss of the capital was a devastating psychological blow to the French.

On 14 June, advance guards from the German Eighteenth Army entered the city without resistance. The German occupation was orderly and restrained, and within a couple of days the inhabitants of Paris began to go about their normal business while thousands of German soldiers wandered around the city as sightseers.

Continued German success

As the infantry marched into Paris, the panzers exploited their breakthrough. Hoth's XV Panzer Corps secured Normandy and Brittany; Panzer Group Kleist crossed the Seine at Romilly and headed by the Massif Central and Burgundy; and Panzer Group Guderian advanced south-east to out-flank and then isolate General Prételat's Army Group Number 2, deployed behind the Maginot Line.

In conjunction with Guderian's advance, Leeb's Army Group C began its offensive, mainly directed at the Maginot Line fortifications. The Germans made relatively slow progress; French forces withdrew in some areas, but only to confirm with the new defensive lines being set up because of the German breakthrough on the Aisne.

Throughout this short period of hostilities, the Germans were unable to capture any of the main fortifications of the Maginot Line, despite shelling by German heavy artillery and repeated Stuka attacks with armour-piercing bombs. The Maginot Line had proved its durability, but its defence had little bearing on the campaign as a whole.

Panzer Group Guderian – now under the command of Army Group C – pushed on towards the Swiss border. Belfort was captured on 16 June, and on the following day, the 29th Motorised Division reached the border with Switzerland at Pontarlier. The French Army Group Number 2 was now trapped between the Maginot Line and the ring of steel that was Guderian's panzer envelopment. As a result, 400,000 French troops were captured. It was one of the easiest and most complete encirclement battles in history.

As Guderian completed his encirclement, Kleist's panzer group forged into central France, reaching Dijon on 16 June, while separate columns advanced to Clermont-Ferrand and Lyons. The only serious obstacle to the panzer advance came near Saulieu when the XVI Panzer Corps was engaged in a fierce but brief fight with the Polish 10th Armoured

BELOW
A battery of German artillery takes the salute from a senior officer as it rides through Paris along the Champs Elysées. German propaganda was swift to release pictures like this to the world's press, to underline the completeness of their victory.

The humiliation of defeat: disconsolate Parisians watch the German take-over of their city.

The symbolic importance of the French capital was lost on no one. During World War I the Germans had failed to take Paris during four years of fighting; in 1940 it had taken less than six weeks. The French armed forces were in a state of total collapse, and many believed Britain would soon follow.

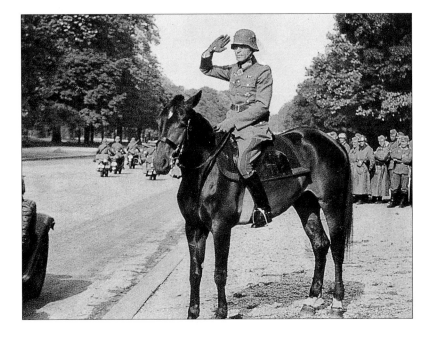

Brigade and the remnants of the French 3rd Armoured Division. The Germans found that organised resistance had almost completely ceased, and the advance was now a test of mechanical reliability rather than fighting prowess. A last act of defiance came from the cadets of the military academy at Saumer on the River Loire. Refusing a call to surrender on 19 June, the cadets (and some other locally based troops) – armed only with ancient weapons from the academy armoury – kept up a spirited defence that lasted two days, and only ended when their ammunition ran out.

French political collapse

The collapse of the French army was paralleled by the disintegration of the French Government. Reynaud headed the 'war' faction and was joined by de Gaulle (recently brought into the government as Under Secretary of State for War). They were opposed by the 'peace' faction lead by Weygand and Pétain. On 11 June, Churchill had made his fourth and last crisis-visit to France, and had typically urged the French to carry on the battle. Again, Weygand asked him for aircraft and troops. Churchill's inability to offer substantial forces met with a cold response from the peace faction, who now believed that, as they had been abandoned by Britain, they had no alternative but to ask the Germans for an armistice.

Reynaud and his dwindling band of supporters attempted to maintain some sort of organised front against the Germans, arguing that if France fell then the war should be carried on from the French possessions in North Africa. A despairing plea for armed support from the United States was inevitably rejected by a government which was then pledged to neutrality. One last attempt to prop up France's military will came from the British Cabinet and de Gaulle, who was then in London, in the form of the 'Declaration of Union' between the British and French peoples (an extraordinary constitutional device to bind the two nations together). Reynaud presented the Declaration to the French Government on the afternoon of the 16th, but the idea of Anglo-French union was promptly rejected. By now a virtually broken man, Reynaud offered his resignation to the French head of state President Lebrun, who then appointed the 84-year-old Marshal Pétain in his place.

On 17 June, Pétain sent emissaries to the Spanish Government to ask for peace negotiations to be opened with the Germans. Some of those who opposed an armistice with the Germans prepared to leave France to carry on the fight from overseas. On the evening of the 17th, de Gaulle joined the British liaison officer General Spears in a light plane and both flew to Britain. Once in Britain, de Gaulle would raise the standard of a 'Free France', around which would rally a growing body of French. Others attempting to escape were less successful and ended up first in French prisons and then in German concentration camps. For the British and other non-French Allied troops in France, this was also a desperate period, with military units scrambling to get out in time. Some 145,000 British troops of the 'second' BEF, along with substantial numbers of Poles and Czechs, managed to slip away before the onrushing Germans.

Hitler accepted the offer of peace talks from the representatives of the Spanish Government. Although the German armed forces had inflicted a crushing victory over France, Hitler did not demand total surrender, as he wished to avoid the risk of the French government-in-exile carrying on the war from its colonies in North Africa, where the French still had powerful military and naval forces. The German terms accepted the continuing sovereignty of France, and that its extensive overseas territories should remain under French jurisdiction (in case they were tempted to go over to the British cause). France itself was to be divided into an occupied zone (in the north and west) and an unoccupied zone (in the south) which would come under direct rule by the new national government led by Pétain. Although the French army was to be demobilised, the French Government was permitted to maintain local military units as a means of ensuring order. The powerful French fleet, much of it based in the Mediterranean, would remain in French hands but would only exist on a neutral basis, and be subject to German or Italian supervision.

ABOVE

Near the famous cathedral of Notre Dame, a German officer browses through one of the book stalls lining the banks of the River Seine. A posting to Paris was eagerly sought after by German soldiers.

LEFT

German soldiers man a checkpoint. Although the fighting was over, a large army of occupation was required to supervise Germany's new-won gains.

Hitler poses for the cameras
in front of the Eiffel tower.
The German leader was so
delighted with his victory
that he took a short holiday
in France, sightseeing in
Paris and visiting the
battlefields he had fought
over in World War I.

Although the peace terms were relatively lenient, Hitler was determined to ensure that the armistice negotiations themselves would be painfully humiliating for the French. On 20 July, Pétain received instructions to send a delegation to Paris, which arrived in the capital the following day. Led by General Huntziger, the delegation was driven to Compiègne on the 21st and taken to a forest clearing, which contained the railway carriage in which the armistice of 1918 had been signed (the carriage had been hastily removed from a museum in Paris).

A delighted Hitler was present at the preliminary phase of the negotiations, determined to enjoy this ritual revenge over the victors of the previous world war. Huntziger was handed the armistice convention and told that no discussions would be entered into. After conferring with his political masters in Bordeaux, the French delegation signed the armistice at 0850 hours on 22 June 1940. As a consequence of the Italian intervention in the campaign, a second armistice was signed in Rome on 24 June, with all hostilities in France ending at 0135 hours on the 25th.

Hitler's victory

Adolf Hitler, the former World War I corporal, had defeated his great enemy France in just six weeks, a feat that his former commander-in-chief, the Kaiser, had failed to do in four years. And while the German casualties on the Western Front during 1914–18 ran into the millions, German losses in 1940, according to OKH estimates, amounted to a relatively light figure of 27,074 killed, 111,034 wounded and 18,384 missing (most of these being fatal casualties). Daily German casualty rates were twice as high for the period of the 'Battle of France' in June than during the fighting in May, reflecting improved French tactics and greater French determination to fight in this second phase of the campaign.

French losses were proportionately heavier than those of the Germans, with at least 90,000 killed and 200,000 wounded. The figures for French prisoners captured by the Germans varied, ranging from a minimum of 1,450,000 to as much as 1,900,000 (most of whom remained in German POW camps as a bargaining tool for 'good behaviour' from the French Government – in other words as hostages).

The German campaign against the Allies in the west was one of the great triumphs of modern military history. The two opposing reasons for Hitler's victory lay in the quality of the German armed forces – in planning the campaign and in its execution – and the corresponding failure of the French armed forces at every level, from the lowliest infantryman to the high command. The ineptitude of the French came as a surprise to both their fellow allies and their German opponents. How could an army that fought with such conviction during World War I (and again later in World War II) fall apart so easily in 1940?

The political malaise that ran through so much of France during the inter-war years was contributory factor which corroded French resolve. But in the end blame had to be laid against the French military system. The army was inadequately armed and equipped; its strategic deployment was fatally flawed; its

tactical ability owed nothing to 1940 and everything to 1918; and its commanders had little faith in victory. The French had lost the battle in the first few days of fighting.

Germany triumphant

The Germans now dominated most of Europe. Only the British remained at war and, according to most estimates, it would only be a matter of time before they too succumbed to Hitler's will, either through a negotiated peace or by force of arms. But Churchill's defiant refusal to treat with Nazi Germany and the RAF's victory in the Battle of Britain ensured that the war would continue. Britain and the new German 'empire' were separated by the English Channel, and while air operations could be (and were) conducted directly across the Channel, the ground war would move elsewhere.

ABOVE
A German military band in the Channel Islands, the only piece of British soil to fall to the Germans. They were to remain occupied until the end of the war, after being bypassed by the Normandy landings.

LEFT
Hitler surveys the railway carriage in which both 1918 and 1940 surrender ceremonies took place. German victory in 1940 overturned the humiliation of the Versailles treaty for Hitler and the Germans.

CHAPTER EIGHT

Italy's African Disasters

The dramatic German successes of 1939–40 persuaded
Mussolini that his forces could emulate Hitler's European
conquests elsewhere, and create a new Roman Empire in Africa.

Ever since taking power in Italy in 1922, the fascist leader Benito Mussolini had dreamt of accumulating new possessions in a bid to emulate the great empire of classical Rome. But Italy lacked the economic and military resources to achieve il Duce's grand aims, which moreover found little support among the majority of the Italian people. To the established Italian colonies in Libya, the Dodecanese islands, Eritrea and Italian Somaliland, Mussolini added Abyssinia (Ethiopia) in 1936 and Albania in 1939. Both these nations lacked the means to defend themselves against the Italian armed forces, but when Mussolini decided to extend his operations, against France and Britain in June 1940 and Greece the following October, he took Italy out of its military depth and over-committed the slim Italian resources, with disastrous consequences. This military adventurism would be the direct cause of the destruction of the Italian fascist state and the subsequent deposition and imprisonment of Mussolini in 1943 by his compatriots.

Germany's extraordinary military triumph over France in 1940 had encouraged Mussolini to act. By declaring war on France and Britain, Mussolini hoped to receive his share of the pickings, which he believed would follow the defeat of these major powers and the dismemberment of their extensive overseas colonies and possessions. Unfortunately for Mussolini, Britain was not defeated, and the Franco-German armistice talks established a new state (Vichy France) in southern France which left French colonies in Africa intact and under French supervision, the very areas in which Mussolini had hoped to make substantial territorial gains. But as Italy was very much the junior partner in the Axis, Germany invariably disregarded Italian interests if they were not to Germany's advantage.

Italian command structure

Marshal Pietro Badoglio was chief of the general staff for the armed forces, but his position as Italy's senior soldier was undermined by Mussolini, who acted as minister for all three armed forces. Mussolini had a controlling voice over the entire military machine but at the cost of efficiency, as the three services operated independently of each other. Badoglio was replaced by General Ugo Cavallero at the end of 1940, who attempted to reform the entire high command (*Commando Supremo*) on more coordinated and efficient lines.

Command of Italian troops in Libya was the responsibility of Marshal Italo Balbo, until he was shot down and killed by his own

ABOVE
*Mussolini (here
photographed with German
foreign minister Joachim
von Ribbentrop) liked to see
himself as a man of destiny.
Events would soon prove
otherwise.*

troops in a 'friendly fire' incident on 28 June 1940 and replaced by Marshal Rodolfo Graziani, also the army chief of staff. The Duke of Aosta was commander-in-chief of Italian forces in East Africa, where, as a result of the colony's isolation and distance from the Italian homeland, he was at least able to exercise a degree of real control over the men under his command.

Further problems faced by the Italian supreme command included the series of impetuous decisions made by Mussolini to deploy his forces where he thought they might bring him most influence and glory. During the Battle of Britain, Mussolini despatched an expeditionary force of fighters

and bombers which were badly mauled by the RAF. The same was done during the German invasion of the Soviet Union. In the latter case, Mussolini sent a large military force as well as aerial units. Mussolini's contribution to the 'crusade against Bolshevism' was a disaster: of the 230,000 Italian troops despatched to the Eastern Front, over half became casualties. The net result of Mussolini's attempt to impress Hitler was to stretch Italy's already meagre military resources to breaking point.

Army strength

In 1940, the Italian army had 73 divisions at its disposal, totalling 1.6 million troops. The army had a notional aim of raising 126 divisions, but this was never realised, not so much for want of manpower but through shortages of equipment and the inability to train and organise such a large number of recruits. The vast bulk of these troops were organised into infantry formations, although 17 infantry divisions were termed 'self-transportable', which gave them a degree of mobility similar to the standard (motorised) British infantry division. The Italians had a limited armoured capability, comprising just three armoured, two motorised and three light divisions, equipped with poorly armoured and undergunned tanks which were effectively obsolete for the period. This deficiency would be ruthlessly exposed in the Western Desert campaigns, where armoured formations had a tactical importance beyond that found in other theatres of war.

Among the better troops available to the army were the six alpine divisions, trained in mountain warfare and deployed in northern Italy and the Balkans. Fighting alongside the Italian army was a fascist militia – commonly known as the black shirts – which were organised into legions of two infantry battalions. Each army infantry division was augmented by a black shirt legion, partly to increase levels of manpower (most Italian divisions only had two rather than the more usual three infantry regiments) but also to introduce right-thinking fascist troops into the army. In addition, three small divisions of black shirts were organised for service in

Libya, their organisation based on the colonial division of around 8000 men as against the regular infantry division of 13,500.

The Italian air force (the *Regia Aeronautica*) had gained a deserved reputation for innovation in the 1920s and 1930s, but by 1940 it had become an organisation in decline. Chronic and prolonged under-funding of the Regia Aeronautica ensured that on the outbreak of war most of its aircraft, like the army's tanks, were obsolete. This was especially true of the fighter arm, where the Fiat CR-32 and CR-42 biplanes were outclassed by the Hurricane fighters of the RAF, which in themselves hardly represented the cutting edge of fighter design at the time. Numbers were also in short supply, and as the war progressed the German Luftwaffe began to take over Axis aerial responsibilities as a whole, leaving the Italian air force to carry out mostly home defence, reconnaissance and minor bombing duties.

Italian aims

Mussolini hoped to use the colony of Libya as a springboard for conquest in Africa. Libya was surrounded from the west and south by French possessions, and in the east by British-controlled Egypt. Originally, the Italians adopted a defensive position, but with France out of the war – and its colonies protected by the Franco-German armistice – the Italian high command began to look towards invading Egypt, the cornerstone of British influence in the Middle East and North

LEFT
The Suez Canal was Britain's lifeline to India and the Far East. Accordingly, the Axis attempted to wrest it from British control, while Britain prepared to defend it with the utmost determination.

Africa, whose conquest would bring German respect and admiration for the Italians.

Egypt protected British territories in Palestine and Jordan, and conferred influence and control over a far wider area, including Syria, and oil-rich Iraq and Iran. The port facilities in Alexandria allowed the Royal Navy to dominate the eastern Mediterranean, and the Suez Canal was the British lifeline to India and the Far East. The loss of Egypt to Britain would have been a strategic disaster of the first order, while for the Italians, the conquest of Egypt would open up the Sudan and forge a direct link with their possessions in East Africa.

The Italian military presence in Libya in 1940 consisted of nearly 250,000 men, 1800 guns, 350 light tanks and some 8000 trucks. Italian air strength was comparatively weak but its 150 front-line aircraft compared favourably with anything the RAF could deploy at the time, the Battle of Britain being

an understandable priority. The Italian forces were divided into two armies. In Tripolitania, in the west, was the Fifth Army (General Italo Gariboldi) with six regular (metropolitan) infantry divisions plus two smaller black shirt divisions. The Tenth Army (General Francesco Berti) was deployed in Cyrenaica in the east and comprised three metropolitan infantry divisions, one black shirt division and one Libyan native division (with another due to arrive). The disparity in allotment of troops to the Fifth Army reflected earlier Italian intentions to secure Tunisia from the French, but now that Egypt was the prime target, Berti's Tenth Army was reinforced to a strength of nine and later ten divisions.

British forces in Egypt

British forces in Egypt came under General Sir Archibald Wavell, commander-in-chief in the Middle East. Wavell had fewer than 100,000 troops to cover a vast area that

ABOVE

British troops train in Egypt in preparation for the coming offensive against the Italian Army. Although outnumbered by the Italians, the British were better trained, armed and led, and would comprehensively outfight the Italians in the coming campaign.

OPPOSITE

British and Commonwealth troops cheer as they arrive at the docks in Alexandria, part of a convoy of reinforcements to the British Middle East Command in Egypt.

BELOW

General Sir Archibald Wavell, Commander-in-Chief of British Forces in the Middle East. His area of command involved too great a geographical area and too great a responsibility for one man. In the early part of the war, Wavell chalked up a number of successes, including the Italian defeats in Cyrenaica and in East Africa, but failures in Greece and against the better trained and armed Germans in North Africa led to his dismissal.

stretched from Iraq down through Jordan, Palestine and Egypt to the Sudan. In Egypt, Wavell was able to muster a total of some 36,000 troops, and facing the Italians along the Libyan border were two under-strength divisions: 4th Indian Division (Major General Noel Beresford-Peirse) and the infamous 7th Armoured Division (Major General O'Moore Creagh). Although both short of men, vehicles and guns, the divisions were of the highest quality, and formed part of the newly instituted Western Desert Force under the command of Lieutenant General Richard O'Connor.

The 4th Indian Division contained a solid mix of Indian and British troops with long experience of desert conditions which would stand them in good stead in the coming months. The 7th Armoured Division, which would play a major role in the Desert War,

had been raised in Egypt in 1938 by Major General Percy Hobart, one of the pioneers of armoured warfare in Britain.

In contrast to many other tank officers in the British army, Hobart understood how armoured forces should be organised and deployed. He was also a tireless trainer of the troops under his command, and he welded the various tank, infantry, artillery, signals and administrative units of his forces into a coherent formation, well versed in the complexities of travelling and fighting in desert conditions. The jerboa – or 'desert rat' – was adopted as the soldiers' divisional insignia, an indication that they were at ease in a desert environment. The normally reserved O'Connor paid tribute to the commanding officer and men of the division in 1939, when he said he considered the 7th Armoured Division, 'the best-trained division I have ever seen'.

British dispositions

The 7th Armoured Division was deployed along the border, mounting small raids into enemy territory which not only inconvenienced the Italians but actually led them to overestimate the size of the British troops facing them. Before his appointment to command in Libya, Marshal Graziani had urged offensive action against the British, with D-Day for an Italian invasion of Egypt set as early as 15 July 1940.

Once in Libya, however, Graziani became more cautious, and began asking for time to prepare supplies for the advance (which would have to take place along a single coastal road). Mussolini on the other hand urged immediate action, and a series of increasingly angry telegrams winged their way between

Italy and Libya before the offensive finally got underway on 13 September.

While the Italian generals vacillated, the British War Cabinet in London made a difficult and courageous decision. Throughout the summer of 1940 the threat of German invasion remained very real; the Battle of Britain was raging overhead, and the German army was assembling an invasion fleet of converted Rhine barges on the other side of the English Channel. After the recent disasters in France and Belgium, and the evacuation at Dunkirk, the British army was acutely short of weapons and equipment for home defence, but if Egypt was to be defended and the lifeline to Britain's colonies preserved, Wavell would need reinforcements, especially in tanks, artillery and vehicles.

ABOVE

An Egyptian Army British Mark VI light tank, part of the inadequate force that defended Egypt against the Italians in the autumn of 1940. Reinforcements would provide the British with a stronger force capable of taking the war to the enemy.

On 15 August the decision was made to
reinforce the Egyptian command with three
tank battalions/regiments (154 tanks in total),
48 anti-tank guns, 48 25-pounder gun-how-
itzers, and other infantry weapons and
ammunition. Despatched to Egypt via the
Cape they steamed into the Red Sea on 19
September, preparatory to entry into the Suez
Canal. Churchill wrote afterwards: 'The decision to give this blood transfusion while we
braced ourselves to meet a mortal danger was
at once awful and right. No one faltered.'

The invasion begins

On 13 September 1940, four divisions and an
armoured group from the Italian Tenth Army
invaded Egypt. Progress was slow as a consequence of the high temperatures – at times
over 50°C (120°F) – as well as the absence of
a proper road, anti-tank mines, and Graziani's
almost innate sense of caution. After four days
of marching – some 105km (65 miles) over
the border – a black shirt division occupied
Sidi Barrani, and there the Italian 'invasion'
was halted by Graziani. The advance cost the
Italians 120 dead and 410 wounded; the
British 7th Armoured Division, which had
been ordered to conduct a fighting withdrawal, lost only 50 men.

Rather than press on to Mersa Matruh,
where Wavell had built a defensive line,
Graziani ordered his men to dig-in, and continue construction of the Via Balbia – the
main road that ran across Libya – from the
border to Sidi Barrani, where the British road
to Alexandria began. The Italians stocked Sidi
Barrani with provisions and ammunition, and
construction was started on a fresh-water
pipeline. Graziani was an experienced colonial general and, working on the assumption
that the British had deployed substantial
forces in Egypt, his methodical approach to
invasion was sensible if not inspired. But the
British did not have substantial forces ready
for action in Egypt during September and
early October, and an opportunity for
Graziani to push on towards Alexandria and
Cairo while the opposing British forces were
at their weakest was lost. Throughout
October, the reinforcements sent from Britain
began to come up to the line and join other
British units in the field.

The British counter-attack

When Wavell realised that Graziani's decision
to halt at Sidi Barrani was more than just
temporary, he decided to employ O'Connor
to expel the Italians from Egypt, and if

progress was good, to extend the operation into Libya. The first planning stage was begun as early as 21 September, although it was not until mid-October that 'Operation Compass' began to take shape.

Wavell's problem was to know what troops he would have available for the attack, for while the planning was in progress events outside Egypt widened his range of responsibilities and drained away resources. On 28 October, Italian forces based in Albania suddenly invaded Greece, and Wavell was instructed by British high command to offer the Greek armed forces military support. At the same time, the Royal Navy was heavily engaged in the eastern Mediterranean, and an offensive against the Italians in Abyssinia was also being prepared.

British reconnaissance had revealed the faulty nature of the Italian Tenth Army's positions around Sidi Barrani. The Italian positions were divided into a coastal and an inland group of camps, separated from each other by a gap of around 24km (15 miles). The imaginative British plan of attack would exploit the gap between the Italian camps and would begin with a secret overland march by O'Connor's Western Desert Force; the infantry would overrun the main Italian coastal group, while the armour would cut off any chance of reinforcement. The proposed attack was kept secret from all but a handful of senior officers, and they were told it was little more than a five-day raid, although at the last moment Wavell informed O'Connor that if the 'raid' proved successful then it might be exploited to the full.

Selby Force

The British were able to deploy 30,000 troops from the 4th Indian Division, 7th Armoured Division and a secondary formation called Selby Force, commanded by Brigadier A.R. Selby. Selby Force, around 1750 men strong, consisted of three columns of motorised infantry supported by a small complement of armoured cars and anti-aircraft and field guns, its role being to advance along the coast and pin down the enemy's troops with a limited frontal assault, while the other two divisions would skirt round the Italians and outflank their positions.

BELOW

British light tanks advance into the desert. The terrain encountered in Egypt and Libya provided great scope for armoured operations by both sides.

Italian aerial reconnaissance had reported signs of increased British motor traffic but interpreted this as merely a move to strengthen their defences in the light of a possible Italian attack. When O'Connor's troops moved forward on 8/9 December 1940 – in the bitter cold of a desert winter night – they found the gap in the Italian centre. Surprise was total.

Victory at Sidi Barrani

The 4th Indian Division, supported by a battalion of Matilda tanks, overwhelmed the Italians around Sidi Barrani. The Italian commander, General Maletti, fought on although wounded, and was killed bravely leading from the front. By 0830 hours the fighting was over and, for the price of 63 dead, the 4th Indian Division had captured 2000 prisoners. The 7th Armoured Division undertook a more wide-ranging sweep which reached the coast well to the west of Sidi Barrani, preventing the arrival of reinforcements and cutting off any means of retreat for the enemy in Sidi Barrani. The British victory was complete: after only a couple of days' fighting, Italian losses amounted to 38,000 prisoners, 237 guns and 73 tanks. Those Italians who escaped the British net quickly scuttled back over the border into Libya.

At this point, O'Connor suddenly lost the 4th Indian Division – withdrawn in order to participate in the invasion of Italian East Africa – from the forces under his command, and he had to await the arrival of Australian reinforcements before he could continue to harry the retreating Italians. 'It came as a complete and very unpleasant surprise,' said O'Connor, who had been unaware of this change of plan. 'The 6th Australian Division had never been trained in desert warfare and had to be rearmed with modern artillery. The

BELOW

An Italian field gun mounted on a lorry. Italian motorised forces made considerable use of such portable artillery; in practice, however, it did not prove particularly effective.

net result was that the removal of the 4th Indian Division led to a serious delay before we could attack Bardia and by so doing we lost surprise completely.'

Bardia besieged

As the Australians were being transported up to the battle front, O'Connor led his remaining forces into Libya on 14 December, and then swung round to invest Bardia, a strongpoint held by 45,000 Italian soldiers. After the arrival and deployment of the Australians, the assault on the Bardia perimeter started on 3 January 1941 and was a true all-arms affair, led by 23 Matilda tanks and supported by fire from Royal Navy ships (accompanying the landward advance) and from the RAF. The 6th Australian Division would provide the infantry to take Bardia. The Australian advance was supported by fire from a 25-pounder battery of the Essex Yeomanry. Gunner L.E. Tutt described the attack:

We moved our guns to a new position for our attack on Bardia. We fired off out first big programme and then moved through the wire surrounding the place to be able to engage fresh targets. We came across a battery of Italians. It became the fashion to decry Italians as soldiers; this may have been true of their infantry but not their artillery. In this instance they had died at their guns. Their bodies were scattered close to their firing positions and they must have remained in action until out infantry tanks [Matildas] and the Australians had overrun their gun sites.

Once the Australians had penetrated the anti-tank ditch that formed the basis of the perimeter defence of Bardia, they advanced forwards to the shore line, cutting the Italian force in two. After some sporadic fighting the garrison surrendered on 5 January. Fully aware of the necessity for speed, O'Connor had led the 7th Armoured Division along the coast towards Tobruk during the fighting for Bardia. Tobruk was one of the few deep water ports in the region, and of great strategic importance for the movement of supplies along the Libyan–Egyptian coast. Its loss would seriously harm the Italian war effort in North Africa.

The first battle for Tobruk

The British armour cut communications around Tobruk, and once the Australian infantry had arrived, the attack went in at dawn on 21 January. As there were only 12 Matilda tanks still operable after the long British advance along the coastline, O'Connor supplemented his armour by 'mechanising' a squadron of Australian cavalry and supplying them with captured examples

ABOVE
A vast crowd of Italian prisoners assembles in the distance, before being taken to the rear. Although few Italians tried to escape once captured, they remained a logistical nightmare for the British.

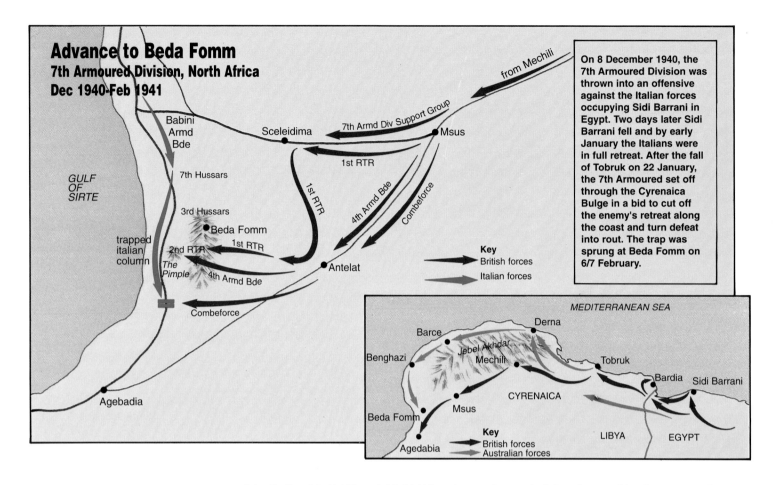

Advance to Beda Fomm
7th Armoured Division, North Africa
Dec 1940-Feb 1941

On 8 December 1940, the 7th Armoured Division was thrown into an offensive against the Italian forces occupying Sidi Barrani in Egypt. Two days later Sidi Barrani fell and by early January the Italians were in full retreat. After the fall of Tobruk on 22 January, the 7th Armoured set off through the Cyrenaica Bulge in a bid to cut off the enemy's retreat along the coast and turn defeat into rout. The trap was sprung at Beda Fomm on 6/7 February.

of the Italian M-11/39 and M-11/40 tanks. Now they were in Libya, the Italian defenders fought harder than in previous engagements to protect the Italian colony. Captain Baker, an officer commanding a troop of Matilda tanks in the action, describes the battle to penetrate the Tobruk defences:

Approaching a wadi, we'd been shelled for about three miles without being able to tell where the fire came from. I spotted a gun flash from behind stones on the wadi edge. I ordered my troop to attack, ignoring machine guns and anti-tank fire from the flank. It was the guns we were after. Then I heard a whoof of shells passing at point-blank range. It was a question of which would knock out the other first. I just kept straight on and told the gunner to let go when we were near. Although we yawing and pitching all over the place he hit the emplacement with his first shot.

Then we went for three other guns. I turned quickly, which threw up a cloud of dust, drove round the cloud and took them by surprise. When we were only yards away we could see the men in their dark green uniforms with their coats open, sweating as they tried to hump their guns round and train them on us. We simply went straight towards them, firing; we would have gone straight over them if we hadn't knocked their guns out. The we drove the loaders and odds and ends into a

dugout. And then the next thing I saw was a white flag surrendering.

The speed and aggression of the British advance to Tobruk caught the Italians defenders off-guard, and despite a few energetic counter-attacks, the Tobruk defence was broken by nightfall on the 21st. The following day the Italian garrison surrendered. The advance had been so rapid that Tobruk's seawater distilling plant fell undamaged into British hands and the vital strategic port installations were up and working again within a few days.

A major problem facing the British was the large number of Italian prisoners who had to be rounded up, counted and sent back to the rear. One of the features of this campaign was long columns of prisoners marching back towards Egypt and POW camps. Most of these prisoners seemed not to be particularly dejected at the prospect of captivity and escaping from the dangers of combat, and they occasionally provided moments of humour for their captors. Corporal Hoffman, a former journalist who had enlisted in the 6th Australian Division, described one such incident he witnessed:

Fascist flamboyance was exhibited by a captured major in a column of prisoners. When it had reached a safe spot he rushed to the head of the column and baring his chest to them, cried (in Italian): 'Shoot me ... and save my honour.' This brave Roman exhortation must be read with the obvious knowledge that whatever the prisoners had, they certainly had nothing with which to shoot anybody.

The 'suicidal' major repeated his gesture of honour several times until an Australian sentry approached with a bayonet levelled at the seat of his pants, and said: 'Get back, you mug, before I shoot you.' The terrorised fascist major skipped back into line at the double.

The British offensive continues

The five-day raid to expel the Italians from Egypt was transformed into an invasion of Mussolini's North African empire. The dilemma now facing the British was whether to extend this offensive to capture Benghazi and the great 'bump' of Cyrenaica (eastern Libya) or go onto the defensive. Churchill was mindful of supporting the Greeks in their battle against the Italians on the Albanian border. He wrote to the chiefs of staff committee on 6 January: 'It is quite clear to me that supporting Greece must have priority after the western flank of Egypt has been made secure.'

For the time being, however, O'Connor was allowed to continue with his offensive against the Italians. Despite the wear and tear on troops and equipment (compounded by shortages of petrol), the pace of the advance did not falter. Derna was captured on 30 January, the Italians falling back without putting up a fight. O'Connor now saw a chance to destroy the Italian Tenth Army in its entirety. If he continued to advance along the coast he would certainly push the enemy out of Cyrenaica, but the bulk of the Italian troops would escape back towards Tripoli, and thus remain a threat to British interests in North Africa. If, however, he sent the

BELOW

A Bren carrier from a Sikh unit advances over rough terrain in Africa. The British Army in North Africa relied heavily on experienced troops from the Indian subcontinent.

remnants of the 7th Armoured Division in a short cut across the desert to swing around the mountains of the Jebel Ahkdar, he might cut off the Italian retreat, prevent their escape, and pull off a stunning feat of arms.

O'Connor's gamble

O'Connor was told that such a route was impassable for motor vehicles, but he decided to give it a try. Time was of the essence: the British had to reach the coastal road at Beda Fomm before the retreating Italians passed through to safety. Despite a shortage of serviceable machines, the 7th Armoured Division drove through Mechili, over rock-strewn terrain to Msus, and then on to the coast at Beda Fomm on 5 February. They were there just in time, as they encountered the leading elements of the Italian Tenth Army streaming south to Tripoli. All the while, the Australian infantry on the coast road were pushing the Italians towards the trap which was now set at Beda Fomm.

Seeing their way blocked to Tripoli – and safety – the Italians tried to break through the barricade of British armour, but despite their superiority in numbers their attacks were uncoordinated and failed miserably. The artillery and tanks of the 7th Armoured Division reaped a rich harvest of blazing Italian vehicles. Following the British armour was the celebrated journalist Chester Wilmott, who observed the rout. Having destroyed 46 tanks with little cost to themselves, the British blocking force thought there could be little left of the enemy armour which was battleworthy:

After lunch, reports came in we could hardly believe. One spoke of 15 tanks leading along a transport column. The next reported 25 medium tanks at the rear, and a third said there were 30 mediums interspersed through the column. That made 70 all told but by fast manoeuvring we were able to take them on piecemeal. It was a really hard job, and we fought them all afternoon. By dark there couldn't have been more than 30 left.

BELOW

A British convoy moves up to the front. In North Africa, the soldier had to be supplied with everything, including water, and consequently logistical demands were greater than in other theatres of the war. As each side advanced, their supply lines became stretched, forcing them to slow their progress.

Nevertheless, by that time more than half our medium tanks were temporarily out of action, owing to mechanical trouble, for they had been going without stop for days. Tanks of one regiment ran out of ammunition twice during the afternoon and had to come back for supplies. Apart from this the fighting went on continuously.

The Italians capitulate

The collapse of this last despairing effort to break through the British line was followed by white flags as the remaining Italians gave up the struggle. The British offensive had advanced 800km (500 miles), destroyed an army of 10 divisions and captured over 130,000 prisoners, all for the loss of only 500 killed and 1373 wounded. O'Connor signalled Wavell, back at his HQ in Cairo: 'Fox killed in open.'

It was a glorious success for the British army, the first since the opening of hostilities in 1939. Understandably, O'Connor wished to exploit the victory and, by keeping up the momentum of the advance on the Libyan capital, inflict a complete victory over the Italians. The demands of the wider strategic picture quashed any hope of a follow-up, however. The pressure from Churchill to send troops to aid the Greeks prevailed, and the first desert campaign was allowed to fizzle

ABOVE
Troops from the York and Lancaster Regiment discover the importance of good-quality water, always in short supply in the desert.

**Fiat CR 42
Italy**

The Italian Fiat CR 42 biplane was a useful fighter by the standards of the mid-1930s but by 1940 aviation had progressed so rapidly that this aircraft was obsolete when matched against the Hurricanes of the British Royal Air Force. It was armed with two 12.7mm machine guns, with provision for two 100kg (220lb) bombs, and had a top speed of 274mph (441kph).

Two British soldiers examine the burnt-out wreck of a CR 42 in the desert. The air forces of both sides in the early stages of the desert campaign were relatively small, and neither side possessed air superiority.

out. O'Connor was bitterly disappointed at the loss of this opportunity to clear the Axis from North Africa in one fell swoop, but he loyally accepted the decision of British high command without remonstration.

As British advance guards carried on to El Agheila, this first British offensive of the war in the desert came to a close. It was unique in character, both sides having to come to grips with the problems of waging war in the wilderness of North Africa. The extremes of climate came as a shock to all but the most experienced desert hands: in summer it was possible to fry an egg on the bonnet of a truck; in winter the desert could be covered with a hard frost followed by snow showers. Distances were enormous, and all supplies for the troops in the front and rear areas – including fuel, ammunition, food and water – had to be laboriously transported to the front from depots hundreds of miles to the rear. Apart from the extremes of climate, the troops had to endure the misery of sand storms, the only thing in the desert that could be guaranteed to bring hostilities to a stop. Bob Sykes, a British soldier new to the desert, found his first sand storm a frightening experience:

The sand storm came at us like an express train at about 40mph [65kmph] with increasing gusts of wind. All oxygen seemed to go out of the air, and the flies were maddening and swarming. The heat was terrific and I sweated so the sand caked on me – in my eyes, nose and ears. I sat down in my dugout and waited, thinking it would be over in a few minutes, but suddenly I nearly panicked – the sand was coming through every crack. I thought I

would be buried. I fought my way out. I could hardly stand up in the wind. The sand was whipping the skin off my face and hands. It was almost pitch dark and I felt entirely alone. Then a light appeared and the sun began to look like a dirty orange. The noise slowly abated and the wind died down: I had ridden out my first sand storm. As we brushed off the sand off our faces so they bled.

Desert discomforts

For the hardened desert soldier, the sand storms, the heat and the flies were borne with an almost stoic equanimity. For other servicemen, newly arrived in the desert, adjusting to the rigours of a new way of life took time. One RAF pilot, who had been withdrawn from the relative comfort of Malta, was less than enthusiastic when describing his new billet in the sand:

I soon discovered that desert life was no picnic. Drinking distilled sea water, which was hot and salty, didn't quench our thirst but just kept us alive. There was nothing we could get that would quench our thirst; in fact, we had a perpetual thirst that almost drove us crazy. Thirst is a terrible thing, but the imagination is worse: we would lay awake at nights thinking of milkshakes, lemonades, cider and ice-cold water from mountain streams. In the daytime we were nearly driven crazy by the terrific heat and the thousands of flies. At nights the lice, bugs and cockroaches tormented us and the sand storms arose covering our mouths, noses and hair with fine sand.

Sometimes they got so bad it was considered unwise to venture from your tent. One night a friend of mine went to see a friend of his in a

BELOW

Italian conscripts on the quayside in Naples cheer before their departure to Italian Somaliland. There they would mount an invasion of Abyssinia and overthrow the government of Haile Selassie.

tent a hundred yards away. He missed it and was lost for fourteen hours.

While sand storms were relatively short-lived, if violent, flies were a perpetual nuisance, and were a pest that no one could get used to. 'There were thousands of them,' complained one veteran soldier. 'They were hardbacked green things, very large. They'd be in your eyes, your ears, everything, and you couldn't do anything about it.' Another British soldier revealed a common problem for troops trying to relax in the desert: 'Flies were a terrible nuisance. More often that not you'd be drinking a cup of tea and you would have to put your hand over the top and sip it between the thumb and finger to stop the flies, otherwise they would be lining up around the rim to dive in.'

Italian conscripts on the quayside in Naples cheer before their departure to Italian Somaliland. There they would mount an invasion of Abyssinia and overthrow the government of Haile Selassie.

But if many men found the desert a hostile and unfriendly place in which to fight and live every day, others developed an appreciation for its sense of space and its rugged grandeur. 'I liked being in the desert,' wrote one veteran of his experiences in northern Africa. 'It was a good, healthy life. I can't explain the peace on a night, the sky – how marvellous it was.'

British Somaliland taken

For Mussolini, the blow of the Italian defeat in Cyrenaica was followed by the loss of Italian East Africa. The Horn of Africa in 1940 consisted of a number of colonial possessions. The Italians held Eritrea, Italian Somaliland and Abyssinia (which they had seized in 1936, after ejecting its ruler Emperor Haile Selassie). French Somaliland had been demilitarised following the Franco-German armistice, leaving British Somaliland vulnerable to attack.

On 1 August 1940, an Italian force of five infantry brigades moved across the border into British Somaliland. The small British force was only able to offer token resistance, and on advice from British Middle East HQ in Cairo, the British garrison prepared to withdraw from the ports of Zeila and Berbera. When the Italians arrived on 19 August they found the ports abandoned. The conquest of British Somaliland was the first and only Italian military victory of the war.

Mussolini ordered the Duke of Aosta, the commander of Italian forces in East Africa, to adopt an offensive strategy and attack northwards into the British-controlled Sudan. Short of resources, Aosta rejected the Duce's exhortation to launch an offensive against Khartoum, preferring to build up his forces to defend East Africa against the possibility of any British counter-attack.

BELOW
An Italian signals unit broadcasts radio messages during the invasion of Abyssinia, while local tribesmen look on. The Italian forces proved far too strong for the poorly armed Abyssinian troops.

RIGHT

A rare picture of a German volunteer unit fighting in East Africa on the Italian side being awarded its colours. Although German forces were not officially involved in this campaign, volunteers were not discouraged from fighting for the Italian cause.

BELOW RIGHT

Hailed as a triumph by Mussolini when it first appeared in 1936, in combat the Breda Ba.88 was a failure. Attacks on Sidi Barrani had to be aborted in September 1940, as the sand filters caused the engines to overheat, and the aircraft were unable to maintain formation and altitude. By November most examples had been stripped of any useful equipment and left as decoys for any attacking British aircraft.

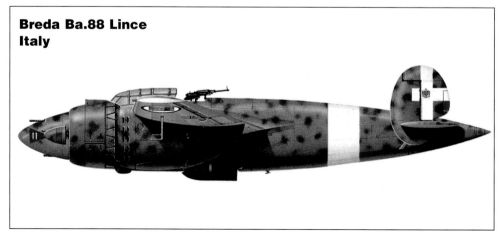

**Breda Ba.88 Lince
Italy**

Early in 1941, the British began the process of ejecting the Italians from the Horn of Africa, despatching invasion columns from all points of the compass to secure their possessions in the Middle East. The 4th Indian Division, which had been withdrawn from O'Connor's offensive in the Western Desert, and the 5th Indian Division provided the backbone of a force commanded by Lieutenant General William Platt, which would attack from Sudan into Eritrea. The Anglo-Indian troops were joined by a battalion of Free French troops from Senegal and a regiment of the French Foreign Legion which had joined the Free French cause. From Kenya, in the south, British and South African troops invaded Italian Somaliland. Another British column attacked northwards from Kenya, while, finally, British forces based in the Aden Protectorate crossed the Gulf of Aden and landed at the port of Berbera in British Somaliland.

Terrain difficulties

The harsh mountainous terrain of East Africa made all movement extremely difficult, and both sides relied heavily on mules, and even camels, to transport their equipment. And in contrast to the situation experienced in the Western Desert, the Italians fought with considerable determination. Platt's attack opened on 15 January 1941, and was directed against the mountain fastness of Keren, which controlled communications in Eritrea and northern Abyssinia. The Italians had constructed a formidable defence, and the two Indian divisions had to scale the peaks that surrounded Keren before they could even come to grips with the enemy. The Allied forces were repeatedly beaten back by fierce counter-attacks, and only after further reinforcement and heavy aerial and artillery bombardments were the Italians forced to retreat; after a siege lasting 53 days, Keren was in Allied hands. Platt then pushed forward to the Eritrean capital of Asmara, which was secured on 1 April.

Southern thrust

In Kenya, Lieutenant General Sir Alan Cunningham led a force comprising the 11th and 12th African Divisions and the 1st South

BELOW
An Italian L3/35 light tank advances into view. Armed only with machine guns, this vehicle was too light to be effective in anything but a police or reconnaissance role for the Italian forces.

African Division. Advancing into Italian Somaliland in February, Cunningham's army broke through the Italian line along the River Juba on 19 February. The British then marched swiftly along the coast to capture Mogadishu five days later. From Mogadishu, the British column drove directly northwards into Abyssinia, and on 29 March it reached Jijiga and there met up with the British force that had landed at Berbera in British Somaliland on 16 March. The combined force, under Cunningham, broke through the Marda Pass on 30 March, cut the Djibouti railway line at Diredawa, and entered the Abyssinian capital of Addis Ababa on 5 April. Emperor Haile Selassie was returned to his capital, while Cunningham wasted no time in advancing north to meet up with General Platt, then moving south from Eritrea.

Aosta refuses to surrender

Italian rule in Abyssinia had effectively collapsed, although the Duke of Aosta refused to surrender to the invading forces. With what remained of his army he decided to adopt a new defensive position in the high terrain around Amba Alagi. On 3 May, South African troops, supported by Ethiopian guerrillas, reached the area and began to advance up the Amba Alagi heights – 11,200 feet high – and there set siege to the Italian positions on the heights. On 12 May, Cunningham and Platt met, and their two forces combined to tighten the screw on Aosta's men.

Inevitably short of ammunition and water, and under heavy bombardment from South African artillery, the Italian position was hopeless. Aosta began to consider surrender to the regular British forces (the fact that the Ethiopian guerrillas had slaughtered Italian prisoners during a mountain-top attack was a further influencing factor in his choice of which forces to surrender to). Negotiations were begun, and after the agreement of terms, on 19 May, Aosta and his remaining 5000 men marched out of Amba Alagi. They were given full military honours by the British and South African soldiers.

The Italian surrender at Amba Alagi brought the total number of captured Italian troops to a figure of no less than 230,000, but a further 80,000 enemy soldiers remained active. They were based in two separate regions: south-west of Addis Ababa in Galla-Sidamo province was General Gazzera's force, about 40,000 strong, while north-west of the capital, based around Gondar, was a similar-sized force led by General Nasi. Most of the British and South African troops at this stage were withdrawn for service in other theatres of the war, leaving this last phase of the campaign to the African troops in Abyssinia. However, the African troops were relatively few in number, the distances to be travelled were very great, and with the onset of the rainy season, progress was inevitably slow as mud hampered the army's advance.

The campaign's final stages

The British command concentrated its resources against Gazzera's troops. The torrential rain and rough terrain made all movement

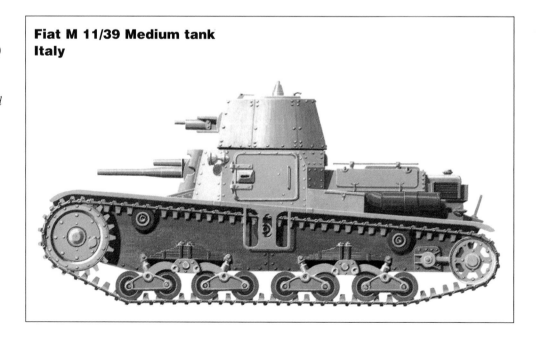

**Fiat M 11/39 Medium tank
Italy**

extremely difficult, but the African troops pursued the Italians into the Galla-Sidamo province with great doggedness. On 21 June, British African troops entered Jimma, while the Italians retreated deeper into the country-side to escape their advance. But unknown to the Italians, a Belgian force sent from the Congo was moving directly towards the Italians to intercept them. The two sides col-lided on 3 July, and after a short engagement, Gazzera's exhausted men laid down their arms and surrendered to the Belgian commander, Major General Gilliaert.

The end of Italian East Africa

In the north-east, General Nasi's troops had established themselves in the mountainous region above Lake Tana, with their head-quarters at Gondar. Although the Italian position was strong, they were running short of supplies. Attacks by Indian and African troops were repeatedly repulsed, and the

Italian garrison of Wolchefit only surrendered on 27 September when its food supplies had been completely exhausted. The main Italian force in Gondar continued to resist until they were overwhelmed by a whole series of British attacks, so that it was only as late as 28 November 1941 – little more than a week before Pearl Harbor – that Italian resistance finally ended in East Africa. It had been a long and arduous campaign, but Mussolini's East African empire had ceased to exist.

Apart from safeguarding the southern flank of Egypt, and other British possessions in East Africa, the conquest of Abyssinia enabled President Roosevelt to lift the embargo on United States shipping using the Red Sea, which had been imposed on 10 June 1940 to avoid American casualties. American mer-chant ships could now unload at Suez itself the increasing number of supplies being sent from the United States for use by the British army in the Middle East.

ABOVE
Italian troops march into captivity after the surrender of the Italian stronghold of Amba Alagi, May 1941. The resolute defence of this position earned the Italian garrison the respect of British and Commonwealth forces.

A further consequence of the British victory in East Africa was the full and safe establishment of the 'Takoradi route', an aerial highway which ran from West Africa, through Takoradi and Fort Lamy to Khartoum and then Cairo. The route was organised by the Free French, and played a vital role in the transport of thousands of aircraft of all types and supplies to the Middle East. W.B. Kennedy Shaw, one of the pioneers of the British Long Range Desert Group (LRDG), remarked: 'While we were waiting at Fort Lamy for transport to Cairo, I saw every day dozens of aircraft on the Takoradi-Khartoum-Cairo route. I then realised the great service our French allies had rendered in securing this vital line of communications.'

Rommel arrives

The two great victories in Cyrenaica and East Africa boosted British morale, but they were soon overshadowed by events elsewhere. The destruction of the Italian Tenth Army during O'Connor's invasion of Libya had forced Mussolini to swallow his pride and accept a German offer of direct military assistance. On 12 February 1941, the appointed commander, Lieutenant General Erwin Rommel, arrived in Tripoli, to be greeted by his Italian allies. With him were advance elements of what was to become known as the Africa Corps. On 24 February, German reconnaissance units clashed with the British screen in front of El Agheila for the first time in North Africa.

This was to be the first step of a major German offensive. But even more worrying to the British high command in Cairo was the German expansion into the Balkans. Churchill had promised aid to Greece, the only state in mainland Europe still actively opposed to the Axis. As the Germans began to become involved, however, this offer would soon backfire, bringing disaster to both Greeks and British.

OPPOSITE
A part of the Italian stronghold at Amba Alagi, showing the rugged, mountainous terrain fought across by both sides in the campaign.

BELOW
Local people gather to hear a speech to be delivered by the Emperor Haile Selassie on his return to Abyssinia. Throughout the period of occupation the Abyssinian people had maintained an armed resistance against the Italians.

CHAPTER NINE

BALKAN BLITZKRIEG

The fall of France left the bulk of Europe under Axis control or favourable to its cause. Only the traditionally unstable Balkans remained to threaten Germany's Romanian oil supply.

During the first year of World War II both the Axis and the Allies had refrained from military involvement in the Balkans. Britain had no strategic interest in the area and lacked the resources to conduct operations far from British bases in Egypt and Palestine. The Germans did have a strategic interest in the Balkans, but were content to impose economic and diplomatic control over their southeast European neighbours. The Balkan states were right-wing dictatorships (whatever their notional constitutional system) and the majority accepted their subordinate position within a zone of German influence. As a region, however, the Balkans were notoriously unstable; their apparent equilibrium could easily be disturbed by internal discord or by outside interference.

Germany was dependent on Romanian oil for its economy and war machine, and Hitler was fearful of any factor which might effect Germany's supply of fuel. A connected anxiety was the possibility that the British might launch bombing raids against the oilfields. Although during this period the British lacked the resources to hit these targets, their security remained a concern to Germany. In October 1940, Hitler secured the right to station troops in Romania to safeguard these essential assets.

Another factor which began to influence German policy towards the Balkans, from the autumn of 1940 onwards, was Hitler's overwhelming determination to invade the Soviet Union in the near future. Hitler, and his army high command, reasoned that the southern flank of their proposed invasion would need to be secure before the attack could be safely launched and, to ensure this, military action might be required. The compliant regimes in Hungary, Romania and Bulgaria posed no threat to German interests in the region, but Yugoslavia and Greece were not a part of the Axis system and as such remained a potential threat to Hitler's schemes.

Mussolini's ambitions

Mussolini deeply resented German dominance in the Balkans, an area of Europe he believed should come under Italian influence. In 1939 he had occupied Albania without resistance. The next stage in his programme of conquest was an invasion of Greece. Italy's population of 45 million against Greece's seven million was reflected in the numerical superiority of Italy's armed forces. Greece also lacked modern weapons and equipment, being reliant on stock which dated back to the previous world war. Mussolini believed that the small and poorly equipped Greek army would not cause him undue problems,

OPPOSITE
An anti-aircraft gun fires into the night, Greece 1939. Mussolini's decision to invade Greece precipitated a political and military crisis in the Balkans, which drew in Britain and Germany.

ABOVE

A Greek field gun prepares to fire on Italian positions. Hardy and highly motivated, the Greek Army was more than a match for the Italians, who had little enthusiasm for this latest scheme in Mussolini's foreign ventures.

but his habitual vanity blinded him to the failings of his own army and the residual hardiness of his opponents.

Italian plans for the invasion of Greece were kept secret from the Germans, who would almost certainly have vetoed such a potentially risky move. Hitler was in France (conducting negotiations with the Vichy government) when he first heard news of an impending invasion, and he hurriedly rerouted his train to Florence in an attempt to dissuade his Axis partner from attacking Greece. He was too late. When they met at the station on 28 October, Mussolini proudly boasted: 'We are on the march! At dawn this morning our Italian troops victoriously crossed the Albanian-Greek frontier!' Hitler was not impressed, but the die had been cast and there was little he could do in the short term except to wait on events.

The Italian ultimatum, which immediately preceded the invasion, had been rejected by the Greek Government, which in turn declared a general mobilisation. King George II was the head of state of a constitutional monarchy, although power in the country lay in the hands of the prime minister, General Ioannis Metaxas. General Alexandros Papagos was commander-in-chief of the Greek army, which could deploy 15 infantry divisions (nine of which had some training for mountain warfare), plus a further four mountain brigades and a cavalry division.

The Italian plan

Under the command of General Visconti-Prasca, the Italian assault would be conducted by four divisions in the Epirus region in the west, with a further two divisions protecting the main attack. Given the ambitious nature of the plan, it was a surprisingly small force, possibly reflecting the over-confidence of the Italian high command. The Italians had hoped to break through the Greek frontier defences before Greek mobilisation could come into effect, but atrocious weather – which turned streams into torrents and the ground into mud – slowed the Italian advance and grounded the Italian air force. The combination of bad weather, mountainous terrain and

**P.Z.L P.24
Greece**

Although obsolete in comparison with the latest fighters, the Royal Hellenic air force's P.24s gave a good account of themselves against the Luftwaffe and Regia Aeronautica. Developed from a 1930 Polish design, Greece's 36 P.24s were virtually her entire fighter strength.

increasingly determined resistance brought the Italian advance to standstill within the space of a week.

Impatient at the lack of results, Mussolini dismissed Visconti-Prasca on 9 November, and replaced him with General Ubaldo Soddu, the army's deputy chief of staff. Soddu's problem was to reorganise his over-extended forces and provide them with reinforcements but these were slow in coming. Meanwhile, the size of the Greek army along the Albanian–Greek border was growing steadily, so that by 12 November its infantry outnumbered the Italians by a figure of around two to one. Rather than adopt a defensive strategy, Papagos was determined to exploit the errors made by the Italians and counter-attack before the arrival of Italian reinforcements could reduce the Greek numerical advantage. On 14 November, the Greeks went over to the offensive along the entire front, from the Adriatic Sea to the border with Yugoslavia.

The Greek V Corps – reinforced to five divisions – achieved the breakthrough on the right of the line, badly mauling three divisions and throwing them back into Albania. This attack was followed by more Greek successes; by the end of November, not only had the Italians been ejected from Greece, they seemed in danger of loosing Albania as well.

But during early December, the Greek offensive began to slow. The Greek army's lack of tanks and paucity of anti-tank guns made it less effective in the valleys and low-lying areas. Accordingly, the Greek commanders preferred to confine operations to the mountains where their tough infantry could be at their most effective. In addition, the already bad weather got worse, as temperatures began to drop as low as -20°C (-4°F), rendering offensive operations virtually impossible. Both Greeks and Italians suffered terribly in these conditions, short of supplies and medical support. On 10 January 1941, the important town of Klisura was taken by the Greeks, but from then on a stalemate ensued. The two sides dug in and waited for better weather in the spring.

German intervention

The Italian disaster in Greece had enraged Hitler, not because he had any sympathy for Italy's territorial aspirations but because it had upset the complex diplomatic balance in the Balkans. When the Italians invaded, the British were invited to establish air bases on Crete and in mainland Greece to provide a degree of air support for the hard-pressed Greeks. The arrival of the RAF in Greece – albeit in small numbers – was Hitler's chief concern, as the Romanian oil fields around Ploesti were now vulnerable to attack. Hitler decided that Germany would have to come to the rescue of the Italians, and on 12 November 1940 he instructed OKH to prepare an invasion plan for the Balkans which would eliminate the Greek 'nuisance'.

But before any military plan was to be put into effect against Greece, the Germans set about bullying the other Balkan states into submission through diplomatic means. Hungary and Romania were already firmly in the Axis camp. Pressure was applied on Bulgaria – which lay between Romania and Greece – and on 8 February 1941 an agreement was signed to allow German

A lieutenant in an artillery regiment in the Greek Army at the time of the Italian invasion in 1940. He wears a kepi, baggy riding breeches and riding boots, and he carries a map case and binoculars for spotting. In combat all ranks would wear a steel helmet of either the British pattern or a new Greek model. The Greek soldiers fought bravely during the campaign, and their repulse of the Italian invaders surprised the world.

troops into the country. General List's Twelfth Army advanced through Bulgaria to take up positions along the Greek border, while the Luftwaffe established forward air fields in readiness for action against Greece. Bulgarian involvement in the Axis was confirmed on 1 March, when it became a junior partner of the Tripartite Pact.

The Germans had more difficulty bringing Yugoslavia into the Axis fold. Yugoslavia came into being as a consequence of the Versailles Treaty, and was made up of six major ethnic groupings, most violently opposed to the other. The Serb-dominated government had long emotional and religious ties to the Greeks, and they did not want to lose their special treaty rights in the Greek port of Salonika (Thessaloniki), which would be denied them in the event of an Italian victory. In addition, they correctly suspected that Italy also had territorial designs on Yugoslavia. Popular sentiment in Belgrade favoured the Greek cause.

Prince Paul, the regent of Yugoslavia, and his government were generally well disposed

ABOVE
Italian dead, killed during a battle in the rugged mountains along the Greek-Albanian border region. The Italian Army was not properly equipped for the conditions it would encounter in Greece.

RIGHT
An Italian heavy machine gun is prepared for an anti-aircraft role during the fighting in Greece.

towards the Allied cause, but they were well aware of their vulnerability to any German military action. As German diplomatic pressure increased on Yugoslavia to join the Tripartite Pact, Prince Paul and his ministers accepted that they had no other option but to bow to Hitler's demands. On 25 March, Yugoslavia reluctantly became a signatory to the Tripartite Pact. The way was now clear for the German armed forces to move through the Balkans and deal with Greece. Code-named Operation Marita, the invasion of Greece was set for early April.

British offers of help

Although the Greek Government was resolute in defending the country from Italy, it did not wish to provoke Hitler, in the full knowledge that German military involvement could destroy Greece. The British, however, wished to develop an anti-Axis alliance in the southern Balkans. Churchill – and his foreign minister Anthony Eden – had hoped to bring in Turkey, Greece and Yugoslavia on the Allied side. Turkey was determined to stay neutral,

however, and Yugoslavia and Greece needed the reassurance of massive military support before committing themselves to overt opposition against Germany, a commitment that Britain was clearly unable to provide.

Greece accepted air support from Britain to attack the Italians, but initially refused offers of full military aid in case this was deemed sufficient provocation to force Germany to take military action against them. Although it was likely that Hitler would have invaded Greece anyway, to ensure the stability of his southern flank prior to the invasion of the Soviet Union, the very fact that the Greeks had allowed the presence of RAF bases in Greece was sufficient to worry the Germans towards intervention. When the Greek Government became aware of German troop movements towards the Bulgarian–Greek border, the fear of German invasion became a reality. As a consequence, Greece accepted the offer of British military assistance.

Why the British should have wanted to become embroiled in the Balkans – when

BELOW

RAF personnel disembark in Athens as part of the first wave of British military aid for the Greeks. Britain encouraged the Greeks to oppose the Axis, even though there were insufficient numbers of British troops in the Middle East to make this a viable strategy.

resources in the Middle East were so stretched – remains a controversial point. Churchill favoured British involvement in Greece simply because it was a way of fighting back at the Germans. Churchill was man whose enthusiasms regularly exceeded sound strategic decision-making, and usually his military advisors reined-in his wilder schemes for intervention. But during the early months of 1941, General Archibald Wavell, commander-in-chief in the Middle East, and other senior military officers surprisingly went along with the idea of intervention laid down by Churchill and Eden.

Logistical problems

Apart from the fact that despatching an expeditionary force to Greece would remove troops from the vital North African theatre of operations, the British did not have sufficient resources to make an intervention succeed. The long supply line across the Mediterranean from Egypt to Greece was exceedingly vulnerable to aerial attack, and the British in the Middle East lacked the necessary aircraft – both in terms of quantity and quality – to defend this link. By contrast, the

Waffen-SS troops drive through the streets of Belgrade. The city fell without much of a fight, so complete was the German victory over the Yugoslav Army.

Axis forces had more than sufficient aircraft to dominate the skies over the Balkans and the surrounding coastal waters. The British army and navy would pay heavily for this deficiency in air power.

Under the command of Lieutenant General Sir Henry Maitland Wilson, a British and Commonwealth force was despatched to Greece on 5 March 1941. Wavell had originally told the Greeks that he would send two Australian infantry divisions, a New Zealand division, a brigade of Polish infantry and an armoured brigade plus artillery and supporting units, totalling over 100,000 men. In the event, the expeditionary force was considerably reduced to 58,000 soldiers. The infantry was supplied by the 2nd New Zealand Division and the 6th Australian Division (totalling nearly 34,000 men). Also included was the 1st Armoured Brigade (around 100 tanks) and two regiments of artillery.

Before the British could assume their positions in northern Greece, however, the Italians launched their spring offensive. The slow but steady volume of reinforcements that had crossed the Adriatic from Italy enabled the Italians to assemble 28 divisions for the attack, which were organised into the Ninth and Eleventh Armies, under the overall command of General Ugo Cavallero (who had replaced Soddu at the end of December). Italian confidence was such that Mussolini himself crossed over to Albania to oversee the impending victory.

The Italian offensive begins

The Ninth Army (General Pirzio-Biroli) opened the attack on 9 March 1941, its 11 infantry divisions supported by an armoured division. As the infantry surged forward, they were caught by a fierce bombardment from the well-sited Greek artillery which caused heavy casualties and prevented the Italians from making any real headway. On the evening of the 9th, Cavallero noted in his diary: 'The Greek artillery is powerfully deployed. All elements of the defending forces are well organised in depth, using positions of strength which enable them to contain and to counter-attack immediately and vigorously.'

For the next two days, the Italians fought hard to dislodge the Greeks from their defences, but to no avail. The attack was eventually called off, the three corps that had led the assault suffering 12,000 killed and wounded. Mussolini returned to Italy with his military reputation further tarnished. The only positive advantage for the Axis was that the offensive had worn down the Greek army, using up most of General Papagos's remaining troop reserves.

Cape Matapan

Italian defeat on land was followed by defeat at sea. The Germans had encouraged the Italian navy to adopt a more aggressive posture in the Mediterranean and attack the convoys of British shipping carrying the British expeditionary force to Greece. The Germans promised support from the newly arrived X Flightcorps – based in Sicily – and the Italian agreed to conduct a two-day sweep as far as the island of Gavdhos, 50km (31 miles) south of Crete. The British were alerted to the Italian plan through the decoding of their naval signals, which were based on the German Enigma pattern. This Ultra intelligence enabled the British naval commander-in-chief in the Mediterranean, Admiral Sir Andrew Cunningham, to assemble a strike force to intercept the Italian fleet. During the night of 28 March, the British ships caught the Italians unawares off Cape Matapan, and by using radar sank three Italian cruisers and damaged the battleship *Vittorio Veneto*. The expected German air support failed to arrive and the Italian fleet scuttled quickly back to port, where it remained for the rest of the war.

Although the British victory at Cape Matapan safeguarded British shipping in the eastern Mediterranean from naval attack on the surface, the German Luftwaffe was gathering in strength to attack British vessels in the Mediterranean and to support the German invasion of Greece. But before Hitler

BELOW
Italian mountain troops march into a Yugoslav town. Although the Germans spearheaded the advance, large numbers of Italian troops were employed as an army of occupation.

could put his plan for conquest into effect, events in Yugoslavia forced a dramatic change.

The news that Yugoslavia had joined the Tripartite Pact was greeted with dismay by many within the country, and on 27 March a military coup led by General Bora Mirkovic overthrew the Yugoslav Government headed by the regent, Prince Paul. A new administration under General Dusan Simovic was installed in Belgrade, while the regent's place was taken by Prince Peter, crowned King Peter II. The coup proved highly popular in Belgrade, with crowds thronging the streets chanting pro-Greek and British slogans. 'Better war than pact; better grave than slave,' ran one typical slogan. In Britain, Churchill was delighted, declaring: 'the Yugoslav nation had found its soul.'

Hitler's fury

Despite British hopes that the coup would mark the start of anti-Axis alliance, the new government was not openly hostile to Germany, but wished only to preserve Yugoslav neutrality. Hitler, however, looked on the coup in Belgrade with fury. In his eyes, not only was it a personal insult, it also threatened his plans for Greece and preparations for the invasion of the Soviet Union. On the day of the coup, Hitler issued a directive which reflected his anger towards the Yugoslavs: 'The Führer is determined, without waiting for possible loyalty declarations from the new

ABOVE

German infantry look upwards as Stukas prepare to bomb another ground target. The closely integrated nature of German air–ground operations was combined with superior material strength to great effect.

government, to make all preparations to destroy Yugoslavia militarily, and as a national unit. The attack will start as soon as the means and troops suitable for it are ready. Politically, it is especially important that the blow against Yugoslavia is carried out with pitiless harshness and the military destruction is done with lightning rapidity.'

German plans

There was to be no declaration of war; military operations would begin with attacks on Yugoslav airfields and the aerial bombardment of Belgrade. The plans for the invasion were to be made in conjunction with Operation Marita, the invasion of Greece. As ever, the military skills of the German general staff proved capable of the new demands, and a new plan was swiftly drawn up to deal with both states. Hungary, Bulgaria and Italy would be expected to provide assistance, for which they would receive territorial rewards from the dismembered Yugoslavia. And to encourage the political break-up of the state, the Croats and other ethnic groups in the region

were encouraged to rebel against the Serb-dominated Yugoslav Government.

In order to ensure the 'lightning rapidity' demanded by the Führer, the German army included a large armoured component within its overall deployment. The combined invasion of Yugoslavia and Greece would draw upon two German armies totalling 32 divisions, of which 10 would be panzer formations and four motorised, or their equivalent. Events moved so swiftly, however, that eight of these divisions would not get to the front in time to see action.

The German Second Army (Colonel-General von Weichs) was stationed in Austria and Hungary and, in tandem with the Italian Second Army, it would attack through Slovenia and Croatia and secure Bosnia. Resistance was not expected to be severe, as Croats and Slovenes had little sympathy for the Belgrade government. The main German attack on Yugoslavia would be made by Panzer Group Kleist, the armoured spearhead of General List's Twelfth Army. The XLI Panzer Corps would take the direct route to

Belgrade from Timisoara in Romania; the XIV Motorised Corps and XI Corps would drive on Belgrade and central Serbia from Bulgaria; the XL Panzer Corps would also attack from Bulgaria to secure Yugoslav Macedonia, in preparation for the attack on Greece. The defeat of Yugoslavia would take the battle-hardened units of the Wehrmacht just 12 days to accomplish, a text-book application of blitzkrieg tactics.

The Yugoslav army

The Yugoslav army was in no position to repel the German attack. Its small peacetime army of 150,000 men could be mobilised to

approximately 1.4 million troops, but many of its conscripts were not in place when the Germans struck along the long Yugoslav border.

On 6 April 1941, Stukas of Air Fleet IV (Colonel General Alexander Löhr) attacked Belgrade, which for the next two days and nights was subjected to an almost continuous aerial bombardment, which inevitably caused heavy civilian casualties, perhaps as many as 17,000 killed and wounded. The German land attack was launched first in southern Yugoslavia, as armoured units of the Twelfth Army crossed into Macedonia, an area which was poorly defended. The

BELOW
Dusty German mountain troops march through the town of Larnia. For most German troops, hard marching was the means with which they outflanked the British and Greek defenders.

Greek peasants, along with an Orthodox priest, present flowers to German troops. Despite the intent of the picture, fraternisation between Greeks and Germans was limited.

SS troops smile for the camera as they advance into Greece. The Waffen SS scored a number of well-publicised triumphs during the Balkans campaign.

bulk of the Yugoslav army was deployed in central and northern Yugoslavia, but, apart from some isolated exceptions, the Yugoslav troops did not fight with much conviction.

The German Second Army found its progress even easier than expected, with whole Croatian regiments going over to the Germans without a shot being fired. On the second day of the Second Army's attack, the

German chief of staff, General Halder, was able to report: 'Information gathered during the course of the day gives the impression that in the north of Yugoslavia the front is breaking up with increasing rapidity. Units are laying down their arms or taking the road to captivity, according to our airmen. One cycle company captures a whole brigade with its staff. An enemy divisional commander radios

his superior officer that his men are throwing down their arms and going home.'

Wietershiem's XIV Motorised Corps (which comprised two panzer divisions and one motorised division) drove from Sofia to Nis and advanced over 500km (300 miles) up the Morava valley in less than seven days, before meeting up with Reinhardt's XLI Panzer Corps in the ruins of Belgrade on 13 April. With the capital and much of Yugoslavia in German hands, most organised resistance ended.

The other Axis nations now moved in for the kill. The Italians advanced behind the Germans along the Dalmatian coast, and on 17 April marched triumphantly into the undefended city of Dubrovnik. A Hungarian force reached Novi Sad, while a division of Bulgarian infantry followed the German panzers into Macedonia. As ever, the real fighting was done by the Germans, who accepted the Yugoslav surrender on 17 March.

Yugoslav resistance

Following the surrender, 6028 Yugoslav officers and 337,684 other ranks became prisoners of war, but almost 300,000 managed to slip away and avoid captivity. Many of these were Serbs who would form the nucleus of a resistance movement, divided between the

BELOW

A New Zealand officer is led into captivity by a German soldier. The large contingent of Australian and New Zealand troops sent to Greece suffered heavy casualties under British command; this caused some ill-feeling among ANZAC troops who believed they were being sacrificed in a hopeless cause.

southern Slovenia, the Dalmatian coast south of Split, Montenegro and the western part of Macedonia (Kosovo). Germany seized northern Slovenia and Serbia.

The disintegration of Yugoslavia unleashed the ethnic hatred that had only just been constrained during the brief existence of the Yugoslav kingdom. The scale of slaughter was prodigious; millions were killed during the course of the Axis occupation. Both Germans and Italians acted with the greatest brutality, but were surpassed in cruelty by local ethnic groups. The Croat Ustase militias killed 250,000 people (mainly Serbs) in just three months; Bosnian Muslims murdered Bosnian Christians; and monarchist Serbs set upon communist Serbs. The killing in Yugoslavia only stopped after Tito had imposed communist rule over the country, but the hatred and resentment remained.

Operation Marita

While the Germans were overrunning Yugoslavia, their forces were simultaneously invading Greece. The Anglo-Greek forces put up a better defence than the Yugoslavs, but they too would succumb to the German armed forces, superior in numbers and matériel, and better trained and led.

The main focus of the Greek defences in the north of the country was the Metaxas Line, which was designed to repel an attack from Bulgaria. Inherent in the Greek defensive plan was the belief that Yugoslavia would be able to defend its border with Bulgaria, and as a consequence the Metaxas Line ended at the Bulgarian-Yugoslav border, leaving Greek Macedonia vulnerable to attack down the mountain valleys from Yugoslavia. The British had strong reservations about the Greek commitment to the Metaxas Line, and General Maitland Wilson would have preferred the Anglo–Greek armies to deploy the bulk of their troops behind the Aliakmon Line, which was shorter and easier to defend. This, however, would have meant abandoning the key port of Salonika to the Germans without a fight, and Greek attachment to the city prevented them from accepting the British plan.

Although the deployment of large numbers of troops behind the Metaxas Line was arguably a strategic mistake, the biggest problem facing the Allied forces lay in the air. The Greeks had no effective air force to speak off in April 1941, and the RAF had 192 air-

Royalist Chetniks of Colonel Draza Mihalovic and the communist Partisans of Josip Broz, better known as Marshal Tito. Reflecting the ease and speed of the German conquest of Yugoslavia, German casualties amounted to 392 wounded, 15 missing and 151 killed in action.

Hitler made good his promise to destroy the political basis of Yugoslavia. As early as 10 April, Zagreb's radio station broadcast a message proclaiming the formation of a 'free and independent Croatia' which was to be led by the brutal Ustase leader Anton Pavelic. The Hungarians acquired the Voivodina, a triangle of land formed by the Drava, Danube and Tisza rivers, and which had a Hungarian minority. Bulgaria occupied much of Yugoslav Macedonia, while Italy assumed control of

craft, of which only around 80 could be flown at any one time. And nor were they the latest models which could have put up some sort of fight against the modern aircraft leading the Luftwaffe attack. Even the small number of Hurricanes the British had sent to Greece were now no match for the Messerschmitt Bf-109s that had been uprated since the Battle of Britain. But it was in sheer numbers that the aerial discrepancy was most telling, as the combined German and Italian air forces were able to deploy about 1100 front-line aircraft.

The German Twelfth Army struck at 0515 hours on 6 April 1941. The five infantry divisions of XXX Corps (General Ott), deployed in formation in eastern Bulgaria, crossed the border and captured the undefended province of Thrace, before turning westwards to assault the sector of the Metaxas Line running along the River Nestos. The XVIII Mountain Corps (General Böhme) consisted of two mountain divisions, plus the 2nd Panzer Division. Its mission was to attack the Metaxas Line directly from the north.

Tough Greek resistance

Supporting the offensive were the bombers of VIII Flightcorps. As the German dive bombers swooped down on the Greek defences they were disconcerted to met by heavy anti-aircraft fire, for alone amongst the great European fortifications of the time, the defences of the Metaxas Line included turret-mounted 37mm anti-aircraft guns. And unlike the poor-grade fortress divisions that manned the Maginot Line, the Greek defenders were members of high-grade units. The German XXX Corps was thrown back when it attempted to cross the Nestos, suffering heavy casualties. The German mountain troops, fighting their way down the Rupel Pass, were also forced to retreat. Eventually, the XVIII Corps was able to make some progress against the Metaxas Line, bringing up high-velocity

BELOW
Having commandeered a fishing boat, SS troops (from the Leibstandarte Adolf Hitler) *prepare to cross the Corinth canal. This was an audacious move which outflanked British defences in southern Greece.*

RIGHT
SS-Obergruppenführer Sepp Dietrich photographed during negotiations leading to the surrender of the Greek Army.

BELOW
German troops attend a ceremony to celebrate the defeat of Allied forces in the Balkans, and the conquest of Greece. The campaign had been another stunning example of German military prowess.

guns in order to fire directly into the embrasures of the Greek defences.

The German breakthrough did not come on the Metaxas Line, however, but through the outflanking actions of the 2nd Panzer Division and the XL Panzer Corps (General Stumme), which had invaded Yugoslav Macedonia before turning south into Greece.

German breakthrough

Lieutenant General Vieil's 2nd Panzer Division – which had played a prominent role in forging the Panzer Corridor in France in 1940 – advanced into Yugoslavia on the 6th, eliminating the Bregalnica Division and capturing Strumica. It then turned south down the Axios valley and entered Greece on 8 April, encountering only limited opposition. An attempt to block the progress of the German panzers at Kilkis was brushed aside, and after a dash of some 90km (56 miles), the port of Salonika was in German hands. As a consequence, all the Greek troops holding the Metaxas Line were cut off from the rest of Greece, and at 1400 hours on 9 April, the Greek commander holding the line, General Bakopoulos, instructed his 70,000 men to lay down their arms.

The main thrust into Greece was made by the XL Panzer Corps, having first destroyed the Yugoslav army in and around Skopje (20,000 troops and seven generals taken prisoner). The main axis of advance lay through the Monastir gap, which ran through the high

BELOW
Greek general officers are escorted to the surrender conference in a German staff car. Greece would be garrisoned by German and Italian troops.

Shortly afterwards, the reconnaissance battalion of the *Leibstandarte* found itself engaged in a tough battle with Greek troops holding the Klisura Pass. The battalion commander, Kurt Meyer, sent two of his companies to attack the position from the flanks, while he led a detachment up the main road to the pass. During his advance, the Greeks let off a series of demolition charges and raked the advancing SS troops with machine-gun fire. Meyer and his soldiers were pinned down by heavy fire, seemingly unable to move. Meyer recounted how he solved this problem, using 'dynamic' SS leadership:

A feeling of nausea tightens my throat. I yell to [Untersturmführer] Emil Wawrzinek to get the attack moving. But the good Emil just looks at me as if he has doubts about my sanity. Machine-gun fire smacks against the rocks in front of us. How can I get Wawrzinek to take that first leap? In my distress, I feel the smooth roundness of my 'egg' hand grenade in my hand. I shout at the group. Everybody looks thunderstruck at me as I brandish the hand grenade, pull the pin, and roll it precisely behind the last man. Never again did I witness such a concerted leap forward as at that second. As if bitten by tarantulas, we dive around the rock spur and into a fresh crater. The spell is broken. The hand grenade has cured our lameness. We grin at each other, and head forward to the next cover.

Allied withdrawal

The reconnaissance battalion overran the pass and next day captured the town of Kastoria, taking 11,000 Greek prisoners in the process. The progress made by the XL Corps made the position of the British and Greek troops holding the Aliakmon Line untenable, and in order to avoid being outflanked, the British commander, General Maitland Wilson, ordered his troops to begin a withdrawal to new positions. An attempt to hold the Germans around Mount Olympus had to be abandoned on 18 April, as the British were again in danger of being surrounded by the fast-moving panzer columns. The next defensible line was across the isthmus around Thermopylae, where Maitland Wilson hoped to hold the German attack.

As in previous campaigns, the German panzer divisions did the most damage, and the 100 or so British tanks thrown into the fray were no match for them. The experience of the British 3rd RTR (Royal Tank Regiment) shows just how far behind the British were in this unequal contest. Before going to Greece,

ABOVE

A wounded British soldier is helped by one of his comrades, after their capture by the Germans. Over 7000 British and Commonwealth troops were taken prisoner during the Greek campaign.

mountains into Greece. Spring had not reached this region, and the Germans were forced to battle through snow and freezing temperatures.

The German advance had been spearheaded by the 9th Panzer Division and the *Leibstandarte-SS Adolf Hitler*, a reinforced motorised brigade that had won its spurs in the fighting in France. On 10 April, the *Leibstandarte* was ordered to take the Klidi Pass, the main route into Greece. Instead of Yugoslavs, the SS troops faced better-trained Australians and New Zealanders of the British expeditionary force. Germans casualties mounted but after two days of hard fighting the defenders were prised from their positions, and the Germans made their way into the heart of Greece.

the 3rd RTR had been forced to exchange its already-poor A13 cruiser tanks for the older and slower A10 models, whose tracks were exhausted through operating in the desert. One officer in the regiment, Bob Crisp, revealed the machines' unreliability during an attack to counter a possible German advance:

Sleet battered my eyelids as the tank ploughed through cultivated mud and I ordered my tank commanders not to attempt any turns until they were on firm ground. The squadron nevertheless left behind a trail of broken-down tanks and when, after a freezing night, news came that the enemy armour report had been a false alarm and we went back, we counted the toll of the purposeless advance. Five tanks were left lying with hopelessly broken tracks, two more had fractured pistons. There were no more spare parts so the tanks were destroyed.

All of the 3rd RTR's tanks would be left in Greece: out of total of 52 tanks, 51 broke down and only one was knocked out by enemy fire. The frustration felt by the British tankmen was intense.

The British decide to withdraw

The German breakthrough towards central Greece spelled disaster for the Allies, and on 19 April a conference was held in Athens to assess the situation, attended by King George II and his commander-in-chief, General Papagos, and the British generals, Wavell and Maitland Wilson. All parties agreed that the battle was lost and that the British expeditionary force should withdraw from Greece. From then on, the holding operations at Thermopylae and Thebes were conducted with the intention of gaining time for the British and Commonwealth forces to be evacuated to Crete and Egypt. After the disasters in Norway and France, the British were now to be ejected from the mainland of Europe for the third time in less than a year. It was a bitter blow to the British, but far worse for the Greeks who would now face years of brutal Axis occupation.

Shortly after the decision to evacuate was made, the German XL Corps struck

ABOVE

British military and naval personnel survey defences on the island of Crete, which would become the next battlefield after the fall of Greece. For Germany, Crete would be a useful staging post for attacks against the British in Malta and North Africa.

westwards across the Pindus mountains, isolating the Greek forces facing the Italians in
Albania. On 21 April the *Leibstandarte* captured Yanina to the rear of the Greeks. One of
the subordinate commanders from the Greek
Army of the Epirus, General Drakos, took it
upon himself to surrender his forces to the
Germans. The capitulation took place at
Larisa, and 16 Greek divisions laid down their
arms, leaving the way clear for the Germans
to race southwards through western Greece.
On 23 April, King George and his government left the country, as organised resistance
to the German invasion collapsed.

Typical of misfortune that had dogged the
Allies in the Balkans was the sinking of the
ammunition ship *Glen Fraser* in Piraeus harbour on 6 April by German bombers. The
massive explosion – which shattered windows
in Athens some 11km (7 miles) distant – sank
11 ships in Piraeus and rendered Greece's
main port inoperable. This misfortune had

prevented the landing of supplies for the
Allied advance; now it meant that the port
could not be used to evacuate the British. As a
result, minor ports around Athens and in the
Peloponnese had to be used in its stead.

The evacuation begins

As the British held their positions along the
Thermopylae line between 22 and 24 April,
the evacuations began. Under the command
of Rear Admiral H.T. Baille-Grohman, the
Australians and New Zealanders, falling back
from Thermopylae, were evacuated from the
small fishing ports of Rafina, Porto Rafti and
Megara. The evacuation was going well, but
on the 25th a detachment of German paratroops was dropped behind the main bridge
across the Corinth Canal. The defenders
were too few in number to repel the
Germans, although the charges on the
bridge were blown and the bridge fell neatly
into the canal. The following day the

LEFT
German mountain troops, in a Ju-52, fly towards Crete. Their role was to reinforce the paratroopers, who had captured airfields on Crete to allow the Ju-52 to land.

BELOW
General Bernard Freyberg VC, commander of British forces on Crete. A much-wounded veteran of both world wars, he was renowed as a fighting soldier but was unable to save the island from German conquest.

Germans captured Corinth. Meanwhile, men from the Leibstandarte had assembled makeshift boats and had managed to cross the Gulf of Corinth at Patras. Reinforced by the 5th Panzer Division, they now began to advance into the Peloponnese. On 27 May, German soldiers marched into Athens and the swastika flew over the Acropolis.

The British position was becoming increasingly desperate, but most of the troops were able to retreat to the southern Peloponnese before the Germans cut them off. There they were evacuated by the Royal Navy, who managed to save just over 50,000 British, Australian and New Zealand service-

BELOW

A German paratrooper of the 7th Air Division on Crete. He wears the distinctive pale green/grey cotton Luftwaffe parachute smock and trousers, and a cut-down helmet; he is armed with an MP-39/40 sub-machine gun. The smock was designed to prevent any of the wearer's kit or clothing from becoming entangled in his parachute. Crete was the last major Axis paratroop operation of the war.

men. Only at Kalamata did the embarkation break down, leaving 7000 troops stranded on the Greek shore. Most of the men were captured, although some managed to break out of the German encirclement, and with the aid of the local population evade capture.

For the British, one of the few heartening things in the whole campaign had been the attitude of the Greeks, who applauded their efforts whether in victory or defeat. A gunner colonel attached to the 1st Armoured Brigade described the Greek reaction to the departure of his men: 'We were nearly the last British troops they would see and the Germans might be on our heels; yet cheering, clapping crowds lined the streets and pressed about our cars, so as to almost hold us up. Girls and men leapt on the running boards to kiss or shake hands with the grimy, weary gunners. They threw flowers beside us crying: "Come back – You must come back again – Goodbye – Goodluck".'

Allied and Axis losses

British and Commonwealth losses in this campaign amounted to over 12,000, of which three-quarters were prisoners of war (the majority of these taken at Kalamata). As at Dunkirk, all heavy equipment had to be abandoned, which amounted to 104 tanks, 400 guns and 8000 other vehicles. The RAF had 72 aircraft shot down with a further 137 destroyed on the ground. Two Royal Navy destroyers and four transport ships were sunk, plus another 21 smaller vessels.

The entire six-month campaign had cost the Greeks 15,700 killed or missing; 218,000 men were taken prisoner, although many of these were released a short while later. German losses amounted to just 1684 killed and 3752 wounded. Italian losses were far greater, many of them a consequence of frostbite and illness that resulted from the harsh conditions encountered in the Greek and Albanian mountains. The total casualty figure was just over 100,000: 13,755 killed, 63,242 wounded (including 12,368 severe frostbite cases) and 25,067 missing (most of whom were dead).

The British decision to support the war in Greece had been a military disaster. For a very small price in casualties, Hitler had secured his southern flank and inflicted another humiliating blow against Britain. On the debit side, Hitler had been forced to postpone the start

date of Operation Barbarossa by a month. The only advantage accruing to Britain came in the political sphere, where opinion in the United States, shocked by the German invasion, swung towards Britain for coming to Greece's assistance. The US Congress passed the Lend–Lease bill and American aid began to flow towards Britain.

The only remaining piece of business in the eastern Mediterranean was the future of the island of Crete, which Hitler decided must come into the Axis orbit. Even before victory had been gained in mainland Greece, he had instructed his commanders to prepare Operation Mercury, the conquest of Crete.

The German high command remained fearful of the presence of the Royal Navy in the eastern Mediterranean, and it was decided that the attack should be spearheaded by a vast airborne landing. Planning was entrusted to General Kurt Student, one of the pioneers of airborne operations and commander of XI Flightcorps which contained the 7th Airborne Division (13,000 paratroops), reinforced by three regiments from the 5th and 6th Mountain Divisions (9000 men).

Air support would be provided by General Wolfram von Richthofen's VIII Flightcorps, which had available 228 bombers, 205 dive bombers, 119 single-engined fighters and 114 twin-engined fighters, and 50 reconnaissance aircraft. The first wave of paratroops would be carried in 493 Ju-52 transport aircraft and 72 gliders. The mountain troops would be delivered in subsequent waves, although a naval force was assembled which would brave the presence of the Royal Navy and, under the guard of heavy German air cover, transport artillery and the remainder of the mountain troops to Crete.

Although the British had the advantage of knowing German intentions through good Ultra intelligence, in other respects they were at a distinct disadvantage. The island garrison consisted of around 28,000 British and Commonwealth troops and two under-strength Greek divisions totalling around 10,000 men. Most of the British troops had recently been evacuated from Greece and thus lacked heavy weapons and equipment. Besides a shortage of artillery and tanks, the British were also very short of suitable anti-aircraft guns, a shortage that would prove costly. Worse still, the small RAF contingent was hounded mercilessly by the Luftwaffe, and on 19 May the four remaining

Hurricanes and three Gladiators left for the safety of Egypt to escape total destruction.

General Bernard Freyberg was appointed to command the British forces in Crete, although he had just arrived from Greece and had little time to familiarise himself with his new command. A much-wounded and decorated veteran of World War I (where he won a VC), Freyberg spread his forces along the northern coastline of the island in preparation as much for a sea-borne landing as an airborne assault. The abandoned airfields were obstructed rather than being permanently put out of use, due to a shortage of time and because of the British intention to reuse them in the near future.

Airborne attack

The three airfields of Maleme, Retimo and Heraklion, spread out along the northern coast of Crete, were the targets chosen by Student. On the morning of 20 May – after a heavy bombardment by the Luftwaffe – the first paratroops were dropped, with orders to take the airfields and secure nearby port installations. They would then await progressive reinforcement from air and sea.

The British troops were ready for the Germans, and although short of anti-aircraft guns, they killed large numbers of paratroops either as they landed or while they were still in the air. By the end of the first day's fighting the Germans were at the point of defeat, although Student continued to send in troops to reinforce the scattered detachments of paratroops attempting to advance on the airfields. Only at Maleme, in the west, had the Germans made any progress. Student decided to send in his last parachute reserves the following day. Fortunately for the German cause on Crete, the commander of the New Zealanders defending the airfield withdrew his forces from the area that evening to regroup, believing that the Germans clinging on around Maleme were stronger than they actually were.

ABOVE

General Kurt Student (kneeling with map), the German airborne commander-in-chief, discusses the situation with staff officers. For the first few days, the German grip on Crete was tenuous in the extreme.

German air reconnaissance on the morning of the 21st confirmed Student in the necessity of reinforcing Maleme if his forces were not be wiped out. During the day he sent in his remaining paratroops and flew in a mountain battalion in the afternoon. The airfield was now cleared and firmly under German control, allowing consolidation and the prospect of an advance against the British and Commonwealth forces once enough reinforcements and equipment had been safely landed.

The Royal Navy withdraws

At sea, the Royal Navy had braved the gauntlet of German aerial attack and attempted to intercept or turn back the German sea-borne invasion force. But rising losses, particularly from the German air cover, eventually forced the navy to withdraw from the waters north of Crete on 24 May, thus allowing Germans a secure maritime link with the island.

On 25 May, troops of the 5th Mountain Division managed to break out of the Maleme perimeter and push on through

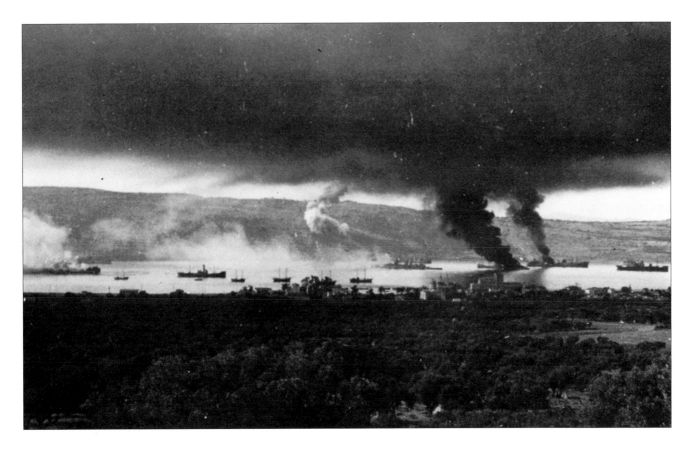

Galatas to Canea, a short distance from the main naval harbour at Suda Bay. By now, the Germans had approaching 20,000 well-armed, high-quality troops on Crete, supported by overwhelming air power. Furthermore large numbers of reinforcements were arriving every day. Freyberg reasoned that the island was lost, and on 26 May he recommended the evacuation of his troops, which commenced the following day. The troops in Heraklion, in the east, were evacuated without difficulty, but the main body in the west had to cross the mountains to the southern port of Sfakia, hounded by the Germans on land and from the air.

A costly evacuation

The Royal Navy would again have to enter the hostile waters around Crete to take off the British contingent. Admiral Cunningham signalled to his fleet: 'We cannot let the army down.' And when one of his staff raised the objections on the grounds of danger, he retorted: 'It takes the navy three years to build a ship. It would take 300 years to rebuild a tradition.' For four days from 28 May, the navy rescued as many of the men as possible, incurring heavy casualties in the process from the Luftwaffe's attacks. Three cruisers and six destroyers were sunk, and 13 other ships were

badly damaged, including the cruiser *Orion*, which lost 260 men killed and 280 wounded through a single German bomb.

British and Commonwealth losses on Crete were 1742 killed and missing, 2225 wounded and over 11,000 captured. Royal Navy losses included nearly 2000 killed, but they had the distinction of rescuing some 18,000 British and Commonwealth troops and transporting them back to Egypt .

The Germans had suffered heavily, with some 4000 deaths, which far exceeded the total casualty figure for the entire Balkan campaign. The scale of the losses shocked the Germans. General Student wrote that Hitler was 'most displeased with the whole affair'. He told Student that 'Crete proves that the days of the paratroops are over.' From then on the German paratroop arm was never used in airborne operations and was confined to a ground-fighting role.

The German seizure of Crete was not exploited by Hitler as a springboard for renewed conquest in the region, and although it protected the Romanian oil fields from attack from the RAF, this respite would only be temporary. Within two years, long-range American B-24 Liberators would begin to pound Hitler's precious Romanian oil-fields to destruction.

ABOVE
Allied transport ships burn in Suda Bay following a German bombing raid. As in Greece, command of the air was decisive in gaining victory against the Allies in Crete.

CHAPTER TEN

TRIUMPH OF THE DESERT FOX

After their dramatic successes of 1940, the British hoped for further victories in North Africa. However the new year saw the arrival of a new opponent: Erwin Rommel, the Desert Fox.

In December 1940, Hitler began to investigate ways of aiding his Italian ally in North Africa. The X Flightcorps established air fields in Sicily towards the end of the month, although its role was to provide support for Axis operations throughout the Mediterranean area. The destruction of the Italian Tenth Army by the British during the winter of 1940–41 – in Wavell's offensive – made the need for German intervention all the more necessary. On 11 January 1941, Hitler issued Directive Number 22, which ordered the formation and despatch of a special detachment to North Africa. This would act as a blocking force to prevent the British from pushing on to Tripoli. At the time, the German army high command (OKH) had little interest in initiating offensive operations in Libya, but the man appointed to command this body of troops had other ideas.

Lieutenant General Erwin Rommel flew into Tripoli on 12 February. His exploits commanding the 7th Panzer Division in France had earned him the admiration of Hitler and an independent command leading Germany's ground forces in North Africa. After reporting to the new Italian commander-in-chief in Libya, General Gariboldi, he set off on an aerial reconnaissance of the forward areas to personally assess the situation facing the Axis in North Africa.

Lieutenant Heggenreiner, a German liaison officer with the Italian army, had written a memorandum to Rommel explaining the poor state of Italian morale. Rommel noted that Heggenreiner, 'described some very unpleasant incidents, which had occurred during the retreat, or rather the rout which it had become. Italian troops had thrown away their weapons and ammunition, and clambered onto overloaded vehicles in a wild attempt to get away to the west. Morale was as low as it could be in all military circles in Tripoli. Most of the Italian officers had already packed their bags and were hoping for a quick return to Italy.' While this was probably something of an exaggeration, Rommel's comments summed up the pessimistic and defensive-minded mentality of the Italians.

Rommel takes command

The Italian army in Libya now comprised five poorly equipped divisions, of which one, the *Ariete* division, was a mechanised formation that had been assigned 60 light tanks. So rife was the despondency in the Italian camp at this point in the desert campaign that Rommel even had difficulty in persuading Gariboldi that a defensive line should be established well to the east of Tripoli at Sirte, directly opposite the forward British positions at El Agheila.

OPPOSITE

A German soldier surveys the terrain ahead with the aid of stereoscopic binoculars. The arid deserts of North Africa were a completely new area of operations for the German armed forces, but they adapted to the new conditions with remarkable speed.

Although technically under the command of Gariboldi and the Italian high command, Rommel had the right to appeal to OKH if he considered his forces to be endangered by an Italian order. Complicating the command structure further, Rommel was given control over the Italian mechanised forces. From the start, however, Rommel acted in an independent capacity and ignored the directives of his nominal Italian superiors and, at times, even OKH itself.

Two days after Rommel's arrival, armoured cars of the 3rd Reconnaissance Battalion were unloaded at the docks in Tripoli, the advance element of the 5th Light Division (renamed 21st Panzer Division in October 1941). This was the beginning of the renowned Africa Corps, or *Deutsches Afrika Korps* (DAK), which officially came into being on 19 February 1941. The rest of the 5th Light Division was due to arrive by mid-April, while the other German formation promised to Rommel, the 15th Panzer Division, would not be ready for action until the end of May. But in early March, a small force capable of offensive operations had arrived, and in addition to the well-armed

reconnaissance battalion, it included the 5th Panzer Regiment, which was allotted 105 medium and 51 light tanks.

The Luftwaffe provided direct support in the form of a fighter screen plus 20 medium bombers and 50 dive-bombers. More aircraft were on call from the main bases of X Flightcorps in Sicily. And during the course of the next few months, Rommel would receive further aircraft from Europe, giving the Germans the edge over the British in terms of air superiority.

The first German moves

With the forces at his disposal, Rommel decided to test the enemy positions around El Agheila. The first clash with the British took place on 24 February and their negative response to this meeting convinced Rommel that the time was ripe for an all-out offensive. The British position in Cyrenaica was, in fact, more vulnerable than it seemed at first sight. The experienced units of Wavell's offensive had been replaced by troops new to combat: the 6th Australian Division had been exchanged for the 9th Australian Division and the loss of 7th Armoured Division was in no way compensated for by the arrival of 2nd Armoured Division, which was seriously under-strength and lacking in knowledge of desert conditions. O'Connor had been transferred back to Middle East Command, and the new British commander, Lieutenant General Philip Neame, failed to measure up to his predecessor.

Supported by the Italian mechanised *Ariete* Division, the newly-formed Africa Corps struck on the 24 March. The British fell back in disorder. Capitalising on British disarray, Rommel pressed his advantage and raced forward along three axes of advance, further confusing his opponents. In order to avoid encirclement, the British rapidly gave ground and retreated to Gazala, but this did not prevent the capture of Generals Neame and O'Connor (the latter had been sent up to advise Neame as the situation deteriorated).

The staff car containing Neame and O'Connor was intercepted by a German patrol near Derna on 7 April. O'Connor's capture was a great loss to the British cause, although his wry comment on the incident was typical: 'It was a great shock and I never thought it would ever happen to me; very conceited perhaps, but it was miles behind out own front and by sheer bad luck we drove into the one bit of desert in which the Germans had sent a reconnaissance group, and went bang into the middle of them.'

The Africa Corps surrounded Tobruk on 11 April and Rommel immediately ordered an all-out assault in the hope of gaining the port before the British had a chance to organise a proper defence. The attacks failed and the Axis forces had to set about mounting a conventional siege operation, and so began the epic 242-day investment of Tobruk. Under the command of the tough Australian Major General Leslie Morshead (nicknamed 'Ming the Merciless' by his troops) the garrison of Tobruk was a mixed force comprising Australian infantry (the 9th Infantry Division plus and extra brigade) supported by British artillery, anti-aircraft guns and engineer units, plus a few Matilda tanks from the Royal Tank Regiment. Morshead immediately stamped his authority over the garrison when he declared: 'There'll be no Dunkirk here! If we should have to get out, we shall have to fight our way out. No surrender and no retreat.'

Tobruk besieged

The German failure to overwhelm Tobruk swiftly was an immense irritation to Rommel but he reluctantly accepted that he must wear down the defenders with repeated aerial and artillery bombardments. For the defenders,

BELOW
In the light of dawn, Australian troops advance into battle. Australian, New Zealand, South African and Indian troops would all make major contributions to the British effort in North Africa.

the German bomber raids became the most constant of the many unpleasant features of life in the fortress. This was a period of German aerial ascendancy as the RAF's resources were limited by other commitments and the distance of its airfields from Tobruk. Stuka raids were particularly disliked by the ground troops. One of the Tobruk gunners, L.E. Tutt, described the feeling of being under dive-bomb attack:

A less welcome break in the routine was the occasional Stuka raid on the position. They were stub-winged, almost ungainly in appearance. They looked rather slow-moving in flight until they went into their dive. They came down like a stone, holding their course until it appeared that they were going to dash themselves to pieces on their target, then they would pull out of it with such suddenness that you felt their wings would be torn away.

Under attack, one seemed to have been chosen as their sole target. You could see the bombs leave their racks, wobble hesitantly then straighten up as they gained velocity. We were encouraged to fire at them with our rifles; I think this was solely to help us with our morale. I saw a Stuka that had been brought down by a Bofors team and the area round the pilot was as armoured as a light tank. No rifle bullet could have penetrated it.

Despite the best efforts of the Luftwaffe and the German army, the defenders of Tobruk did not waver, and all Axis attacks were repulsed. Life for the garrison was tough: the repeated artillery and aerial bombardments had to be endured against a background of summer heat with water and food shortages. A series of nightly convoys, conducted by the Royal Navy, maintained a sufficient supply of ammunition and supplies, but almost all luxuries were denied to the fighting troops. The harsh conditions engendered a sense of shared comradeship that bound the men together, and made then formidable opponents.

Australian withdrawal

During August, the British Government received requests from the Australian Government for the withdrawal of its troops from Tobruk. Despite the difficulty of conducting an amphibious withdrawal from a city under siege, the navy began the operation, which was successfully completed by the end of September. A constant problem facing British commanders in the desert was the attitude of the Commonwealth governments, who had the right to withdraw their troops whenever they wished. The earlier disasters suffered by the Australians and New Zealanders in Greece and Crete had made both their governments and some senior Commonwealth commanders wary of British control. These suspicions were made known to the British, with the result that the high command had to be particularly careful when deploying Commonwealth troops.

The Australians in Tobruk were replaced by the British 70th Division, commanded by Major General R.M. Scobie, who also assumed command of the garrison. Accompanying the British was a brigade of Polish troops and a Czech battalion, and subsequently two New Zealand battalions. The

RIGHT

Uprated with a 5cm main gun, the German PzKpfw III Ausf G was capable of out-shooting light armoured vehicles and was far more mobile than the heavy tanks of the British Army. Before deployment in North Africa German tanks were specially converted for tropical use.

**Panzer III Ausf G
Germany**

reinforcement of Tobruk was not carried out merely to replace the Australians but also to provide a force which would break out of Tobruk and link up with a proposed overland British advance from Egypt.

The Axis foray into Cyrenaica in the spring of 1941 had thrown the British out of Libya, so that any British attempt to relieve Tobruk would involve a major battle with the Germans holding a defensive line along the Libyan-Egyptian border. Rommel had been reinforced by the arrival of the 15th Panzer Division, and by the Trento and Brescia Divisions of the Italian army.

Erwin Rommel

Rommel's audacious plan earned him the respect of his fellow officers, and his leadership style brought admiration from the men of the Africa Corps. Major F.W. von Mellenthin was an officer on Rommel's staff throughout most of the North African campaign, and got to know him well. Mellenthin analysed his talents:

He was in my opinion the ideal commander for desert warfare. His custom of 'leading from the front' occasionally told against him; decisions affecting the army as a whole were sometimes influenced unduly by purely local successes or failures. On the *other hand by going himself to the danger spot – and he had an uncanny faculty for appearing at the right place at the right time – he was able to adapt his plans to new situations, and in the fluid conditions of the Western Desert this was a factor of supreme importance. In planning an operation he was thoughtful and thorough; in taking a decision in the field he was swift and audacious – shrewdly assessing the chances of some daring stroke in the ebb and flow of battle. What I admired most were his courage and resourcefulness and his invincible determination under the most adverse circumstances.*

Between Rommel and his troops there was a mutual understanding which cannot be adequately explained or analysed, but which was a gift from the gods. However the battle was going, the Africa Corps followed Rommel loyally wherever he led, and however hard he drove them.

The British response

The loss of Libya was an unwelcome surprise to the British. Any available troops from the Delta were rushed up to the border to contain any possibility of the Germans pushing on into Egypt. But until the capture of Tobruk, with its vital port facilities, Rommel felt he could not advance eastwards. By default, the strategic initiative passed to the

ABOVE
A view of Sollum from the high Libyan plateau showing the coast road that ran from Tripoli to Alexandria. It was over terrain like this that much of the desert war was fought.

RIGHT

A German soldier scans the skies alongside an MG-34 machine gun, adapted for anti-aircraft duties. Under combat conditions, the solar topees worn by soldiers on both sides were soon abandoned for more practical headgear.

BELOW

A situation map drawn by Rommel during Operation Crusader, the British offensive into Libya.

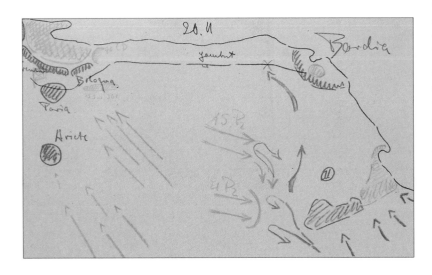

British. Back in London, the prime minister demanded swift action to recover the lost territories and relieve Tobruk. By May 1941, Wavell had assembled the XIII Corps (Lieutenant General Sir Noel Beresford-Peirse) consisting of the 4th Indian Division and a reconstituted 7th Armoured Division, plus the 22nd Guards Brigade.

Wavell remained unhappy at the state of his forces, and did not want to rush into an offensive against the Africa Corps. Such delays did not endear him to Churchill, who continued to press for aggressive action. In May, Wavell acceded to Churchill's demands and assembled a mixed force of armour and infantry under Brigadier Gott to secure the tactically important Halfaya Pass and the strong points around Fort Capuzzo and Sollum. Code-named Operation Brevity, it was hoped that success here would act as a springboard for further offensive action into Libya, including the relief of Tobruk.

After some initial success, the British were halted, and a subsequent German counter-attack unceremoniously chased them back across the frontier. On 27 May, the Germans regained Halfaya Pass, and under Rommel's promptings began to improve their defences in case of a subsequent British attack. The following day, Wavell signalled to the combined chiefs of the Imperial general staff a detailed list of the shortcomings of British weapons and equipment in North Africa:

Our armoured cars are too lightly armoured to resist the fire of enemy fighter aircraft, and, having no gun, are powerless against the German eight-wheeled armoured cars, which have guns and are faster. This makes reconnaissance difficult. Our infantry tanks [Matildas] are really too slow for a battle in the desert, and have been suffering considerable casualties from the fire of the powerful [8.8cm] enemy anti-tank guns. Our cruisers have little advantage in power or speed over German medium tanks. Technical breakdowns are still too numerous. We shall not be able to accept battle with perfect confidence in spite of numerical inferiority, as we could against the Italians. Above factors may limit our success. They also make it imperative that [an] adequate flow of armoured reinforcements and reserves should be maintained.

While Wavell's complaints were largely justified, he understandably failed to make the point that a major reason for British failure lay in the poor tactics adopted by the British and the inability of the separate arms of service to cooperate with each other on the battlefield. While the Germans were swift to adapt to desert conditions, the more experienced British were slow and rigid in their entire operational approach.

Poor British organisation

The British were equipped with the powerful 3.7-inch anti-aircraft gun, which – like the German '88' – was extremely effective against armoured vehicles, but unlike the Germans the British lacked the imagination to use this weapon in an anti-tank role. Another area in which the British lagged behind the Germans lay in the location and repair of broken-down

BELOW
British staff officers prepare orders in a temporary headquarters, an underground well near Bardia.

Italian tank crews are briefed by an officer as they parade in front of their M13/40 medium tanks. The M13/40 was equipped with a turret-mounted 47mm gun, but was not particularly effective in combat, being cramped, unreliable and having a tendency to catch fire when hit by anti-tank rounds.

or damaged tanks. The Germans sent out salvage teams directly behind the main force, and as a consequence were able to get these damaged tanks back into action with minimal delay. The British, by contrast, methodically sent their vehicles back to rear bases to be repaired, which prevented them from returning to the battle, until it was lost.

Operation Battleaxe

In June, a second, larger offensive (Operation Battleaxe) was instigated. The British plan involved a frontal assault on Halfaya Pass and a flanking manoeuvre by the 7th Armoured Division to capture Fort Capuzzo and Hafia Ridge. The British had received a considerable number of tanks as a result of the Tiger convoy which, after much sacrifice as a result of German attacks, had successfully docked in Egypt. Unfortunately, for the British, Rommel had fortified the German line with a screen of dug-in and concealed 8.8cm guns, which could slice through the armour of the

heavy Matilda tanks with ease. And it was the Matilda tanks of the 4th Armoured Brigade which were assigned to attack these German defences. The 7th Armoured Brigade was equipped with the new Crusader medium tanks (Cruiser Mark VI); they had arrived directly from the factory and their crews had not been given time to familiarise themselves with their new vehicles.

On 15 June, the British attack on Halfaya got underway, led by the infantry of the 4th Indian Division, while the two brigades of the 7th Armoured Division advanced through the desert. The attack of Halfaya was repulsed and the British were forced to fall back. German resistance was resolute throughout, and although Fort Capuzzo briefly fell into British hands, a counter-attack quickly ejected them. Rommel now sensed an opportunity to trap the bulk of the XIII Corps, but a timely British withdrawal enabled them to return to their start line by 17 June. Although British casualties were not heavy – around

1000 killed, wounded and missing – of the 180 tanks committed to the battle, about 100 were lost (Rommel admitted to the loss of 12 German tanks). It was a humiliating blow.

The 'dreaded 88s'

Battleaxe was the first time the 'dreaded 88s' had been used in North Africa, and British armoured units would grow to fear its high-velocity shot. Rommel had lured the British armour onto his anti-tank gun line, and destroyed it. This allowed the German tanks to advance against the remnants of the British armour and then carve up the poorly pro-tected British infantry at their leisure. This was a tactic the German army would use repeat-edly during the course of the desert war, a tactical problem the British were seldom able to resolve.

One consequence of the failure of Battleaxe was the replacement of Wavell on 21 June as commander-in-chief in the Middle East by General Sir Claude Auchinleck, a highly regarded officer from the Indian army (one of the few senior officers whose involve-ment in the Norwegian campaign had not tarnished their reputation). The command shake-up was mirrored by other organisa-tional changes, not least the formation of the Eighth Army to take the place of the Western Desert Force. The new Eighth Army com-mander was to be Lieutenant General Sir Alan

LEFT
Knocked out British Matilda II infantry tanks. The Matilda, although very slow and under-gunned, had heavy armour which made it invulnerable to most Axis anti-tank guns of the period. But the high-velocity German 8.8cm anti-aircraft gun could slice through its armour with ease, and many Matildas were knocked out by '88s' during Operation Battleaxe.

Cunningham, the recent victor over the Italians in Abyssinia. Auchinleck and Cunningham found themselves under constant pressure from Churchill to launch a new offensive, but after the disasters of Operations Brevity and Battleaxe they were determined to build up British forces in the desert to ensure numerical superiority.

German reinforcements

During this pause in hostilities, the Germans also reinforced and reorganised their forces. The two panzer divisions (15th and 21st) were reinforced by the arrival of the mechanised 90th Light Division, formed from a nucleus of units already in Africa; it comprised a motorised grenadier regiment and three motorised infantry regiments, one of which included Germans transferred from the French Foreign Legion. The arrival of the Italian XX and XXI Corps and the Savona Division led to a new designation: Panzer Group Africa, an army level formation which contained the Africa Corps.

While the Germans waited, the British prepared to attack. Designated Operation Crusader, the British plan called for a major armoured offensive by XXX Corps (Lieutenant General Willoughby Norrie) to swing round through the desert, take on and destroy the Axis armour and relieve Tobruk. XIII Corps (Lieutenant General A.R. Godwin-Austen) was primarily an infantry formation. Its role in the coming battle was to side-step the Axis defences around Halfaya and Sollum and then advance along the coastal strip towards Tobruk and meet up with XXX Corps.

Auchinleck had insisted upon the tightest security and the Germans were unaware of the Eighth Army's preparations for the offensive. On 18 November 1941, the British tanks advanced into the desert. An intelligence officer in XXX Corps, R.H. Dahl, described the sight of the British armour on the move: 'We gazed ahead at scores of widely spaced vehicles – as far as the eye could see – all spewing up their plumes of desert sand. I was suddenly filled with awe at my first glimpse of the sinews of war.'

Taken by surprise, the German reaction was slow and confused. At first, Rommel assumed that the British armoured offensive was only a reconnaissance. Consequently, XXX Corps's advance was relatively unimpeded, until 19 November when it came upon the *Ariete* Division at Bir el Gubi and the German defences around the airfield at Sidi Rezegh. There the British advance was stopped. The following day the Germans –

BELOW

An Italian anti-aircraft gun in action in North Africa. The Italian Army developed some good artillery pieces, but lacked numbers and sufficiently large supplies of ammunition.

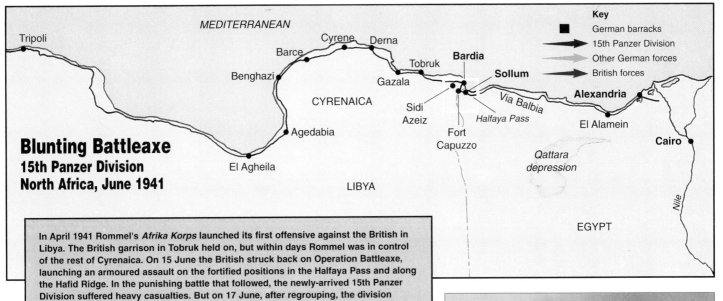

Blunting Battleaxe
15th Panzer Division
North Africa, June 1941

Key
■ German barracks
➤ 15th Panzer Division
➤ Other German forces
➤ British forces

MEDITERRANEAN

Tripoli · Cyrene · Derna · Tobruk · **Bardia** · **Sollum** · **Alexandria**
Barce · Gazala · Sidi Azeiz · *Halfaya Pass* · El Alamein · **Cairo**
Benghazi · CYRENAICA · Fort Capuzzo · Via Balbia
Agedabia · *Qattara depression* · Nile
El Agheila · LIBYA · EGYPT

In April 1941 Rommel's *Afrika Korps* launched its first offensive against the British in Libya. The British garrison in Tobruk held on, but within days Rommel was in control of the rest of Cyrenaica. On 15 June the British struck back on Operation Battleaxe, launching an armoured assault on the fortified positions in the Halfaya Pass and along the Hafid Ridge. In the punishing battle that followed, the newly-arrived 15th Panzer Division suffered heavy casualties. But on 17 June, after regrouping, the division began an outflanking manoeuvre to the south, engaging its opponents south of Fort Capuzzo and forcing them to withdraw.

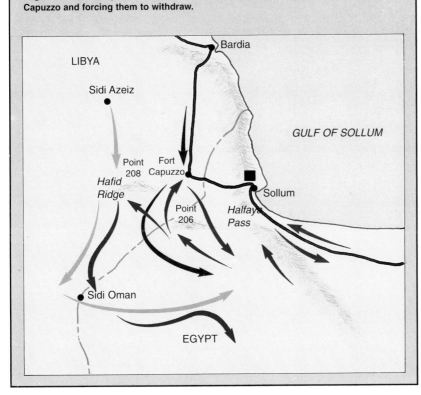

LIBYA · Bardia · Sidi Azeiz · GULF OF SOLLUM · Point 208 · Fort Capuzzo · *Hafid Ridge* · Point 206 · *Halfaya Pass* · Sollum · Sidi Oman · EGYPT

now fully aware of the situation – launched a major counter-attack against XXX Corps with the 15th and 21st Panzer Divisions. This was an extraordinarily confused engagement, later known as the 'multi-layered' battle, where the balance of fortune swung repeatedly from one side to the other.

The fiercest fighting centred around Sidi Rezegh. Bob Sykes, a crew member of a British M3 Stuart light tank, found himself caught up in an enormous armoured mêlée, as each side fought for control of the airfield at Sidi Rezegh:

I cannot describe the confusion of this all-out tank battle; we were here, there and everywhere. I kept switching from tank to tank – out for a breather and some replenishments, and back in again. I do not know who was keeping the score but we were losing a great deal of equipment and men. With our light tanks we were weaving in and out of the battle zone, right in the thick of it. We had developed a tactic of going at the back of the German tank where it was lightly armoured, and piling into it with some pretty disastrous effects to the engine. The noise, the heat and the dust were unbearable.

ABOVE
Rommel observes the progress of his troops through binoculars. Although seen here in a Kubelwagen, he would also use both light aircraft and his personalised half-track, 'Greif', to keep in touch with events at the front.

Australian infantry occupy front-line positions around the Tobruk perimeter. The defence and relief of Tobruk was one of the key factors behind British strategy during 1941.

We were in support of the 8th RTR [Royal Tank Regiment] who were in front of us with heavier tanks but the enemy came in behind us and we were engaged in a fierce battle down to a few hundred yards. We beat then off and continued to assist the 8th RTR but they were later over-whelmed by the onslaught, while we had to retire as we were low on octane and ammo.

Crusader blunted

In two days of battle, the Germans had brought XXX Corps' advance to a standstill and broken its offensive capability. The only ray of hope lay in the advance initiated by XIII Corps. While the 4th Indian Division pinned down the Axis line between Sollum and Sidi Omar, the New Zealand Division made good progress and advanced towards Tobruk. But even here lay danger: if the Africa Corps tuned away northwards from its battle with the British armour the isolated

New Zealanders would be destroyed. It was a moment of crisis in the British camp.

Cunningham's early optimism had com-pletely evaporated and, exhausted by the strain of command, he contemplated a com-plete withdrawal. Auchinleck flew up from Cairo to the front line to confer with his gen-erals, and sensing Cunningham's inability to carry on, he took direct command of the battle. Although the Eighth Army had taken a battering it was not a defeated force and Auchinleck realised that the Germans too had suffered heavy casualties.

As Auchinleck was taking stock of the British situation, events took a new turn. Rather than continue the battle to destroy XXX Corps, Rommel impetuously led his forces directly westwards in an attempt to cut the British supply lines along the frontier wire. Rommel's 'dash to the wire' proved a costly mistake. Under Auchinleck's leadership the British held firm. The Axis forces were repulsed and, short of petrol and supplies, they were forced to retreat in order to prevent XIII Corps successfully linking up with the defenders in Tobruk.

Cunningham replaced

Although the Germans were far from beaten, the tide of battle had turned in favour of the British. Auchinleck decided to continue the offensive. Having lost faith in Cunningham, Auchinleck reluctantly relieved him of his command on 26 November, choosing as his replacement his deputy chief of staff, Lieutenant General Neil Ritchie.

The focus of the battle once again swung back to the area between Sidi Rezegh and the Tobruk perimeter. The German 'dash to the wire' had given time for XXX Corps to re-organise itself and it returned to the fray. During the first week in December the Germans fought desperately to dislodge the British from their forward positions near Tobruk. On 7 December, short of petrol and ammunition, Rommel admitted defeat and decided to withdraw his forces – still largely intact – rather than risk their destruction by continuing the battle. On 10 December, Tobruk was finally relieved by the British. During the remainder of month, the Germans skilfully withdrew from Cyrenaica, the British pursuit hampered by poor weather and the exhaustion of their forces.

Both Axis and British armies had been of a similar size (around 110,000 men each) but casualty figures favoured the British with a total figure of 18,000 as against 38,000 for the Axis, many of them captured during the retreat from Cyrenaica. A major consequence of Operation Crusader had been the relief of Tobruk, but while Auchinleck could take satisfaction in having thrown the Germans out of Cyrenaica, his victory was nonetheless indecisive: the Africa Corps had survived to fight another day, and with the arrival of reinforcements early in January 1942 it would be ready to recommence the battle.

Before the offensive was resumed, Hitler signed Directive Number 38 on 2 December 1941, which was intended to impose a unified command on Axis forces in the Mediterranean and North Africa. The bickering that had developed between the Germans and Italians had compromised Axis effectiveness, and steps had to be taken to resolve these differences and, hopefully, bring Rommel into line. Field Marshal Albert Kesselring, the former artilleryman and Luftwaffe commander, was appointed supreme commander south (*Oberbefehlshaber Süd* – OBS).

Kesselring's brief

Kesselring was instructed in the directive to fulfil a three-fold task: 'To win mastery of the air and sea in the area between southern Italy and North Africa in order to secure communications with Libya and Cyrenaica, and particularly to neutralise Malta. Secondly, to

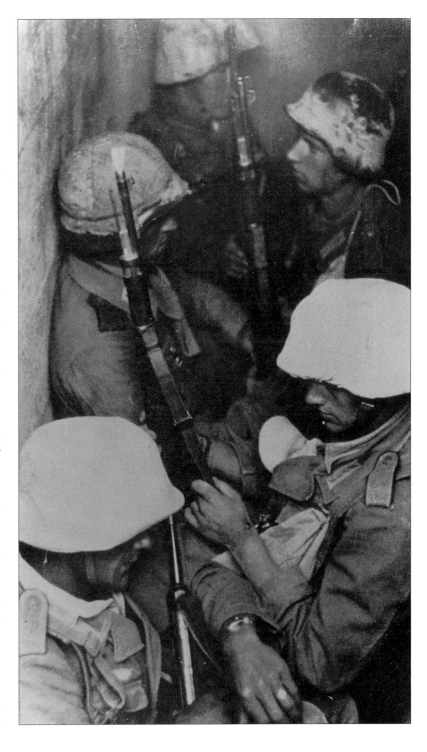

BELOW
German assault infantry crouch under cover, awaiting the signal to launch another attack against Tobruk.

RIGHT

At his post in the Tobruk docks, a British machine gunner, armed with a Bren gun, directs his fire against German aircraft. Although a single Bren had little chance of bringing down an aircraft, sustained fire would put the enemy pilot off his aim.

cooperate with the German and allied [Italian] forces in North Africa. Thirdly, to paralyse enemy movements in the Mediterranean, including supplies to Tobruk and Malta, working in close cooperation with the available German and Italian naval forces.'

Axis command difficulties

The directive was a belated attempt to redress the problems of inter-arm cooperation (army, navy, air force) and the German failure to work effectively with the Italians. Kesselring took command of the Luftwaffe air and anti-aircraft units in the Mediterranean, and received reinforcements with the arrival of Flightcorps II (General Lörnzer), which had been withdrawn from the Eastern Front. Kesselring, however, lacked the real power to oversee all military aspects of the Mediterranean theatre, in a way comparable to an Allied commander like Eisenhower or Nimitz. Consequently, he was unable to improve the key deficiencies that hindered the Axis, above all the supply of men and materials to North Africa, and nor was he able to rein in Rommel, whose refusal to accept outside authority verged on insubordination.

Despite these problems the Germans were in the ascendancy over the British in the Mediterranean during the winter of 1941–42.

Allied convoys had been badly mauled by the Axis. The British position in North Africa was weakened by the withdrawal of experienced British and Australian formations to the Far East, following Japan's entry into the war on 7 December 1941. Like Wavell before him, Auchinleck suddenly saw his army denuded of veteran formations while it was at its most vulnerable, stretched out across the Cyrenaican bulge. Rommel was fully aware of the British problems, and he decided to resume the offensive without delay and catch his opponents by surprise.

Rommel was able to deploy five Axis panzer/motorised divisions for the attack. On the British side, the 7th Armoured Division was being withdrawn back to Egypt, leaving the inexperienced and under-strength 1st Armoured Division to face the Germans. The 4th Indian Division was stationed around Benghazi, too far away to provide support for the forward British armour. The new German attack was launched on 21 January: the British 1st Armoured Division was brushed aside as the Axis division raced forward into the bulge of Cyrenaica, in a repeat performance of the spring offensive of 1941. The 4th Indian Division retreated hurriedly from Benghazi to avoid being cut off and surrounded. The Axis reconquest of Cyrenaica came to a halt against the British defensive line stretching from Gazala on the coast down to the outpost of Bir Hakeim in the south. From early February to mid-May 1942 there was a lull in the fighting as both sides built up their relative strengths for the next round of battle.

The Eighth Army under General Neil Ritchie was divided into two corps. As had been the case in the Crusader battles of the previous year, XXX Corps (Lieutenant General Willoughby Norrie), with 1st and 7th Armoured Divisions, had most of the tanks, while XIII Corps, (Lieutenant General W.H.E. Gott) contained the bulk of the infantry. The infantry divisions were distributed along a defensive line which consisted of a series of boxes or 'hedgehogs', protected by barbed wire and minefields and capable of holding a brigade group.

The development of the box was a typically British response aimed at preventing the panzers from cutting up the infantry in the open desert, as squares had preserved infantry of the Napoleonic era from marauding cavalry. They varied in size but the most usual was one that could hold an infantry brigade of three battalions along with artillery and engineer support. The perimeter would consist of slit trenches to hold the infantry, with some elaborately constructed gun pits for the artillery. Around the perimeter trenches would be a ring of barbed wire and then an extensive minefield.

Flawed British tactics

That the box came to be a regular element of Eighth Army tactical thinking revealed a basic flaw in British military organisation and doctrine. The British army, like all other armies, utilised the divisional system. On paper this was a multi-arms formation able to operate independently on the battlefield; in reality this rarely happened. In fact, the British army was based on the regimental system, which operated as a collection of separate regimental units. Cooperation between these almost tribal units was poor and not properly understood, and in the extremes of combat such cooperation regularly broke down to the detriment of the British fighting effort.

BELOW
Fuel tanks burn in the background as Tobruk comes under attack; in the foreground are rows of captured vehicles parked in the desert.

The German concept of a panzer division comprising an equal and mutually supporting combination of tanks and motorised infantry, artillery and anti-tank guns, plus other mobile supporting arms was not understood by the British. In the Eighth Army, a distinction between the separate arms was invariably maintained, especially between the infantry and armour. A short while after the Gazala battle, Brigadier Howard Kippenberger, commander of the 5th New Zealand Brigade, complained of the at this lack of cooperation: 'At this time there was throughout Eighth Army, not only in the New Zealand Division, a most intense distrust, almost hatred, of our armour.' And it was because the infantry had so little confidence in their own tanks to provide support that the box system gained the support that it did from the British and Commonwealth forces.

A.H.G. Dobson was stationed in the ill-fated 150th Brigade box, and he highlighted one of the chief weaknesses inherent in the Gazala defensive line:

The major problem was that the boxes were too far apart, so that when the attack came at the end of May there just wasn't the coordination between adjacent boxes. The 69th Brigade box to our right must have been five miles away and on the other side, the Free French box at Bir Hakeim must have been another five miles to our south. This lack of support meant one was really fighting an individual battle, which was a disaster if Rommel decided to turn his full might on you — which is exactly what happened to our brigade.

Reinforced from Europe (along with the windfall provided by captured British supplies at Benghazi), Rommel prepared to resume the offensive, not only to complete the capture of Cyrenaica but to press on towards the glittering prizes of Cairo, Alexandria and the Suez Canal. Rommel's plan was simple and direct, relying on speed and aggression to achieve success. Group Cruewell, comprising Italian infantry with German support, would launch a frontal attack against British infantry line to pin down the defenders, while Rommel would lead the Axis armoured divisions in a wide sweep to the south of Bir Hakeim. Outflanking the British line, the Axis tanks would then take on and destroy the British armoured units in reserve, and cut off the bulk of the Eighth Army from its supply lines to the east.

Rommel attacks

On the afternoon of 26 May, Group Cruewell began its assault, and under cover of darkness the German and Italian armoured formations began their outflanking movement. Consisting of the 15th and 21st Panzer Divisions, the 90th Light Division and the *Ariete* Division, it was a formidable force.

Major John Hackett (later to achieve fame at Arnhem) was the commander of a squadron of M3 Stuart light tanks of the 8th King's Royal Irish Hussars. On the morning of 27 May he was ordered forward to investigate reports of enemy activity south of the Bir Hakeim box:

I got C Squadron on the move very quickly — they were a very handy lot. We went up a slope in this typically undulating desert country, and as I reached the top of this rise the commanding officer said to me over the radio: 'Report when you first see them.' I came over the top and there in front of me was the whole bloody German army, as far as I could see, coming my way. I replied to the colonel's

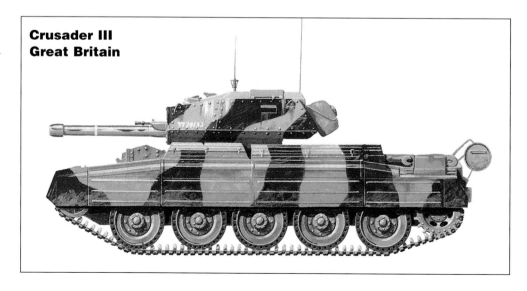

**Crusader III
Great Britain**

transmission: 'I'm engaging them. Out.' I put up a black flag to say 'Attack!' – in those days wireless was not too reliable – and like a mug forgot to take it down again. And any tank flying a flag is of course a control element and attracts fire, so I attracted all the fire there was. I suppose my tank was the first in the Eighth Army to be knocked out that day, which was about three minutes after putting up the black flag.

British confusion

Despite his wounds, Hackett managed to get back to his regiment and was evacuated to hospital. Others were not so lucky, and many British units were overrun in the opening phase of the devastating German assault. Some idea of the confusion and horror of armoured warfare is provided in an account by Harold Harper, an NCO in the South Notts Hussars, which despite its name was an artillery unit assigned to support the 22nd Armoured Brigade. When the German panzers rounded

Bir Hakeim, two armoured cars of the South Notts Hussars were sent forward on a reconnaissance mission. The first contained Harper's battery commander, Major Garry Birkin, and the second his brother, Captain Ivor Birkin, along with Harper:

We had only gone six or seven hundred yards when we heard a garbled message from the commander's radio which immediately told us that something was wrong. Captain Birkin jumped out and dashed across to the [other] armoured car, and I followed him. I've never seen anything quite like it in my life. Major Birkin lay flat on the floor, obviously dead. I went to the back and opened up the doors of the armoured car. Apparently an armour-piercing shell had gone clean through the middle of the battery commander as he was standing in the turret and then chopped off the heads of the two radio operators.

All you could see was the two lads, their hands still holding their microphones – although their heads had rolled off onto the floor. The third

ABOVE

Desert conditions made transportation difficult, and in those areas covered in soft sand, only two or four legged transport was possible. Here, British troops use mules to carry equipment.

operator, who had sent the message, jumped off from the armoured car and raced off.

The catalogue of disasters experienced by the gunners on the ill-fated mission was to continue. While Ivor Birkin remained at the scene of destruction by the first, knocked-out armoured car – distraught at the death of his brother – Harper went back to collect the other vehicle to pick up Birkin and return to report back to his unit:

I put my hand on the driver, who by that time had pulled down all the shutters and was driving blind. We had practised for weeks, whereby I would put down a certain pressure on either the left or right shoulder, and according to the amount of pressure the driver turned the wheel to a varying degree. In the turmoil I put too much pressure on the lad's shoulder and he turned sharply, and just then, out of a cloud of dust, came a Grant tank of the Royal Gloucester Hussars. We hit it head on and literally bounced back five or six yards.

The next thing we saw was our engine on fire. We all had to jump out of the thing. In the meantime, we found we had accidentally run over the laddie who had been the third radio operator in Major Birkin's crew. We'd run over and broken his leg, so we had to drag him with us. The four of us, plus the lad went over to Captain Birkin. And there we were, stranded.

We then jumped on the back of a passing tank of the CLY [County of London Yeomanry] and lay flat on it. The tank commander had no idea we there and kept firing. We had to keep dodging as best we could when the turret and barrel kept swinging round. One of the chaps fell off and we thought he'd been crushed to death, though I found out later that he lived. Most of us received wounds of some sort from the German shelling. I'd crushed my ribs when we collided with the Grant tank and later I got some shrapnel in my left knee. I wasn't aware of it at the time, there was too much happening.

By hammering on the turret hatch, Harper and his comrades managed to attract the attention of the tank commander, who had then sent them back to his regiment's wagon line for treatment. A few hours later, while Harper was having his wounds tended to at a field dressing station, it was overrun by an advancing German panzer unit. The medical staff were permitted by the Germans to carry on with their work caring for the wounded and dying. Suddenly, a light aircraft landed close by the dressing station to reveal a high-ranking German officer, who Harper immediately recognised as General Rommel himself. 'At the height of the battle,' Harper remembered, 'he took time to say that everything possible would be done to make the British prisoners comfortable, and he was sorry that they couldn't get any food through as yet but they would try. I couldn't fail but be impressed by him.'

British failings

Rommel's inspired leadership contrasted favourably with the lacklustre performance shown in the British camp. The Eighth Army's reaction to the German armoured attack had been slow and uncoordinated. Relations between Ritchie and his two corps commanders were not good and there was general disagreement as to what the correct British response should be. At corps and divisional level, few attempts were made by formations to operate in conjunction with each other, so that piecemeal British counter-attacks were defeated in detail by the Germans.

Despite the setbacks suffered by the British on the first day of fighting, the battle was not necessarily lost. Rommel had driven his armoured forces deep behind the Eighth Army's line but the morale of the British soldier held firm and, although poorly planned,

British counter-attacks were beginning to wear down the panzers' offensive capability. After a couple of days of fierce but inconclusive tank combat, Rommel's position began to worsen: the British armour had failed to melt away at the first great onslaught, while German supplies of ammunition and petrol – never large – were on the verge of running perilously low.

The destruction of 150th Brigade

Rommel had hoped to force a supply route through the centre of the British line but he had underestimated the depth of the minefields and was unaware of the presence of the 150th Brigade box astride his proposed route. If this lifeline was to be established then the 150th Brigade would have to be eliminated with the utmost rapidity. Rommel ordered his divisions to withdraw into a defensive position on the edge of the minefields while the 150th Brigade box was destroyed.

The full weight of the Africa Corps was thrown against the hapless 150th Brigade. For nearly 72 hours, three battalions of infantry, supported by the brigade artillery and

BELOW
The staff of a divisional headquarters study their maps alongside an armoured command vehicle. The Germans were masters of radio communication, invaluable in the wide spaces of the Western Desert.

engineers plus a squadron of tanks, weathered the German storm. Sheer weight of numbers and shortage of ammunition told against the defenders, so that on 1 June the position was taken by the Germans. Rommel was deeply impressed by the British stand and later wrote that his troops, 'had met the toughest resistance imaginable. The defence was conducted with marked skill, and as usual the British fought to the end.'

The destruction of the 150th Brigade box allowed the free passage of supplies to the Germans in their defensive perimeter – called the 'Cauldron' – who could then go onto the offensive. Instead, Rommel waited for the

British tanks to throw themselves on his carefully sited anti-tank screen. And this the British obligingly did. Although Ritchie had had several days to plan and execute a thorough counter-attack, nothing had been done. A strange combination of indecision and complacency ruled the Eighth Army's decision-making process. Indeed, Ritchie thought he had the battle virtually won when he heard that the Germans had withdrawn into the Cauldron. But the prompt and concerted attack that might have beaten the Germans never came.

As Rommel built up his strength in the Cauldron during the first few days of June, so

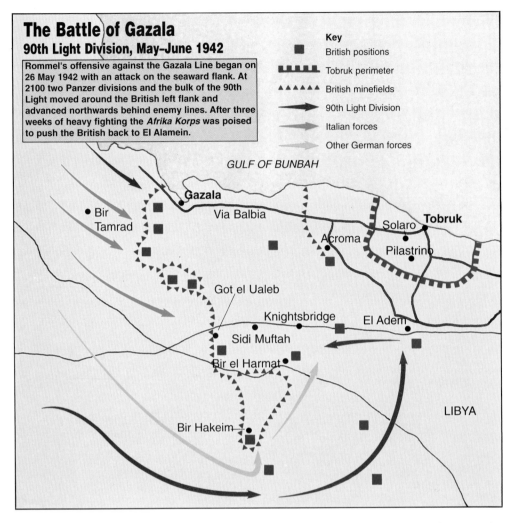

The Battle of Gazala
90th Light Division, May–June 1942

Rommel's offensive against the Gazala Line began on 26 May 1942 with an attack on the seaward flank. At 2100 two Panzer divisions and the bulk of the 90th Light moved around the British left flank and advanced northwards behind enemy lines. After three weeks of heavy fighting the *Afrika Korps* was poised to push the British back to El Alamein.

Key
- ■ British positions
- ▪▪▪▪▪ Tobruk perimeter
- ▲▲▲▲▲▲ British minefields
- ➤ 90th Light Division
- ➤ Italian forces
- ➤ Other German forces

GULF OF BUNBAH

Gazala
Bir Tamrad
Via Balbia
Solaro
Tobruk
Acroma
Pilastrino
Got el Ualeb
Knightsbridge
El Adem
Sidi Muftah
Bir el Harmat
LIBYA
Bir Hakeim

the Eighth Army slowly prepared its counter-attack. Operation Aberdeen got under way on 5 June and was a complete failure. Not only was Rommel thoroughly prepared for it, but the attack was badly organised with infantry and armour operating independently of each other. The failure of Operation Aberdeen was the signal for Rommel to burst out of the Cauldron. On the afternoon of 5 June the tanks of 21st Panzer Division smashed their way through the British, towards the Knightsbridge position, while 15th Panzer Division swung around through Bir el Harmat to the south. The British were now fighting a desperate holding action to prevent the German armour from overwhelming the entire Gazala position.

Bir Hakeim

With the destruction of the British armour virtually complete, Rommel turned directly south to eliminate the Bir Hakeim box. Defended by a brigade of Free French, Bir Hakeim was now vulnerable to German pressure and very exposed. Bombarded from land and air, the French fought on as best they could but running low on supplies their position was becoming untenable. On 10 June the order was given for the French to break out of the box, which with the aid of diversionary attack by the remnants of XXX Corps was a success; 2700 men out of an original box garrison of 3600 made their way to safety.

Tobruk besieged again

What remained of the original British defensive line at Gazala faced encirclement as Rommel reorganised his tired forces to advance on the great strategic prize of Tobruk. In the far north on the coast, the 1st South African Division made good its escape on the night of 13/14 June, but for the two brigades of the 50th Division the situation was more difficult. The 69th Brigade was able to extract itself successfully and retreat directly eastwards along the coast road.

For the 151st Brigade, however, the novel solution was proposed that it should advance westwards (that is, the 'wrong' way) towards the Axis positions before swinging south round Bir Hakeim and then turning eastwards in the direction of Egypt. Although the 151st Brigade lost most of its vehicles and heavy weapons, over 90 per cent of the men eventually managed to get back to British lines. It was a minor epic of the Desert War but only a small compensation for the tragedy about to unfold: the fall of Tobruk.

The Eighth Army had been out-generalled and out-fought in three weeks of intense fighting. On 16 June the British began to fall back towards the Egyptian frontier. This retreat ensured that Tobruk – containing around 35,000 men and a vast mountain of supplies – would again come under siege. Despite the relatively large numbers of troops in Tobruk, a mixed South African, Indian and British force under the command of Major-General H.B. Klopper, the situation was very different from that of the previous year, when the port had successfully sustained an eight-month siege. The anti-tank defences had virtually been dismantled (anti-tank guns were in particularly short supply) and the entire command structure was disorganised as a consequence of the defeat at Gazala.

Rommel wasted no time in this second attempt to secure Tobruk. On 20 June, under the cover of a furious bomber attack, massed German armoured units prepared to fight

ABOVE

The famous German 8.8cm anti-aircraft gun fires against enemy targets during the battle of Gazala. While the British maintained a rigid separation between anti-aircraft guns and other forms of artillery, the Germans combined them successfully.

their way into the south-eastern corner of the
perimeter defences. The staff officer, Major
Mellenthin, witnessed the German attack:

*At 0500 I stood with Rommel on the escarp-
ment to the north-east of El Adem; battle
headquarters had been set up there and when daylight came we had excellent observation as far as the
Tobruk perimeter. Promptly at 0520 the Stukas
flew over. Kesselring had been as good as his word
and sent hundreds of bombers in dense formations;
they dived onto the perimeter in one of the most
spectacular attacks I have ever seen.*

*A great cloud of dust and smoke rose from the
sector under attack, and while our bombs crashed
onto the defences, the entire German and Italian
army artillery joined in with tremendous and well
coordinated fire. The combined weight of the
artillery and bombing was terrific; and as we soon
realised it had a crushing effect on the morale of the
Mahratta battalion in that sector. The Stukas kept
it up all day, flying back to the airfields at Gazala
and El Adem, replenishing with bombs, and returning to the fray.*

Within hours of the beginning of the
bombardment, a breech had been made and

over 200 Axis tanks raced through the shattered defensive line directly towards Tobruk
harbour. Despite gallant but isolated stands by
a handful of units, the defence crumbled
almost immediately. By the evening of 21
June all resistance had come to an end. Not
only did the fall of Tobruk provide Rommel
with nearly 33,000 prisoners and a wealth of
supplies, a grateful Führer promoted him to
the rank of Field Marshal.

The loss of Tobruk was a disaster for
British pride of arms: Churchill called it a disgrace, and rancour over the responsibility for
the failure to hold this vital position was to
continue well after the war.

Eighth Army under pressure

The Eighth Army's troubles were still far from
over, however. In the previous few weeks it
had lost 50,000 men, and as it fell back to the
Egyptian frontier it was still being harried by
the Germans. Rommel had the scent of victory in his nostrils and he pushed his men
ruthlessly: one last effort, he urged them, and
the Delta would be theirs. By the 23 June the

battered Eighth Army had taken up positions on a new defensive line by Mersa Matruh.

Auchinleck takes command

Auchinleck decided that he must take over control of the army himself and on 25 June Ritchie was discreetly relieved of his command. Realising the danger faced by the British forces around Mersa Matruh, Auchinleck began to order a withdrawal to better positions at Alamein. Rommel struck first, however: large numbers of British troops were trapped in the Matruh fortress and those that got away suffered another mauling at the hands of the Africa Corps.

Even though the Eighth Army had suffered badly, discipline and morale held up well during the long march back to Alamein. Certainly there was confusion in many soldiers' minds as to why, yet again, they had been thrown back by the Germans, but the will to fight had not been eroded. One commentator called the Eighth Army 'brave but baffled'. Theodore Stephanides, a doctor acting as medical officer for a labour battalion, made this comment:

What impressed me most was the discipline and order that prevailed everywhere. It was almost impossible to believe that this was a hurried and unexpected retreat. Everybody seemed cheerful and in spite of the numbers and speed of the traffic, I did not see a single collision. Military Police were posted at various points to direct and regulate the traffic and everything proceeded as smoothly as clockwork, rather like a crowd leaving a popular race meeting.

At Alamein, Auchinleck decided to make his stand. His formations were seriously depleted but Rommel's forces were short of supplies – his supply lines ran for hundreds of miles behind his troops – and his men were nearing the point of exhaustion. The two weary gladiators steeled themselves for one last encounter. The first Axis attack on the

BELOW
General Auchinleck talks to Indian troops on a front-line inspection. After the disasters following the defeat at Gazala, Auchinleck took over direct command of the Eighth Army and eventually restored order.

Alamein position came on 2 July. Rommel intended to bypass the position as he had done at Gazala and Mersa Matruh but his advance was checked on the Ruweisat ridge. In their intention to outflank the British, the Axis armoured units were forced further south towards the Sahara.

Suprise at Tell el Eisa

Meanwhile, the Eighth Army had been reinforced with the arrival in the Nile Delta of the 9th Australian Infantry Division, which subsequently took up positions around El Alamein on the coast. On 10 July, supported by British tanks, the Australians launched a surprise attack towards the slight rise known as Tell el Eisa.

The speed of the Australian advance caught the Axis completely by surprise. The Italian Sabratha Division was destroyed and Rommel was forced to divert his armour from his efforts to outflank the British

position on the southern front, to come instead to the aid of his beleaguered troops on the coast. Dug in on the Tell el Eisa, the Australians now had to face the full weight of the German counter-attack. Brigade-major to the 26th Brigade – and one of the planners of the attack on 10 July – Charles Finlay witnessed at first hand the German reaction and Allied counter-measures:

At one stage on 12 July they sent the whole of the 90th Light Division into the attack. Brigadier Ramsay, the Commander Royal Artillery of the 9th Division, was given the artillery of the two divisions south of him to go to work on the Germans. They really tore into them. I think they lost 22 tanks that afternoon. The Germans always used to attack then, out of the setting sun; it was very hard to see them in the desert. The German tanks had to keep going to avoid shell fire, whereas the infantry in the personnel carriers were being blown to pieces. The infantry became separated from their tanks and when they arrived at their objectives

RIGHT

Free French Foreign Legionaries race forward in a counter-attack at Bir Hacheim. The Free French operated on the southern flank of the Eighth Army.

BELOW

Under Allied attack, crew members of an 8.8cm anti-aircraft gun run for cover. Although highly effective in the tank-busting role, the high profile of the gun made it vulnerable to enemy fire once it had been located. Used shell casings lie around on the floor, testimony to the large number of rounds fired in a typical engagement.

there was no infantry support. This set the German back on their heels pretty solidly.

Peak of German success

The inability of the Germans to dislodge the Eighth Army marked the high-water mark of the Axis tide. The initiative passed over to Auchinleck, who handled his forces with considerable skill, although any hopes the British had of immediately throwing the Axis back from the Alamein position were thwarted in turn by some excellent German defensive tactics. On 22 July the battle stuttered to a close, as both sides began to dig in and begin erecting defences across the natural desert choke point, running from Alamein in the north down to the Qattara depression in the south.

The German failure to break through the British line at Alamein despite all his efforts made a deep impression on Rommel. His normal optimism had been worn down in these last failed efforts to secure the ultimate prize of Nile Delta and the Suez Canal, a

prize that he had now been fighting for for a year and a half. On 17 July he had written to his wife in a deeply pessimistic mood: 'Things are going downright badly for me at the moment, at any rate in the military sense. The enemy is using his superiority, especially in infantry, to destroy the Italian formations one by one, and the Germans formations are much to weak to stand alone. It's enough to make one weep.'

Rommel's last gambit

But despite these misgivings, Rommel knew that he must make one last effort to destroy the British before the pendulum of material forces swung irrevocably against him, as the amount of supplies reaching the British and Commonwealth forces increased almost daily. The better-trained and battle-hardened German troops and their superior equipment would soon be swamped by the sheer number of enemy troops and material, particularly since the entry of the United States into the war the previous December.

The British, for their part, knew they had to hang on against the determined German attacks until sufficient numbers of the promised reinforcements from their allies reached the battle front, and an new offensive could be launched to push the Germans out of northern Africa.

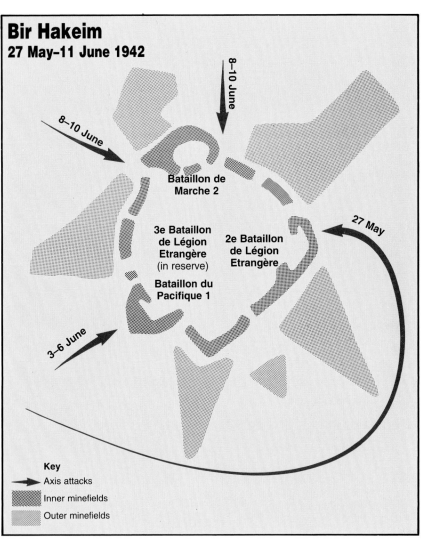

Bir Hakeim
27 May–11 June 1942

8–10 June

8–10 June

Bataillon de Marche 2

27 May

3e Bataillon de Légion Etrangère (in reserve)

2e Bataillon de Légion Etrangère

Bataillon du Pacifique 1

3–6 June

Key
Axis attacks
Inner minefields
Outer minefields

CHAPTER ELEVEN

TURN OF THE TIDE

Alamein marked the high-water point of Rommel's success.
Now, with America joining the war, the sheer weight of Allied
numbers began to push the Germans all the way back to Tunisia.

The Axis defeat at the First Battle of Alamein brought about a temporary lull in the fighting as both sides reinforced their front line in preparation for renewed combat. On 3 August 1942, Churchill arrived in Egypt to attend the Cairo Conference and to see for himself how the Eighth Army was faring in the desert. Churchill was not happy with what he saw. The failures of the summer, combined with what he considered as General Auchinleck's continuing intransigence, made changes at the top inevitable.

General Sir Harold Alexander was chosen to succeed Auchinleck as commander-in-chief in the Middle East on 6 August, while command of the Eighth Army was assigned to Lieutenant General W.H.E. Gott. Before Gott could take up the appointment, however, he was killed when the transport aircraft he was travelling in was shot down by German fighters. He was replaced by Lieutenant General Bernard Montgomery. Brought out from England, Montgomery was a highly abrasive individual who had little time for what he called the 'bad old ways' of the desert generals; either they would conform to his way of thinking or they would be sacked.

Before Montgomery could impose his stamp on the Eighth Army, he was called upon to defend the Alamein position against a last-gasp offensive by the Axis. In what became known as the Battle of Alam Halfa, Rommel followed the well-tried formula of a wide attack around the British southern flank with his armoured formations. The British defensive plan, based on one proposed by Auchinleck and his deputy chief of staff, Major General Eric Dorman-Smith, anticipated the German move. The British were also aided by good Ultra intelligence, which provided them with information of Rommel's proposed attack.

Alam Halfa

The Axis forces were allowed to initiate their flanking attack on the night of 30/31 August without interference, but they were funnelled towards well-defended British positions on the Alam Halfa ridge. As they made their advance, the Axis units were harassed by repeated RAF bomber attacks, while chronic shortages of fuel also slowed their progress. Determined British resistance along the Alam Halfa ridge brought the Axis offensive to a standstill. Rommel's armour was now in a very exposed position, and prudently he ordered a general retreat. By 6 September, the Axis forces were back on their start line.

Alam Halfa demonstrated that Montgomery was an adroit tactician, who was not overawed by the 'Rommel legend' and

OPPOSITE

Wildcats and Seafires on the deck of HMS Formidable *prepare to take-off in support of Operation Torch, the Allied landings in North Africa, November 1942.*

Ground crew prepare a squadron of RAF Hawker Hurricanes for a patrol over the Western Desert. By September 1942 the balance of power in the air had swung significantly in favour of the Allies.

who believed that victory lay only just around the corner. Another portent for the future was the excellent level of RAF–army cooperation during the battle. As the strength and ability of the Desert Air Force continued to rise, the future for Axis ground units looked increasingly bleak.

Churchill, as usual, pressed for an immediate resumption of offensive operations, but Montgomery refused to be rushed. Ever the methodical planner, Montgomery set about building up morale and training his troops for the next major battle, which he believed would be the decisive event of the North African campaign.

Montgomery made great play of the poor morale of the Eighth Army before his arrival, and his disparaging and often inaccurate remarks on Auchinleck's tenure of command reflected badly on Montgomery himself. None the less, the army needed shaking up and Montgomery was certainly the man for such a job. Despite an obvious partisan bias, Montgomery's own views – taken from his 'Review of the Situation of the Eighth Army from 12 August 1942 to 23 October 1942' – are of more than passing interest: 'Gross mismanagement, faulty command and bad staff work had been the cause of the whole thing. But the final blame must rest on General

Wishful thinking: the map on which Rommel marked his intended thrusts towards Alexandria and Cairo should he break through the Alamein defences.

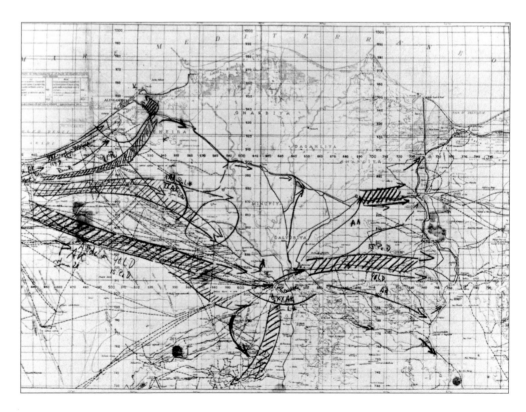

Auchinleck for allowing an inexperienced general like Ritchie to mishandle grossly a fine fighting army, and for allowing a policy of dispersion to rule.'

Even excepting an element of exaggeration – and a complete absence of credit given to Auchinleck for his sure handling of the Eighth Army during the Crusader and First Alamein battles – there was some truth in Montgomery's accusations. On other aspects of the Eighth Army's performance he was equally severe yet very telling:

I was watching training very carefully, and it was becoming apparent that the Eighth Army was very untrained. The need for training had never been stressed; consequently no one ever did any training; most of the officers had come to the fore by skill in battle and because there was no one any better who could be promoted; these officer were not skilled trainers.

There were very few really first-class officers in the Middle East in the higher ranks; most of the number one jobs were filled by second- and third-rate officers. Here again Auchinleck was to blame; he continually refused to have good men sent out from England, preferring the second-rate man on the spot whom he knew.

Montgomery's appeal

Montgomery's skill for self-publicity soon had its effect on the troops. He made repeated visits to the units under his command as part of his mission to create a new Eighth Army spirit. His behaviour elicited mixed feeling from the men, but on the whole they were favourable. If nothing else, the front-line soldier knew who his commander was and knew that he was determined to secure victory. More to the point, Montgomery stressed that he would do all in his power to minimise casualties. One British NCO saw Montgomery several times during this period and passed comment: 'For the first time in the war we had a commander who told us man for man what was happening. It was all very encouraging. He would talk on the same level as the men. He gained great respect from me.'

Montgomery had decided that his great offensive would open on the night of 23 October. During the seven weeks at his disposal – from the blunting of Rommel's offensive at Alam Halfa to the 23rd – Montgomery incorporated reinforcements into the Eighth Army and rehearsed all his troops in battle craft. Patrols and small probing operations were a feature of this period, intended to wear down enemy resolve, to toughen up those inexperienced in combat and gain information on enemy dispositions.

In the Australian sector, for example, these patrols soon developed into a routine, even a way of life, according to J.R. Oates of No. 5 Field Unit:

LEFT
Newly arrived in North Africa, the British commander Montgomery (left) briefs an officer of the 22nd Armoured Brigade. Montgomery's style of leadership was both abrasive and inspirational.

These nightly forays into No Man's Land, and on many occasions into German-occupied territory itself, yielded good results. Not only were casualties inflicted on the enemy and information gained, but in many cases weapons and stores were captured. Working on information gleamed by patrols, parties of engineers made a feature of penetrating enemy lines, stealing dumps of mines, and sowing them in enemy territory.

Allied raids

As well as conducting patrolling missions, the Eighth Army carried out a number of local attacks designed to test Axis resolve and to provide better jumping-off points for the main battle. In the north of the line, an Australian raid (Operation Bulimba) was a partial success, but a larger action conducted by a brigade of the 44th Infantry Division (Operation Braganza) was a bitter failure, causing heavy casualties for no gain. If nothing else, these raids confirmed to the British that the Axis forces were far from beaten and remained a profound danger.

Further to the south were the 'private armies', units of special forces who operated on the flanks of the main force. A British officer who helped organise these units called the desert a 'small raider's paradise', for it was in North Africa that most of these troops – encouraged by Wavell and Auchinleck – came into being. Their basic philosophy was centred around the idea that well-trained and highly motivated men could carry out onerous and often dangerous missions impossible for conventional forces. The private armies

reflected the British enthusiasm for the Boy's Own school of warfare, where derring-do by a resolute officer and his faithful men would win the day against vastly superior odds.

The first of these organisations to see the light of day – and probably the most effective – was the Long Range Desert Group (LRDG). The brainchild of a British officer, Major Ralph Bagnold, who had explored the Western Desert extensively before the war, the LRDG was set up to perform deep reconnaissance missions far behind enemy lines. Bagnold was given permission by Wavell to do as he wished, and he recruited a volunteer force of New Zealanders, who were then at a loose end after having lost their arms and equipment through shipping losses. Later the New Zealanders were joined by Rhodesians, and then troops from the Guards and subsequently yeomanry regiments.

Driving modified Chevrolet and Ford trucks, the LRDG operated from a string of oases deep in the desert, sending out patrols throughout Libya to as far west as the border with Tunisia. Missions could last weeks at a time, and the men not only had to learn the special techniques of desert survival, such as navigating by sun compass, they had to be highly resourceful to survive in these harsh conditions. Self-discipline replaced the spit and polish of conventional army discipline, and each soldier was expected to be able to look after himself.

The professionalism of the LRDG compared favourably with many other private armies, which, in the main, were organised

RIGHT

Men of the Long Range Desert Patrol stand by a truck specially modified for desert conditions. The LRDG were masters of navigation in the open spaces of the Western Desert, and played a valuable role in gaining information of German and Italian movements.

RIGHT

David Stirling,' the founder of the SAS, was one of the most dynamic leaders of special forces in North Africa.

and led by inspired amateurs. The commandos in the Middle East were formed from 8 and 11 Commando, known as Layforce after their commander, Colonel Robert Laycock. Layforce experienced mixed fortunes. Their prime function was to conduct amphibious raids along the North African coast, attacking enemy installations. The commandos achieved some success with relatively modest ventures, where resources were carefully matched to a specific task. The larger, open-ended raids were generally less successful, and disasters were not uncommon. The expedition mounted in November 1941 to attack Rommel's headquarters was one such operation. The leader of the raid, Lieutenant Colonel Geoffrey Keyes, was killed (receiving a posthumous VC) and many of his troops were captured. Faulty intelligence and desperately over-optimistic planning had doomed the attempt from the outset.

While recovering from injuries from a commando raid, one young officer, David Stirling, decided there was a place for small raiding teams to be dropped by parachute behind enemy lines. Supported by Generals Ritchie and Auchinleck, Stirling was given the go-ahead, and in mid-1941 he began recruiting volunteers from the remains of Layforce. Stirling and his 65 recruits gave themselves the title L Detachment Special Air Service (SAS) Brigade, intended to deceive German intelligence that an airborne brigade was being formed in the Middle East.

The first mission undertaken by the SAS was a parachute attack against two Axis airfields (16 November 1941), but the men were dispersed by high winds and the whole affair was a fiasco, the detachment losing 70 per cent of its strength. The survivors were picked up by the LRDG. Stirling saw the effectiveness of the LRDG and immediately abandoned the parachute concept in favour of overland operations in heavily armed jeeps, guided to their targets by the LRDG.

Specialising in attacks against enemy airfields, the SAS achieved some excellent results. On one occasion the SAS second-in-command, Paddy Mayne, led a raid which destroyed 40 Italian aircraft. Stirling was allowed to expand his force, which attracted a

stream of volunteers, incorporating such diverse elements as French paratroops, the Greek Sacred Squadron, the Special Boat Squadron, and the Special Interrogation Group (which comprised native-speaking Germans opposed to Nazism).

Desert patrols

Captain Pleydell, an SAS medical officer, found membership of this unusual organisation an interesting change from more conventional duties:

Although life was free and easy in the mess, discipline was required for exercises and operations. On the operation in which I was involved, our patrol would make long detours south of the battle line and then loop up north to within striking distance of an airfield or similar target. Camouflage had to be expert, so that when you hid up you couldn't be detected – even at close distance. Slow-flying enemy aircraft could follow our tracks to our hiding places and they represented a real threat. It was a hit-and-run, hide-and-seek type of war.

Working alongside the more organised of the private armies were individuals engaged in undercover work in Libya. One of the more colourful of these people was Vladimir Peniakoff, a man of Russo-Belgian descent who, after service in the French army during World War I, ended up as an engineer working in Egypt. On the outbreak of World War II he managed to secure a commission in the British army, and undertook special operations behind enemy lines. Initially, Peniakoff – nicknamed Popski by the British – worked with Libyan Arabs hostile to the Axis, but with

BELOW

Lieutenant 'Tiny' Simpson, a member of the Long Range Desert Group. He wears the heavy knit 'commando' sweater worn by many members of Britain's special forces during the war. His beret is that of the Royal Tank Regiment. Clothing for the LRDG was a mixture of British and Commonwealth issue, later supplemented by American items as these became more widely available.

A British supply column moves forward as part of the preparation for Alamein, under Montgomery's watchful eye. In the lead is a transporter carrying an M4 Sherman tank, which at the time was one of the more effective armoured vehicles available to the Allies.

help from the LRDG he expanded his organisation – which became 'Popski's private army' – and instigated sabotage raids on Axis positions. One of the most successful raids involved the destruction of 100,000 gallons of petrol, the commodity the German panzer divisions so desperately needed.

Montgomery's disdain

Unlike his predecessors, Montgomery did not have a very high opinion of the groups of special forces roaming the desert. In particular, he was not keen on having his best men and NCOs poached by the SAS. John Hackett – after being wounded at Gazala – was appointed to act as a liaison officer between high command and the various private armies. He found their leaders, 'a very varied list of prima donnas. My job was to try and make special operations comprehensible and palatable to senior officers, which took a lot of doing because they were not an easy lot to keep under full control.'

In one attempt to secure volunteers, Hackett and David Stirling met with Montgomery just prior to the battle at Alamein. Montgomery was not impressed with Stirling's entreaties and, according to Hackett, Montgomery replied: 'What makes you think, Stirling, that these men will fight better under your command than under mine. And, anyway, they won't be ready for

the battle [Alamein].' I couldn't resist saying, 'Well, they may not be trained in time for the next battle, but they will be trained for the one after that and the battles to follow.'

This was too much for Monty. He hammered the map at Alamein and said, 'There will be no other battle in Africa. This is going to be the last battle. My mandate is to destroy Rommel, and I propose to destroy him,' he said tapping the Alamein position, 'just here.' David, who was never well known for his obsequiousness, said: 'Oh yes, General, but the last general told us something like that, and the one before him too.'

Not surprisingly, Stirling did not receive his recruits. This anecdotal exchange typified the deep difference between the freewheeling special forces soldier and the professional general. Although the private armies did do good work on the flanks, Montgomery knew that only by defeating the Axis in a major battle could the desert war be won. And as he explained to Hackett and Stirling, the battle would be won or lost at Alamein.

Preparations continue

During September and October, while the British continued to prepare for the offensive, the Axis forces improved their defences, the Germans 'corseting' or supporting the Italian troops in the front line with their own infantry units. Worn-out and ill from the strain of constant fighting in desert conditions, Rommel temporarily left Africa to recuperate in Germany, leaving overall command in the hands of General Georg Stumme, a veteran of the Balkans and the Eastern Front.

Axis dispositions

The Axis armoured formations were withdrawn to act as a mobile reserve, leaving five infantry divisions – including the newly arrived German 164th Division and the Italian Folgore Airborne Division – in fixed positions along the front line. They were reinforced by the Ramacke Brigade, comprising seasoned German paratroops operating in a ground fighting role.

Under the direction of Colonel Hecker, Rommel's chief of engineers, the Axis had constructed a formidable defensive line, which included a series of interlocking strong points, protected by nearly half a million mines, of which 14,000 were anti-personal mines intended to discourage enemy anti-tank mine clearance teams. The lack of manoeuvrability inherent in the Alamein battlefield – between the Mediterranean Sea and the Qattara Depression – made mines particularly useful for the defenders, and the Axis commanders hoped that they would be sufficient to blunt any Allied advance, prior to the arrival of their own reserves.

Six Axis divisions were held back as mobile reserves. To the rear, in the southern sector, were the 21st Panzer and *Ariete* Armoured Divisions; to the rear, in the northern sector, were the 15th Panzer and Littorio Armoured Divisions. The 90th Light Division and the Trieste Motorised Divisions acted as an army reserve, and were deployed further along the coast road.

For the first time in the desert war, the British had a clear numerical and material advantage over the Axis: 195,000 troops against 104,000 (50,000 German); 1029 tanks against 489 (211 German); 2311 guns of all types against 1219 (644 German); and 530 serviceable aircraft against 350 (150 German).

Montgomery's plan maximised his resources. In the past, the desert commanders had attempted to turn the open southern flank of their opponent, but the Alamein position made such a manoeuvre impossible. Consequently, Montgomery decided to attack frontally in the north. The Axis intelligence services were deceived by Allied decoys that

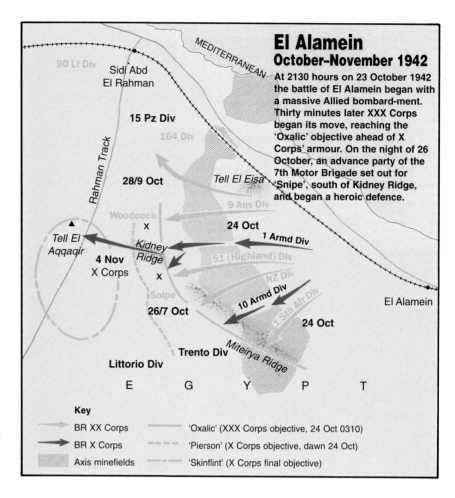

El Alamein
October–November 1942

At 2130 hours on 23 October 1942 the battle of El Alamein began with a massive Allied bombard-ment. Thirty minutes later XXX Corps began its move, reaching the 'Oxalic' objective ahead of X Corps' armour. On the night of 26 October, an advance party of the 7th Motor Brigade set out for 'Snipe', south of Kidney Ridge, and began a heroic defence.

Key
- BR XX Corps
- BR X Corps
- Axis minefields
- 'Oxalic' (XXX Corps objective, 24 Oct 0310)
- 'Pierson' (X Corps objective, dawn 24 Oct)
- 'Skinflint' (X Corps final objective)

there was a large armoured formation in the southern sector, while the most rigorous camouflage discipline was adopted by the main strike divisions in the north, which helped disguise the increasing concentration of forces in this sector. Montgomery had opted for an attritional battle, which played to British military strengths while reducing the advantages of mobility possessed by the panzer divisions.

The arrival of reinforcements had allowed Montgomery to divide the Eighth Army into three rather than the usual two corps. The

BELOW
Veterans of the Africa Corps advance to take up positions along the Alamein line, their exhaustion evident. The Germans would soon be on the defensive, and were about to experience the might of superior Allied resources.

Armoured cars from a New Zealand unit round up Axis prisoners. The majority of troops captured by the British and Commonwealth forces at Alamein were Italians, who lacked the mechanical means to withdraw from the battlefield.

XXX Corps (Lieutenant General Oliver Leese) contained the main strike formations – 9th Australian, 51st (Highland), 2nd New Zealand and 1st South African Divisions, which would smash their way into the enemy front line – and the 4th Indian Division which was stationed on the Ruweisat Ridge.

The Allied plan

Two corridors were to be opened up in the Axis minefields, through which would drive the armour of X Corps (Lieutenant General Herbert Lumsden), comprising the 1st and 10th Armoured Divisions. Instead of attempting an immediate breakout, X Corps would take up defensive positions alongside the infantry of XXX Corps to await and wear down the inevitable counter-attacks from the Axis armoured divisions.

To the south was XIII Corps (Lieutenant General Brian Horrocks) containing the 7th Armoured Division and the 44th and 50th Infantry Divisions, plus a brigade of Free French infantry. Their role was to launch two subsidiary attacks in an attempt to tie down the enemy reserves in that sector, especially the 21st Panzer Division, while the main battle was being fought to the north.

On 23 October the Eighth Army silently took up its battle positions. In order to protect the advancing infantry, Montgomery decided upon a night attack. Major General Douglas Wimberley, the commander of the 51st Highland Division, recalls the moments before the attack:

As we motored forward it was amazingly quiet. Hardly a gun or shell broke the silence. In fact, with memories of the 1914–18 war, I thought it was really too quiet to be true. In the stillness that preceded the storm I stood at one of the gaps in the wire and watched my Jocks in the moonlight. Platoon by platoon they filed past, heavily laded with pick and shovel, sandbags and grenades – the officer at the head, his piper by his side.

At 2140 hours local time, the guns of the Eighth Army fired in unison. The artillery barrage – the biggest in the desert war – was an experience few forgot. Not only was it highly successful in knocking out most of the Axis forward gun positions, it was a great boost to the morale of the advancing troops. One veteran tankman, Bob Sykes, remembered the barrage well:

We sat talking until it became dark, a few outbreaks of firing here and there, and then absolutely dead quiet. Suddenly, way up north a searchlight lit up, pointing straight up, followed by another. Then the night sky lit up with the biggest gun barrage I have ever known. The noise was more than deafening; everything seemed to go round and round.

Parties of sappers then advanced into No Man's Land, using newly arrived mine

detectors to open up paths through the Axis minefields. Alongside the sappers were a number of 'Scorpion' tanks, which had been modified to set off mines with whirling flails attached to a revolving drum positioned in front of the tank. Despite the best efforts of the British engineers, progress was slow and many mines remained in place which would cause casualties to both troops and tanks.

The first stages of Alamein

The sappers were followed by the infantry, advancing with bayonets fixed, and in the case of the 51st (Highland) Division, with pipes playing. In the northern sector, the role of Leese's XXX Corps was to advance along the two corridors in the minefields. The right-hand corridor was assigned to the 9th Australian and the 51st (Highland) Divisions; the left-hand corridor was given to the 2nd New Zealand Division. Initial progress was good but increased resistance from the German and Italian defenders prevented the first night's objectives from being reached. Despite this delay, Montgomery had the satisfaction of knowing that his troops were inflicting heavy casualties on the enemy infantry. The Italian Trento Division was badly mauled and two battalions of the German 164th Infantry Division were destroyed in the first night's fighting.

Because the British infantry had been unable to open up the corridors through the minefields, the armour of Lumsden's X Corps became clogged up inside the Axis front line and further back in No Man's Land. Montgomery ordered Lumsden to punch a way through, but the attempt failed with heavy losses in men and machines. On 25 October, Montgomery ordered both XXX and X Corps to press home their attacks with renewed vigour, but by now the Axis forces had recovered from the first onslaught and their stiffening resistance brought the British attack to a halt.

In the southern sector, the British XIII Corps launched its diversionary attack as planned. The 7th Armoured Division was held back, the weight of the attack falling to the 44th and 50th Infantry Divisions. The Italian troops facing XIII Corps' attack fought with great determination, and the British made little headway while sustaining heavy casualties. The attack by the Free French Brigade against the desert high point of the Qaret el Himeimat at the south of line also came to little. Despite the failure to gain ground, Horrocks' XIII Crops had been successful in their prime objective of delaying the advance of the 21st Panzer Division and Ariete Armoured Division from their positions in the south to support the Axis forces in the northern sector.

On the other side of the minefields, the Axis commanders had been taken off guard by the British attack. Some generals were away on leave, and the acting commander-in-chief, General Stumme, had a heart attack and fell from his vehicle while driving across the battlefield on the night of the assault. His death was a blow for the Axis cause, and time

BELOW
A 25-pounder gun howitzer of the British Eighth Army opens up on enemy positions. Despite Allied air superiority, the gun position is fitted with camouflage nets as a precaution.

was lost until the Africa Corps commander Lieutenant General Ritter von Thoma could take overall responsibility. When Rommel heard news of the attack, he rushed back to the front and by 26 October he was hard at work directing counter-attacks against the British in the northern sector.

The increasing ferocity of the Axis counter-attacks led Montgomery to remove units from the XIII Corps to reinforce the formations fighting in the northern sector. Although the breakthrough had not materialised, Montgomery maintained that the battle of attrition which had developed must eventually work to his advantage due to his superior numbers, as long as his troops held firm. The 7th Motor Brigade was sent forward to absorb the storm of German attacks between the Australian and Highland Divisions. One of the units in the 7th Motor Brigade – the 2nd Battalion, the Rifle Brigade – conducted an epic defence during the battle of a small rise known as Snipe Ridge. Major General Raymond Briggs, commander of the 1st Armoured Division (then controlling the 7th Motor Brigade) recalls the battalion's fight:

The first counter-attack came in at 3am on the 27th, and between then and dusk no less than eight major attacks were directed on the unfortunate but by no means unhappy battalion. Withholding the fire of their twelve six-pounder anti-tank guns until the enemy tanks were frequently within 150 yards [137m] range they did terrific damage.

In the meantime I was listening on my headphones to the course of the battle and to the appeals for tank assistance. I gave orders directing the tanks to their aid but every move across the valley was met by intense anti-tank fire and the loss of my tanks.

There was another factor too, known only to me and which I could not disclose. News had just reached me that the 21st Panzer Division was on the move from the south to join the 15th Panzer Division opposing us. I knew that every tank would be needed at short notice, as they were a few hours later, to take on the two divisions. I had to balance the possible destruction of the Rifle Brigade against the necessity to conserve my tank state. My reluctant decision was that I must leave the infantrymen to fight it out themselves.

The CO, Colonel Vic Turner, was wounded in the head early in the engagement but refused to give up and carried on by sheer guts almost until the end. His award of the Victoria Cross was described by Field Marshal Alexander 'as one of the finest of the war'. After the battle I had an independent survey of the tanks and guns still lying around the position. In the few hours of fighting that unit had brewed up 35 tanks and damaged beyond repair another 20.

Montgomery calls a halt

Considering the pounding they had taken, the Rifle Brigade's casualties were relatively light. But although the German counter-attacks were being held by the Eighth Army, the British were unable to make progress. Montgomery decided to call a temporary halt to the offensive and regroup his now rather disorganised forces. Montgomery's decision was greeted with anger and impatience by Churchill, who initially thought Montgomery

BELOW
British troops carefully scan the ground for mines. Mines were used extensively as an area denial weapon by both sides, channelling the fighting into narrow sectors of the front and preventing enemy forces from outflanking defensive lines.

was fighting a 'half-hearted battle'. In fact, the Eighth Army commander was preparing his forces for the final blow, designated Operation Supercharge.

Churchill's temper would have been further improved if he had been aware of the despondency that the British attack had induced in the Axis camp. Rommel wrote to his wife on 29 October in gloomy tones:

The situation continued very grave. By the time this letter arrives, it will no doubt be decided whether we can hold out or not. I haven't much hope. At night I lie with my eyes wide open, unable to sleep for the load that is on my shoulders. In the day I am dead tired. What will happen if things go wrong here? That is the thought that torments me day and night. I can see no way out if that happens.

Rommel, once the most optimistic of commanders, had was being ground down by the offensive as surely as his own forces were being overwhelmed by the Eighth Army. Rommel's hopes for victory – not only in Africa but as for the war as a whole – faded; for him the war was lost.

Operation Supercharge

The renewed British offensive was launched on 2 November, and was pressed home with the utmost ferocity. Italian anti-tank guns continued to fire on British tanks at 18m (20 yds) range, and the 9th Armoured Brigade, which spearheaded the assault, was badly mauled, losing 70 of its 94 tanks. The 1st Armoured Division, however, was able to inflict heavy casualties on the enemy. In the air, the Desert Air Force dominated the skies

above Alamein, making movement in daylight a hazardous occupation. Although the Axis line was still holding during the night of 2/3 November, Rommel accepted that the battle was lost. He had only 35 German tanks still operable, and these were now acutely short of fuel. Rommel began to prepare orders for a general retreat.

Throughout 3 November, the Axis clung onto their positions, under direct orders from Hitler to stand and fight regardless of consequence. But attacks by the 51st and 4th Indian Divisions ruptured the Axis defences, and on 4 November Rommel began the long retreat back to Tripoli. Montgomery despatched elements of the New Zealand Division and the 1st, 7th and 10th Armoured Divisions in pursuit. The British follow-up was cautious and, aided by poor weather, Rommel was able to make good his escape, although those Axis

ABOVE

Field Marshal Albert Kesselring – commander of the Axis forces in the Mediterranean – lives up to his nickname of 'Smiling Albert'. The situation for the Axis forces was, however, desperate.

BELOW

United States troops wade ashore near Oran in Algeria. The Torch landings transformed the strategic picture in North Africa, and forced the Axis to retreat to a defensive perimeter around Tunisia.

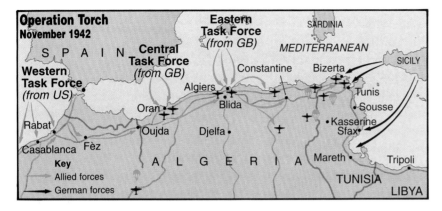

Operation Torch
November 1942

Western Task Force (from US)

Central Task Force (from GB)

Eastern Task Force (from GB)

SPAIN

MEDITERRANEAN

SARDINIA

SICILY

Constantine

Bizerta

Algiers

Tunis

Blida

Sousse

Oran

Rabat

Oujda

Djelfa

Kasserine

Sfax

Casablanca

Fèz

Mareth

Tripoli

A L G E R I A

TUNISIA

LIBYA

Key
→ Allied forces
→ German forces

forces without motorised transport and fuel (mainly Italian) were rounded up and captured within a matter of days.

Operation Torch

Montgomery had won a major victory. The Axis forces suffered around 20,000 men killed or wounded, and a further 30,000 were captured. The Eighth Army's casualties numbered 13,500. The British success at Alamein was followed by news of Operation Torch, the Allied landings in Morocco and Algeria. The Axis forces in North Africa were now faced with a war on two fronts. No longer could Rommel turn back on the Eighth Army for another round of fighting; he had no option but to fall back on Tunisia, where Hitler was belatedly sending reinforcements.

As the Germans and Italians fell back through Libya, they made sure that the British

did not have an easy advance. Rear guard actions had to be overcome and minefields and booby traps dismantled. The Germans made a stand at El Agheila between 23 November and 13 December, but were forced to retire into Tripolitania. As the Axis retreated back through their supply dumps so their resistance increased. The British had to mount attacks to clear the Germans from their positions at Wadi Zem Zem and in the hilly country around Homs. But the orderly British advance was too strong for the Germans to conduct much more than delaying operations.

On 23 January 1943 victorious British troops marched into Tripoli, which for years had been the goal of the Eighth Army's endeavours. Rommel meanwhile retreated further westwards, crossing the border into Tunisia on 4 February. There he rallied his forces behind the newly constructed defences of the Mareth Line. The desert war was over, but the fighting would continue in the mountains of Tunisia.

If the Battle of Alamein turned the tide of war in the Western Desert, then the Allied Torch landings of 8 November transformed the war in North Africa. A combined Anglo-American expedition, Operation Torch consisted of three major amphibious assaults against the coasts of Morocco and Algeria. The Americans provided the bulk of the troops; the British contribution included

RIGHT

General Dwight D. Eisenhower, appointed Supreme Allied Commander in North Africa, inspects British troops. The Americans were beginning to play an increasingly important role in the conduct of operations.

LEFT
*Commonwealth troops
engage in house-clearing
operations in North Africa.
They are armed with SMLE
rifles, first used in World
War I, but still an excellent
weapon of its type.*

substantial naval and aerial forces, plus specialist military units. The Allied commanders thought it prudent to keep the British in the background during the first wave of the assault, as there was till strong ill-will felt by the French towards the British as a result of the Royal Navy's bombardment of Mers-el-Kébir in 1940.

The Western Force (Major General George S. Patton) sailed directly from the United States and landed in Morocco, the bulk of its troops directed to the capture of Casablanca. The Central Task Force (Major General Lloyd Frendendall) and the Eastern Task Force (Major General Charles Ryder) sailed from the United Kingdom through the straits of Gibraltar towards Algeria. Frendendall's troops were to capture Oran, while Ryder's force had the most difficult assignment, which was to capture the seat of the Vichy French colonial government in Algiers, and then press on to invade Tunisia.

The Vichy French government – an ostensible ally of Germany – had been able to maintain control over its North African colonies of Morocco, Algeria and Tunisia after France's surrender, but there were pronounced anti-German feelings within the colonial administration which the Allies were able to exploit to their advantage. As a result, French opposition to the Allied landings was confused, limited and ultimately ineffectual. Once ashore, the Allies suppressed what

remained of Vichy French resistance, and an armistice was arranged on 10 November.

Units of the Eastern Task Force – which along with other Allied troops in western North Africa was absorbed into the First Army – advanced forward into Tunisia, supported by parachute drops. The intention was to capture Tunis, and then advance southwards to cut off Rommel's forces retreating back through Libya.

Although the Torch landings caught the Germans by surprise, they reacted with the utmost swiftness. Although Hitler and OKH had previously regarded the campaign in the Western Desert as little more than a side show, their attitudes changed dramatically after Torch; Hitler was determined that North Africa must be held at all costs. German reinforcements were rushed to Tunisia as the advance guard of the Fifth Panzer Army, to be commanded by Colonel General Hans-Jürgen von Arnim. As a result, the Allied push on Tunis was thwarted by the arrival of German troops in Tunisia. By the end of November mobile operations came to a close – partly a consequence of the bad weather encountered in the Atlas Mountains in winter – and the Allies were reconciled to the preparation of a full-scale offensive to take place in the following spring.

The rough terrain and winter weather made conditions difficult for the Allies, but more problematic still were the complexities

British supply trucks pass by a burnt-out German Ju-52 transport aircraft. The Germans used a large number of these transport aircraft to supply their forces in Tunisia; many of them were shot down by Allied fighters.

of the new command structure. This was the first instance of combined operations between the armies of Britain and the United States. There were a number of heated points of exchange between the commanders of both nations, reflecting differing strategic priorities and military traditions. And yet, on balance, the two armed forces worked surprisingly well together, in contrast to the bad relations that regularly bedevilled Italian–German operations.

More ambiguous was the position of the French in North Africa. After some initial reluctance they were won over to the Allied cause, especially now that the Germans were beginning to look vulnerable. French troops were slowly integrated into the Allied command structure, although some French commanders were unhappy at serving under the British. General Dwight D. Eisenhower was appointed Supreme Allied Commander, although tactical matters on the ground came under the control of British commanders: General Alexander moved up from Cairo to take charge of the newly created 18th Army Group, while Lieutenant General Sir Kenneth Anderson led the First Army, a multinational force of British, American and French troops. Advancing from the south was Montgomery's Eighth Army, which had forced Rommel's forces through Libya and into southern Tunisia, where they took up new positions along the Mareth Line.

Defeat at Kasserine

Before the Allies were ready to mount their offensive, the Germans struck. On 14 February 1943, German armoured columns led by Rommel forced their way across the mountains and routed the inexperienced US II Corps in front of the Kasserine Pass. Von Arnim was also successful in throwing back Allied troops holding positions to the north. Rommel wished to exploit this victory by advancing deeply into the Allied line, but he was overruled by his superiors. Within a few days the Allied line was shored up and the German advance was contained.

Rommel no longer had the freedom of action he had enjoyed in the desert, and his outspoken belief that the Germans should completely withdraw from Africa brought him into direct conflict with Hitler. Rommel despaired over the direction of the war in North Africa, and the following notes he made provide a good summary of the problems facing the Axis forces in early 1943:

We had still received no strategic decision from the supreme German and Italian authorities on the future of the African theatre of war. They did not look at things realistically – indeed, they refused to do so. What we found really astonishing was to see the amount of material that they were suddenly able to ship to Tunisia, quantities out of all proportion to anything we had received in the past. The urgency of the danger had at last percolated through to Rome. But the British and Americans had meanwhile multiplied their supply shipments many time over and were steadily increasing their strategic command over sea and air. One Axis ship after the other was going down beneath the waters of the Mediterranean, and it was becoming obvious that even the greatest effort could no longer hope to effect any decisive improvement in the supply situation; we were up to our necks in the mud and no longer had the strength to pull ourselves out.

The mismanagement, the operational blunders, the prejudices, the everlasting search for scapegoats, these were now to reach the highest stage. And the man who paid the price for all this was the ordinary German and Italian soldier.

Rommel leaves Africa

Despite Rommel's foreboding, the Axis continued to attack. A second, limited offensive was mounted against the Eighth Army opposite the Mareth Line at Medenine on 6 March, but it was a clumsy affair and the British desert veterans – well armed with anti-tank guns – repulsed the attack, destroying many valuable German tanks in the process. Exhausted and frustrated, Rommel left Africa for good on 9 March, passing control of German forces to von Arnim. General Giovani Messe, meanwhile, had assumed command of all Axis forces in North Africa, although his freedom of action depended on German agreement.

Montgomery's own assault against the fotified Mareth Line got underway on 20 March. The British plan called for a major blow to fall on the centre-right of the Line, with a wide flanking manoeuvre on the left to be carried out by the New Zealand Corps (the original 2nd Division augmented by additional troops) to draw away reserves from the main battle. A well-timed attack by the XV Panzer Division, however, stalled the main

ABOVE

Riding in Bren carriers, a column of Indian troops advances through a town in North Africa. Although lacking in armour protection, Bren carriers were used to ferry troops into battle as well as acting as a basic transport.

LEFT

Water supply was always a major problem in the desert. Here barrels of fresh water, transported along the coast from Alexandria, are rolled ashore to the waiting troops by Royal Navy personnel.

British offensive, so Montgomery switched the focus of the assault, despatching the 1st Armoured Division in support of the New Zealanders' left hook. Battered by ferocious attacks from the Desert Air Force, and fearing encirclement, the Axis troops skilfully withdrew from Mareth to new positions at Wadi Akarit, although the panzer units lost much of their armour in the process.

The Axis retreat continues

Montgomery launched a frontal assault against the Wadi Akarit defences on the night of 6/7 April, forcing a breach in the Axis line. General Messe was now also faced by a new threat on his right flank from the rejuvenated US II Corps (now under the command of General Patton); he decided against continuing the fight and withdrew northwards towards Enfidaville. The Axis armies were now being driven back into a perimeter surrounding the ports of Bizerta and Tunis.

While the Eighth Army advanced northwards, the First Army opened its assault from the west. On 22 April, the British struck in the centre of the line, while the Americans advanced along the coast. The Axis troops held on desperately to their mountain defences, notably at Longstop Hill, where the British 78th Division fought a bitter four-day battle to wrest control from the German defenders. As the Eighth Army's attack against Enfidaville had stalled, Montgomery sent troops to support the First Army offensive to break out of the mountains towards Tunis.

During the first week in May, Allied units began to push forward onto the coastal plain:

on 5 May the British 1st Infantry Division captured Djebel Bou Aoukaz and the following day the 4th Indian Division – which had fought continuously in Africa since the beginning of hostilities – drove the Axis off the key Medjez el Bab position.

Tunis captured

The way was open for exploitation by the tanks, and on 7 May the 7th Armoured Division – the original Desert Rats – swept triumphantly into Tunis. Further north, the Americans captured Bizerta, leaving the Axis to make a last stand on the Cape Bon peninsula. But the Allied breakthrough had overwhelmed the Axis command, which was unable to organise effective resistance. On 12 May, von Arnim was captured, and a day later Messe formally surrendered what was left of the Axis armies.

Hitler's reckless policy of massively reinforcing the Tunisian bridgehead bore bitter fruit, for along with 115,000 Italians he lost 125,000 German troops to the POW camps. The vast haul of Axis prisoners was a special bonus for the British, who for nearly three years had fought over desert and mountain for this moment. During the seven-month campaign in Tunisia the Allies suffered just over 40,000 killed and wounded, the bulk of them British casualties.

On 13 May 1943, General Alexander sent his famously laconic despatch to Churchill in London: 'Sir, it is my duty to report that the campaign in Tunisia is over. All enemy resistance has ceased. We are masters of the North African shores.'

INDEX